COMING ABOUT

A Family Passage
at Sea

D0888037

COMING ABOUT

A Family Passage at Sea

SUSAN TYLER HITCHCOCK

SHERIDAN HOUSE

This edition published 2002 by
Sheridan House Inc.
145 Palisade Street
Dobbs Ferry, NY 10522
www.sheridanhouse.com

Grateful acknowledgment is made to the following for permission to
reprint previously published material:

Liveright Publishing Corporation: Excerpt from "maggie and milly
and molly and may" from *Complete Poems: 1904-1962* by E.E.
Cummings, editing by George J. Firmage. Copyright © 1956, 1984,
1991 by the Trustees for the E.E. Cummings Trust. Reprinted by
permission of Liveright Publishing Corporation.

Viking Penguin and Laurence Pollinger Limited: Excerpt from
"Whales Weep Not!" *from The Complete Poems of D.H. Lawrence* by
D.H. Lawrence, edited by V. de Sola Pinto and F.W. Roberts.
Copyright © 1964, 1971 by Angelo Ravagli and C.M. Weekley,
Executors of the Estate of Frieda Lawrence Ravagli. Reprinted by
permission of Viking Penguin, a division of Penguin Books USA Inc.,
and Laurence Pollinger Limited on behalf of the Estate of Frieda
Lawrence Ravagli.

Library of Congress Cataloging-in-Publication Data
  Hitchcock, Susan Tyler
    Coming about : a family passage at sea / by Susan Tyler Hitchcock
      p. cm.
    ISBN 1-57409-135-2
    1. Hitchcock family—Journeys   2. Voyages and travels. 3. Hei
Tiki (Sloop)   4. Caribbean Area—Description and travel.
I. Title.
G500.H57   1998
917.2904'52—DC21   97-24427
                                              CIP

Printed in the United States of America

To the memory of

DAVID WAYNE WATKINS, JR.
without him, there would not have been a boat

and

BOOTON HERNDON
without him, there would not have been a book

ACKNOWLEDGMENTS

Special thanks to Bonnie Herndon, Jeanne Nicholson Siler, Elizabeth Breeden, and Boyd Zenner for generous responses to early drafts. Thanks to my agent, Jane Dystel, and my editor, Elizabeth Zack, for seeing the possibilities and helping make them come real. Thank you to the Virginia Center for Creative Arts for underwriting my two productive weeks there. Thanks especially to my husband, David Watkins, for trusting me to tell our story and for waiting until the book was finished before he even read it.

The pattern of our lives is essentially circular. We must be open to all points of the compass; husband, children, friends, home, community; stretched out, exposed, sensitive like a spider's web to each breeze that blows, to each call that comes. . . . How desirable and how distant is the ideal of the contemplative, artist, or saint—the inner inviolable core, the single eye.

–ANNE MORROW LINDBERGH, *Gift from the Sea*

How long [a wave] will live, how far it will travel, to what manner of end it will come are all determined, in large measure, by the conditions it meets in its progression across the face of the sea. For the one essential quality of a wave is that it moves.

–RACHEL CARSON, *The Sea Around Us*

And they rock, and they rock, through the sensual
   ageless ages
on the depths of the seven seas,
and through the salt they reel with drunk delight
and in the tropics tremble they with love
and roll with massive, strong desire, like gods.

–D. H. LAWRENCE, "Whales Weep Not!"

Why upon your first voyage as a passenger, did you yourself feel such a mystical vibration, when first told that you and your ship were now out of sight of land? Why did the old Persians hold the sea holy? Why did the Greeks give it a separate deity, and make him the own brother of Jove? Surely all this is not without meaning.

–HERMAN MELVILLE, *Moby-Dick*

For whatever we lose (like a you or a me)
it's always ourselves we find in the sea

–E. E. CUMMINGS

CONTENTS

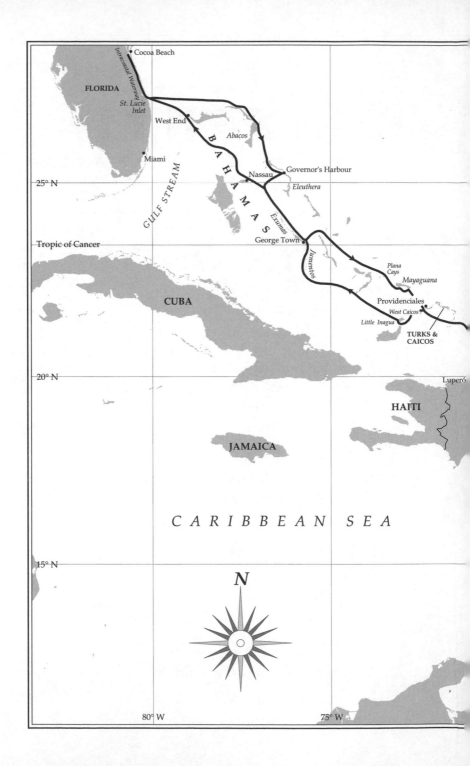

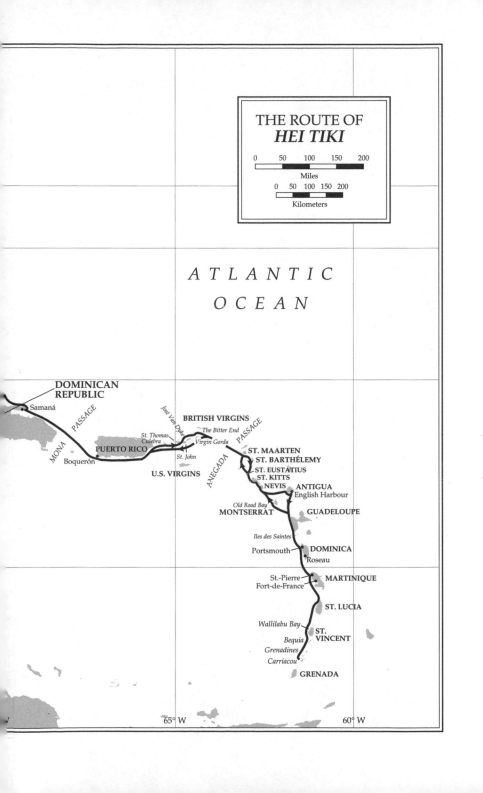

THE ROUTE OF
HEI TIKI

0   50   100   150   200
Miles
0   50   100   150   200
Kilometers

ATLANTIC

OCEAN

DOMINICAN
REPUBLIC
Samaná

MONA PASSAGE

Boquerón

PUERTO RICO

St. Thomas
Culebra

Jost Van Dyke

St. John

U.S. VIRGINS

ANEGADA PASSAGE

BRITISH VIRGINS
The Bitter End
Virgin Gorda

ST. MAARTEN
ST. BARTHÉLEMY
ST. EUSTATIUS
ST. KITTS
NEVIS   ANTIGUA
English Harbour

Old Road Bay
MONTSERRAT

GUADELOUPE

Iles des Saintes

Portsmouth   DOMINICA
Roseau

St.-Pierre   MARTINIQUE
Fort-de-France

ST. LUCIA

Wallilabu Bay
Bequia   ST.
VINCENT
Grenadines
Carriacou

GRENADA

65° W   60° W

Coming About

A Family Passage
at Sea

1

Casting Off

CALL US WISHFUL. CALL US RECKLESS. CALL us escapists, whatever you will. We needed to break free and live new again.

In our twelve years of marriage, we had bought land, built a house, cultivated a garden, and given birth to two radiant children. Both of us had work that we, more than many, could call our own. Yet something was missing. There was no center we could find to hold. So we took to the water. We lived aboard *Hei Tiki* and sailed nine months through the Caribbean.

The boat belonged to Granddad, David's father. Retired from the navy, he bought the deck and hull and constructed the rest himself. He built in fuel and water tanks, laid down the cabin floor, put up cabinetry, installed the engine, strung the rigging, wired the lights. She was a sloop, thirty-four feet long, with a mast that stood forty-four. Some years back, her deck had been repainted a tropic turquoise. Even with diligent upkeep, *Hei Tiki* showed her twenty-five years.

She was a lucky boat, David's family all believed. A wooden effigy of Hei Tiki, the Maori god of fertility, danced on the bulkhead. It had been carved by a Maori tribesman for David's mother, a New Zealander by birth. She was the sailor, even more

than her husband, and although she had died less than a year after David and I were married, I am sure she would have blessed
our plan to sail.

The plan took a year to germinate. After ten days of sailing
together one summer—the first time I had ever spent more than
a weekend on a boat—David and I talked possibilities.

"We could live aboard for a year, sail down the islands,"
he said.

"With the children?" They were barely school-age.

"Of course."

"Leave our house?" We were still building.

"Get someone to live there. Rent it," he said.

"Could we afford it?"

"It would probably cost less than a year at home."

I kept asking questions, but somewhere inside I was already
saying yes.

We needed something to pull us together. Like many American
families, we were spinning out centrifugally.

David often stayed at work until seven, eight, or nine. He
was a mechanical engineer. He liked his hands on the machines.
When federal tax credits for solar heating installations ended
in 1986, his solar contracting business had spiraled down. Now
he worked independently, designing heating and air condition-
ing systems. Sometimes he had to work late to make sure the
heat came on. Sometimes, after work, he had a few beers with
the guys.

I had strung myself out between two offices, teaching
humanities to engineering students and writing for a living—
sometimes essays of my own, but more often advertising and
fundraising pieces. I was the one who broke off work to pick up
the children at day care. I was the one who cooked their dinner,
read them stories, brushed their teeth, and tucked them in.

Now the children were starting to go off in different directions. Both attended the public elementary school seven miles
from our mountainside home in Virginia. But John was playing
soccer, which meant an afternoon of practice and a game every

Saturday. Soon Alison would want to learn gymnastics, or ride horseback, or take art lessons, and I would be driving her around, too.

I was tired. Frustrated. Feeling lonely. David and I were married, but we weren't doing much together.

Still, it wasn't anything out of the ordinary. My husband and I both wanted careers. I thought we were going to raise our children as a team, but when one baby arrived, then another two years later, I saw less and less of David. His truck would thunder up the driveway just as I dozed off. I would try to rouse myself, but my eyelids would sag. I was exhausted.

And I was mad. Some nights I couldn't contain it. "Why don't you call and tell me that you're going to be late? I never know when to expect you. I sit and wait from six o'clock on. Guess I should just assume you'll be home at nine. But you never tell me. Couldn't you just call and say hello sometime?"

Confrontation always shut David down. He looked away. Or he walked outside.

Sometimes I followed him. "I feel like a drudge. I work all day, then I come home and I'm the only one here for hours. Cooking, cleaning, taking care of the children."

He would sit and smoke his cigarette, looking far away.

"We never do anything together. I feel so trapped in this routine. Get up, drive the children to school, work a short day and never get my own work done, because I have to go pick up the children and deal with them until I'm exhausted. You get to stay out as long as you want."

Finally he turned around and let me have it.

"Do you think I want it this way? Don't you see what pressure I'm under, managing a cash flow of half a million? If things go wrong, we could lose everything. I try to talk to you about it, but you don't even listen. You fall asleep while I talk."

I gulped. It was true. He kept on.

"Every time we talk, you let the children interrupt us. You never choose our marriage over them. When I do come home early, you either bitch at me or you consider it your chance to leave. This is no partnership. This is alternate parenting."

Then finally he said it. "This isn't my idea of a marriage. We haven't had sex for months."

By stating the problems, we had taken one step. Solving the problems would take many more. We spent years in limbo, recognizing that this married life wasn't what we had hoped for, but unable to see clear to changing.

Then we started to talk about sailing.

In those first years of marriage, he hadn't told me how much he loved sailing. We shared gardening, hiking, goats, and chickens. My landscape never had boats in it.

David had grown up breathing salt air. He had helped his father build boats, sailed to the Bahamas and back just for pleasure. Sailing was a thing he did with the guys, though, when we first married. That was okay with me, because I got seasick all the time.

Then he took two weeks and sailed to the Bahamas with four men friends. Next he bought shares in a sailboat with three other guys. When friends of ours started chartering boats every weekend, inviting us along, I thought I ought to go. Soon I would be a sailboat widow if I didn't.

I tried scopolamine patches, and they leveled out my nausea. I loved the wind in my hair, the smell of salt and fish and sunshine. David started thinking sailing with women wasn't all that bad. I started thinking, *I might learn to like this.*

David's father sailed *Hei Tiki* to the Bahamas every summer. One year, David suggested we go along. We spent ten days aboard. We started from Florida, crossed the Gulf Stream overnight, and spent seven jewel-like days in the Abacos.

"Come up on deck with me," said David late one afternoon as Granddad sailed us into Hope Town. "Let's douse the jib. When I let loose of the halyard, pull the sail down." Our bodies stretched, reached, and pulled down in unison, folding the stiff white sail. "Great teamwork," he said.

Fresh from those ten days, he proposed a family journey. Devote a year to sailing. Nothing to do but be together, take care of ourselves, our children, and our boat, and travel from island to island. I felt things begin to loosen deep down inside.

With a mixture of hope and disbelief, I kept our plan secret for months. I borrowed a Caribbean travel guide from the library. Some names were familiar—Martinique, St. Maarten. Others were new—St. Eustatius, Dominica, Montserrat. David pinned a chart of the Mona Passage on the living room wall. We would cross that body of water to get from the Dominican Republic to Puerto Rico. It just looked like water with lots of numbers and arrows. I didn't understand what he saw as he studied it.

At first I only told one friend, the one who believed in miracles. "Keep it a secret," I whispered. I gave her a pair of earrings, tiny, mother-of-pearl palm trees. I wore a matching pair. "Help me believe," I asked.

Those earrings became my amulet. I would quietly finger their firmness and wish our dream true. When I saw my friend wearing hers, it felt like validation. Someone else believed. Maybe we would save up and spend a family year on a sailboat.

We started practicing a more frugal style of life, both to save money and to ready ourselves for life on board. I imposed new household efficiencies. I no longer hired a woman to clean our house. No new winter clothes; we could get by with what we had. Besides, next winter, we wouldn't be wearing any. We started using cloth napkins. I cooked less meat.

We started saving money. We needed ten thousand dollars, David estimated. We worked hard through the fall and winter, feeling less resentment toward one another. We shared a goal.

The more people I told, the more the trip became a reality. One by one, I arranged for jobs to end. No teaching past summer term. Finish fall publications early. Leave behind articles for winter. To the editor of the magazine for which I wrote a column, I also offered to write ahead.

"Write from the boat instead," she said. "You'll be our Caribbean correspondent. We call your column 'Letters from Home' now. It will be 'Letters to Home' for the year."

I made an appointment with my children's principal and outlined our plans. They would miss first and third grade. I wanted to be sure they came back into second and fourth. "I don't see any problem," he said. Then he added, to my surprise, "They'll learn more out there than they will in a classroom."

Those who knew us well applauded the plan. From others, we heard a litany of reactions.

"How do you get to do that?"

We're in charge of our life.

"Will they let you take your children out of school?"

They're our children.

"I couldn't stand to be with my husband that long."

I'll learn.

"I couldn't stay cooped up with my children."

We'll find out how.

"That's something we've always dreamt about, but I just know we'll never do it."

Why not?

After a certain point, there was no turning back. I knew it when I got the phone call from my mother.

"I don't think you've thought this thing through clearly," she said. "There are people out there, floating around in boats. You see them all the time on the news. They are animals, trying to escape. Pirates. Desperadoes."

I listened, but I didn't answer.

"You have two growing children to take care of. Where will you buy groceries? Where will you find food that's safe? And water. There's the risk of cholera, malaria. All sorts of intestinal bugs. How will you do laundry? Why now, of all times, take your children out of school? First and third grade? These are very important years."

That's just why, I thought, but said nothing.

"What if someone gets sick? What if something happens to David? Or to you? What on earth would you do in an emergency?"

I kept listening. She kept talking.

"Isn't there some other way of regenerating your life without taking on this plan to become—to become . . . boat people . . .

and put yourselves out of commission entirely? It's simply not fair to your children or yourself. You seem to be trying to escape."

She stopped. She wanted an answer, but I couldn't begin to speak.

"One more thing," she said.

"Yes?"

"How can you leave everything behind? What will you have when you get back? I should know. I've been there."

I glimpsed through to her core concern. When I was four, our family lived in Italy, supported by my father's Fulbright scholarship. Things didn't go well. They sent me back to my grandparents after a few months. My mother then returned, and finally my father. They argued through the birth of a second child and too many more years of a bad marriage, then they divorced when I was thirteen. To Mother, leaving home meant a breach in the marriage. To me, it could, instead, mean healing.

"What will you have accomplished when it's all over?" she continued. "If I could see anything good coming of this plan, I would feel differently."

She ran out of steam.

"I've written down your comments, and I'll think about all of them," I said.

"Please do." She hung up.

That conversation sealed the plan for me. Not a one of her nightmare visions could change my mind. Food, water, laundry? It's not a no-man's-land out there. Cholera, malaria? From the University of Virginia's international health clinic, I already had received a country-by-country analysis of our itinerary. In an emergency? "Look at the map," said David. "We'll rarely be out of sight of land." Haitian boat people? "I agree," he said. "Better not go near Haiti. Too damn many U.S. Coast Guard clippers."

One of my mother's comments did haunt me, though.

"Are we escaping?" I asked David.

He paused, then asked, "What do you think?"

"It feels just the opposite to me," I answered.

"What do you mean?"

"By going sailing together, we'll have to be together. We can't escape. That's what we're choosing."

"There's your answer," he said.

At the ages of six and eight, the children weren't sure what they were in for. Alison, my youngest, had never been on a boat before. John had been sailing once, and all he could remember was how scared he felt when the boat heeled over. They were more aware of what they would miss than what they would gain.

"No school? Yay!" John said.

"We'll still do schoolwork, though. We'll take books and papers, and your father and I will be your teachers. I'll teach reading and writing and Dad will teach math."

"Will you stay with us?" Alison asked.

"We'll be together every day."

"Dad, too?" asked John. I nodded.

"What about Ahab and Pirate?" Alison worried about our dog and cat.

"We'll find someone who will take care of them while we're gone. They'll be here when we get back."

"Can't we bring them with us?"

I shook my head. "It's going to be different in a lot of ways. We can't bring everything with us. You'll have to choose a few special toys. We'll have to be very careful about things we don't even think about at home, like water and electricity."

I watched John's face as thoughts flashed through his mind. Then he said, "No TV?"

Thank goodness, I thought to myself, but I just echoed his words. "That's right. No TV."

By spring, David was spending weeks in Florida, working on the boat with his father. When we had asked Granddad's permission for a year aboard *Hei Tiki*, he had answered, "Needs a new motor if you do." He and David installed a brand-new, twenty-six-horsepower inboard. They rewired everything. They rebuilt the galley. Piped in a new refrigerator. Mounted a photovoltaic cell off the stern and tied it into battery storage.

Sailing projects crowded our workshop at home, too. On one trip home from Florida, David hauled back a beat-up little rowboat. "It's a Dyer dinghy," he said. To me, the name meant nothing. To sailors, David explained, Dyers were top-of-the-line hard-bottom dinghies. "People these days like rubber inflatables. Not me," said David. "This thing will plane like crazy. Makes it easier to tow."

The nuts and bolts of sailing were already real for David, but they were still unknown to me. I had only sailed three weekends before those fateful ten days in the Bahamas together, and I figured I ought to know more. I went out on a twenty-eight-footer into the Chesapeake with two woman friends, one a seasoned merchant mariner. She put me to the test. "Come about," she commanded, then she sat back and watched.

It still was not second nature. *Turn into the wind,* I told myself. I gripped the mainsheet with my right hand, turned the steering wheel with my left. I pulled the line in as the boat eased over. The boom swung across with just the right momentum—not too violently, not too lazily. The sail picked up wind on the other side. We glided on in a new direction.

"Right!" she said. "If you can do that, you can sail."

Still I worried over how much the three of us would have to depend on David. He had the knowledge, the skill, the experience. One night's dream said it all. I dreamt that all four of us had ventured into a field of tall grass, just in sight of home. Two copperheads muscled by; one bit David on the ankle, and he collapsed. I shouted to the children to jump onto a nearby tractor. I could barely lift David onto the hay wagon that was attached. Then, panicked and inexperienced, I had to figure out how to drive the machine.

I knew so little, when it came down to it. I had never anchored, never navigated. I could steer the boat and I could tack—but in a crisis, I wouldn't know what to do. I wanted to be strong and equal, but how could I when David knew so much and I knew so little about sailing? In my darker moments, I feared the plan was all wrong. In my darkest moments, I

imagined the worst. The sea has swallowed up many boats and
sailors.

I moved on through the summer, keeping faith in our plan.
Farmed out our pets. Packed away books, dishes, furniture, and
clothing—everything except the few things we could take with us.

A group of business students rented our house for the
school year. That six hundred dollars per month would cover
monthly bills at home and then some. I asked Kathy, a close friend
and neighbor, to open mail, collect rent, pay bills, and mind business. She agreed, as long as I would phone every month and invite her and her husband to fly down and sail with us for a while.

We sold a little piece of property we owned. I taught and
wrote. David finished his last two heating systems. We saved
and didn't spend. By June, we had six thousand dollars in hand.
I was owed $5,000 more by August, with another $1,750 due in
January. The magazine articles I wrote from the boat would
bring another two hundred dollars every other month. We were
well over our goal of ten thousand dollars.

In August we left Virginia. I cried as I climbed into the car.
Friends hugged, then waved as we curved down our driveway.

"When will we come home again?" Alison asked.

"Less than a year. Not too long. Don't be sad," I said, piling on the consolations. To her, at the age of six, a year was an
unfathomable unit of time, stretching into the future forever.
Just last night, she had sobbed and clung to Kathy, refusing to
say goodbye.

"Don't cry, Alison," said John. An eight-year-old brother
could sometimes be a comfort, sometimes a pain. For the moment, he was choosing to comfort. "When we get to Granddad's,
we can swim in the pool and take the canoe out." It was easier for
him to let go and look forward, even if only a week into our future.

In Florida, every action pushed us closer to casting off. David
and Granddad bent for days over a greasy outboard motor. The
old British Seagull had sat unused in the garage for years. They

took the whole thing apart and soaked it in engine cleaner. They replaced every part they could buy at the store, then they put it back together. Of course it didn't start, so they started fiddling again. Finally, its high-pitched blare seared through the neighborhood. Our dinghy now had an outboard motor.

I bought twenty yards of marine canvas and sewed a new cockpit awning, which sailors call a "bimini." Granddad had designed the frame years before, bending aluminum tubing into collapsible arches over which stretched an eight-by-eight-foot shade. Fore, aft, and side curtains tied or snapped on. I had to sew curves and corners, hammer in snaps and eyelets. When I finally stretched the bimini on the frame, Granddad examined it. "Almost as good as mine," he winked, and it felt like approval.

We bought cases of food at a discount warehouse. Pinto and kidney beans. Beef stew, chicken à la king, and chili con carne. Tuna, corned beef, and sardines. Green beans, peas, and corn. Peaches, pears, and pineapple. Ten pounds of rice. A dozen boxes of pasta. A huge bottle of ketchup. Ten pounds each of sugar and flour. Six pouches of instant Gatorade. Two jars of instant iced tea. Worcestershire sauce. Dill pickles. I felt as if I were choosing blindly. I had so little sense of what food we would need. What could we buy in the islands? What could we catch? What would we want? Faint with uncertainty, I bought a big bag of chocolate bars.

Granddad kept the boat at the Eau Gallie Yacht Club, a twenty-minute drive from his Cocoa Beach home. Through two weeks of sewing the bimini, provisioning the galley, and moving belongings on board, I began to feel at home on *Hei Tiki*.

The cockpit would soon become the hub of our world, our open-air living room. Cushioned benches, seven feet long, faced each other and connected like two arms of a narrow "U." At the helm, the driver gripped the wooden wheel, read the hemispheric compass mounted on the binnacle, and drove. From the helm, you could lift a hatch behind you and reach into the lazarette, a broad, deep storage compartment that we had already filled with docking lines, snorkeling equipment, water jugs, fuel jugs, fishing tackle, life jackets, and cases of beer and soda.

Hei Tiki measured thirty-four feet in length. Of those thirty-four, the lazarette and cockpit took ten. You had to climb from the cockpit up onto the deck, walking the foot-wide deckways on either side to where the forward hatch popped open like a cigar box. The largest swatch of empty deck lay at the forward peak, where one could sit, lie, or stand, leaning up against the forestay, and gaze out beyond the confines of this little dwelling. Plastic-coated lifelines, knee- and hip-high, strung from stanchion to stanchion all around the deck. Shrouds and stays stretched from decksides up to the mast and its crosspiece, the spreaders, so that even if the walkways were narrow, there were plenty of things to grab.

The deck would be our yard, the cockpit our living room. Kitchen, bathroom, and bedrooms were in the cabin below.

Four steep wooden steps, called the companionway, led to the galley. To the right—or should I stay starboard?—counters, refrigerator, sink, cupboards, stove. To the left—port—a five-foot table and a six-foot settee, long enough and cushioned so it worked as a bed—better, in fact, than it worked for dining, since the four of us would have to slide in side by side to eat at the galley table. We would eat out in the cockpit most of the time.

On the wall above the galley table hung a clock and the Hei Tiki. The clock had a classic oval face with graceful hands, indicating hour and minute. Hei Tiki had an eerie insect face, with lidless eyes and tongue stuck out. Holding knees wide apart, the Maori god displayed ambiguous genitals. Even from the helm, one could see this pair of wall hangings that symbolized the sailing life: precisely measured, yet wild and free.

The spaces were small as one moved through the cabin. Two people could not fit side by side in the passageway that connected the galley to the forward berth. On one side of the passageway was the head, on the other, the locker. The head, as I was already trying to call the bathroom, would fit inside a small shower stall. It contained a toilet, a sink, a medicine chest, and a showerhead with a flexible hose. You could sit on the toilet and take a shower.

Across the way, so close you could reach out and touch them, were a small hanging locker and a bank of cubby spaces.

We each got one cubby, in order of height. They were deep, but not very wide—each held the volume of a dresser drawer—and they represented the space we allowed ourselves for almost all of our clothing.

The forward berth looked like the bed of choice to me. This was *Hei Tiki*'s master bedroom, so to speak. Shaped into the bow of the boat, it was broader than a double bed at one end and tapered at the other—which is why, I supposed, this bed was also called the V-berth. The forward hatch opened up just above the broad end, so you could lie there and look at the stars. A blue nylon airscoop could fit over the hatch; tied to the rigging, it swept air down into otherwise closed quarters. But this space, as every other space inside *Hei Tiki*, was cramped in all directions. Two feet of headroom, shrinking foot room, and nothing but the bed filling the space.

Every corner that could store things did. Two little shelves at the foot of the V-berth had been assigned, each to a child, for toys. They could only bring as many as would fit into those spaces. Cupboards under the V-berth held storage items like sheets and towels, soap and toothpaste, and pharmaceuticals. Under the galley sink, there was a little space to squeeze sponges, scrub brushes, soaps, and cleaners.

Behind the galley settee's back cushions, you found cupboards. Lift the settee's bottom cushions: more storage. Above the settee was *Hei Tiki*'s only bookshelf. It followed the contours of the boat, narrowing down to a space smaller than the smallest paperback. Readers that we were, we needed more space for books, so we bought two plastic tubs that fit, one atop another, under the head of the V-berth. Floor-level galley cupboards stored tools and spare parts—everything from nuts, bolts, and washers to backup pumps, alternators, and propellers. Many sailboats have a table dedicated to navigation. Not *Hei Tiki*. Under sail, the galley table became the navigation table. Charts were stowed in another cupboard. There was a place for everything, and everything had to be put back in its place.

Aft of the galley, under the cockpit benches, ran two quarterberths, each designed to sleep an adult comfortably. Above the

port quarterberth, electronics were mounted: the VHF radio—
in essence, our phone—and the GPS instrument, which reads
latitude and longitude signals off satellites. From the starboard
quarterberth, a door slid open to reach the back of the engine
and the propeller shaft.

David nurtured a minimalist vision of a boat, everything
stowed behind closed doors. But we just couldn't strip down
that far. Finally he agreed to dedicate one quarterberth to storage. "As long as you guys keep your stuff back away from the radio and the GPS," he said, "and as long as nothing gets shoved
into the other quarterberth. I've got to be able to get at the engine in an emergency."

Under ordinary circumstances, he would check the engine
from its front. You could tip the companionway staircase panel
open from the top and look in at the engine, or you could pick
the whole panel up and lean it elsewhere to get two hands on the
engine.

In lockers under the cockpit benches, we stowed our sails:
the mainsail, the jib, and a storm sail, a special small-scale main
that David had ordered for our trip. "You get out there in the
middle of a hurricane, and you don't want the big mainsail, even
reefed down," he had said.

"Hurricane?" I had asked. I thought we were going to sit
out bad weather.

"Got to be ready for anything," he had said. "It can come
up on you without your knowing it."

The day to sail finally came. Granddad drove us to the yacht
club. We hoisted our last bags onto the deck. "Bags below,"
commanded David. "I want the deck clear."

"Yes, sir," I said, half joking.

"She pulls a little to port in reverse now, remember,"
Granddad said as David turned the key to start the motor. He
seemed to have more to say, more advice to give, more little idio-
syncracies of this boat of his to tell us about. But he held back.
He had said yes long ago, and now we were on our own. He

walked down the finger dock and pulled a bow line off the pylon. "Catch, John," he called, and threw the line onto the deck.

"Susan. Stand back here and fend off," David called. I stood on the stern behind him, ready to push, but *Hei Tiki* backed slowly out of the slip without coming close to a pylon. David shifted into forward, and we were moving out of the marina. I looked back to the land we were leaving. John and Alison held close on either side. It was midmorning, and the air still smelled new. Granddad stood at the end of the dock, slowly waving. Waving and waving, until we couldn't see him anymore.

Eight hours into our journey, my face glowed, fresh from a day in the sun and salt wind. We had traveled forty miles down the Intracoastal Waterway, a one-day sail into our nine-month journey. We were cruising.

"Over there," David said, pointing to a sliver of an island in the middle of the waterway. A few trees straggled for existence. A heron preened. What made this a good place to stop for our first night out, I didn't know.

"Throw out the anchor," he told me.

I walked up the sky-blue deck of the boat and unfastened the anchor that lay on the bow. I could barely leverage it out over the water. It splashed down and sank fast. Rope slid through my palms.

"Is it hooked yet?" David yelled.

Hooked? Rope kept sliding. *What's hooked?* I hated to admit to David that I had no idea how to use the anchor. No idea how it worked, or what I was supposed to do to make it work. I looked down into the water. Brown and murky. I couldn't begin to picture what was happening down there. More rope kept sliding, faster.

David bolted up out of the cockpit, leaving the boat without a driver. He yanked the rope out of my hands, jerked on it, drew fifteen feet back onto the deck, then pulled up hard. I saw the line tighten, sensed the boat snap to.

I just stood and watched his motions. First of many lessons.

How to set the anchor. "You can't just throw it out and expect it to hold," he was saying.

I wanted to sass back, *How should I know?* But I also didn't want to admit any ignorance. He had been sailing all his life. I had been out—what?—five or six times, and always under the tutelage of someone more experienced. Here we were, intending to sail through the next nine months of our life together. I was excited, I was happy, but I was also terrified. *Would it always be like this moment, where he knows all and I know nothing?* I stashed that worry out of sight for the time being.

We had seen a lot of boats earlier that day, but once we anchored, it felt as if we were the only boat in the world. David stripped to swim trunks and dove in without saying another word. His slow, relaxed freestyle carried him toward the island. John bombed into the water and swam after his dad, his stroke jerky and awkward. He was still learning. Alison leapt right in, too. She bobbed up to the surface and looked back at me.

"Come on, Mom. Jump."

I stood on the bow of the boat, looking down into the water. How did I know what lurked beneath? A twisted tree stump, a sunken boat, some toothy water creature lying in wait? Irrational fears, but real. I was scared to jump into the water.

I stood on the edge of the deck of the boat, and the feelings washed over me. All the decisions leading up to this moment. All the planning, all the explaining, all the putting everything in order. All the late night conversations, all the weeks spent apart, working, we believed, toward the same goal. I had never lived on a sailboat. I had never sailed more than ten days straight. Would I like it? Could I do it? Was this journey a solution, or would it turn out to be just a new rendition of the same old problems?

I breathed deeply, and I jumped in.

No stump, no wreck, no creature. Just velvet, cold salt water enveloping my body, shocking off the hot day's sweat.

My new element.

2

Aground

On THE MORNING OF SEPTEMBER 9TH, WE struck out to the east to cross the Gulf Stream. It had taken us two days to move down the Intracoastal Waterway from Cocoa Beach to St. Lucie Inlet. Two nights we had anchored and slept aboard. Each one of us drove the boat for a while. We dropped and pulled up anchor. It all felt like a practice run until I saw the Gulf Stream blue.

Florida water, no matter how deep, no matter how broad, stayed a thick, murky brown. Two hours after leaving Florida behind, we seemed to cross a watery line, and suddenly we were sailing through deep sapphire blue. We were in the Gulf Stream, and it would take all night to cross it.

The Gulf Stream has a muscle to it. Like a maritime river, it runs up the coast of Florida. We were sailing across the grain, working to gain as little northerly direction as possible. I took my share of time at the helm. "We want to get due east, but we need to head more like one-oh-five or one-ten degrees to get there," David said, sliding out from beside me and going below to check our position.

The compass needle floated between 90° and 120°. As long as I steered the boat, I could rise above my nausea. I was wear-

ing a scopolamine patch just in case. I didn't want to succumb
to seasickness on our first overnight passage.

A light wind from the southeast gently filled the sail. I
leaned back so the sun touched my face outside the shade of the
bimini. The sail fluttered. "Fall off!" David cried from below.

Fall off? What was he talking about?

He pointed urgently left.

I looked at the compass: 128°. The sail was flapping. The
boom balanced precariously, as if ready to shift sides. I rammed
the wheel over to the left. The compass swung back to 100°,
90°, 86°. The sail refilled. The boom stiffened. David, standing
at the GPS, poked buttons and shot a look my way. "Keep it on
one-oh-five," he said.

"I'm trying." I stared at the compass. The needle swayed:
102°, 106°, 113°, 117°. I inched the wheel back over: 109°,
102°, 94°.

"Try spotting on something outside the boat," David said,
climbing up into the cockpit beside John. Alison stretched full-
length on the other cockpit bench, numbed by our movement
through the water.

I looked ahead. Nothing but sky and water. "Spot on what?"
I asked. It would be daylight tomorrow before we saw land.

"Find a cloud," said David.

Dense billows lined the horizon. Stray puffs floated closer.
"But they move," I said.

"Use one, then find another," said David. "The point is to
not watch the compass. You'll drive straighter that way."

I began to get the hang of it. It was two in the afternoon. We
had twelve or fourteen hours, David said, until we crossed onto
the Bahama Bank, then another eight or so across the Bank to
Powell Cay in the Abacos, the northernmost cluster of islands in
the Bahamas, where he wanted to anchor. I would drive for an
hour or two while David lay down and rested. Then he would
take the helm and I would lie down and try to sleep. Nervous,
excited, unsure of everything, I doubt I slept more than four
hours. David, too: he would rest on the galley settee, pulling his

knees up and lying on his side. Then he would jerk straight, look around, pull himself up to his feet, brace himself to balance, tip open the companionway, and shine a flashlight down into the engine. He was looking at the engine every half hour. Every time he did, the smell of diesel and the clatter of pistons and pulleys flooded out into the cockpit.

"Everything okay?" I yelled down.

He nodded. "You?" he asked. I nodded, and he lay back down. Although his eyes were shut, I could tell from his face he still wasn't sleeping.

After dark, I could use the stars as guides. Even they shifted, as the hours turned around, but they shone more steadily than the fleet clouds. Or maybe I was just driving more steadily. I held the helm from ten to two-thirty while everyone slept. I felt in control.

David took the helm before daylight. When I woke up, the colors, the proportions of the water had all changed. We had left the Gulf Stream. We were in the Bahamas, named by the Spanish for their "baja mar"—shallow waters. White sand, visible just twenty feet beneath us, reflected the light as a vivid turquoise. Gray-green chunks of island scratched the surface at a distance. The air smelled sweet and warm.

We let out our fishing line, trolling a spangled lure a hundred feet behind us. The line zinged around noon.

"It's a tuna!" John shouted.

"It's not a fish," Alison said, leaning astern. "It's a piece of trash caught on the line."

"It's a marlin!" John insisted. "Reel it in, Dad."

David planted his feet on the aftdeck and reeled in the fish. "Come here, Alison," he said, and he cupped his body around hers, letting her crank the reel. It was a shimmering, silver barracuda, sharp teeth bared as it fought against the hook.

"Can we eat it?" asked Alison.

"You don't eat barracuda," David said. "Ciguatera."

"Why not?" she asked.

"Ciguatera," he repeated. "It's a disease that some big fish carry. Eating barracuda can make you sick."

It wasn't dinner, but it was our first catch. David held the fish as each child posed for the camera. The barracuda dangled almost as long as they were tall.

"Now let's write about it in our journals, Alison," said John. This was the kid who always screwed up his face and acted as if to write was to thread thick yarn through a fine needle. Now he had something to write about.

Today we couhgt a "Barracuda" about 20 inches 3 to 4 pound Alison thouht it was a coke can. I spoted it and Alison reald it in and we took two pictures.

We reached Powell Cay just after 2 P.M., exhausted from lack of sleep yet invigorated by the prospect. Everything felt new, and all ours. Bright hot sun, cotton-ball clouds, an occasional gull. We anchored behind the crescent of an island, thirty feet out. A tumbledown bungalow, its timbers halfway to driftwood, was the only sign of any habitation. From the deck, we could gaze down through the water, ten feet deep, to a clear sand bottom. A fish swam by, crossing under our prow. Not another boat around.

Soon John splashed into the water, fins and snorkel on. Alison hesitated. He dove below, then crashed back above the surface, waving a starfish in the air. Alison applauded. She couldn't resist. She jumped in, too.

Between lack of sleep and the brisk salt air, we all felt hungry early. I scanned the cans. Cooked a cup of rice, then stirred in a can of tuna, a can of mixed vegetables, and a can of mushroom soup. Bland and salty, easy to eat. Just right.

Then it was time to do the dishes.

"This dishpan doesn't fit in the sink," I said to David. The blue plastic dishtub was twice as big as the galley sink. How could I fill it with water if it wouldn't squeeze under the tap?

"Doesn't matter," David said. He squirted in detergent, carried the tub up to the forward deck, and filled it with a bucket of seawater. "Endless supply," he said as he ruffled up suds and started scrubbing.

I rinsed, following his lead. As I tossed out the dirty water, I caught a glint of silver. I gasped. Our one and only serving spoon had fallen into the drink. I could see it, settling down to the sand. Warm light spread over the evening. The water was crystalline. I slipped on my bathing suit, plunged in, and recovered my loss.

The rhythms of our new life began rocking us gently. We slept and woke when we wanted. We dove right into the turquoise sea. We sailed to nearby Green Turtle Cay. We anchored amidst a dozen sailboats. To the west, vast sky and water; east, the little pink and white town of New Plymouth.

Going to town meant balancing four bodies in our shell of a dinghy. *Hei Tiki* was our house; the dinghy was our car. We always carried oars, but David was committed to the Seagull motor that he and Granddad had brought back to life.

He pulled the dinghy up by the bow line, right alongside the cockpit, and assigned seats. "Kids in front, Mom in the middle." One by one, we climbed over the lifelines and into the dinghy. One misstep could flip it over. John and Alison jostled onto the front seat. I dangled a foot from the coaming of *Hei Tiki* and stepped onto the dinghy's gunwale. "No! No! Middle!" David yelled. To pull myself back up, I grabbed the GPS antenna.

"Not that!" David yelled.

"What *can* I grab onto?" I snapped.

The kids giggled. I felt so stupid, and David wasn't helping at all. I slopped one foot straight down into the middle of the dinghy. Fiberglass creaked under me. Motor oil and saltwater sloshed into my sneaker. That couldn't be the way to do it, I thought, but at least I was in the dinghy.

"You hold the boat," David said. Chop in the anchorage kept the dinghy bouncing. I held onto the mother boat while he fiddled with the outboard. He wrapped the pullcord, primed the carburetor, choked the engine, and opened the throttle. I could feel him concentrating, as if intensity would help this temperamental motor start. With one percussive move, his hand whipped the pullcord and his elbow socked me square in the jaw.

I blurted out some noise of distress, but David's attention didn't swerve. He was already wrapping the cord for another pull.

"Are you okay, Mom?" Alison asked quietly.

"I will be," I gulped. I felt violated, and David hadn't even noticed.

David jerked again. This time I ducked and the greasy pull-cord thrashed him, striping his white T-shirt with motor oil. The old Seagull grunted into action. David tuned it to a high-pitched roar. I let go of *Hei Tiki*. Off we went to town.

New Plymouth, Abacos, Bahamas, traces its history back to the eighteenth century, when citizens loyal to King George fled a newly independent America. The town fills eight little city blocks, articulated by cracked concrete roadways and whitewashed stone fences. In early September, croton leaves and hibiscus flowers threw a green and red glow against all that white.

John and Alison kept asking questions.

"Why are the cars so small?"

"Where are all the other cars?"

"Did you see how many people were riding bicycles?"

"Why did a can of juice cost four twenty-five?"

"Do you think there were more black people or more white people there?"

"I saw lots of kids, and only one was wearing shoes."

"They had chickens in their backyards. What were those other birds, Mom? Turkeys?"

Their education had begun.

As had mine. David gestured over to a large metal buoy, a channel marker between us and shore. "Here's something interesting," he said quietly. It was early in the morning, before the children were awake. "Take a look at that buoy and tell me which way the current is flowing."

A light wind was ruffling waves up on the water. They traveled from right to left across the ball. I pointed left.

"Look again," said David.

I looked and shrugged my shoulders.

"The waves make it look as if the water is moving from right to left, but it isn't. The waves are moving in that direction, but not the water. But the water *is* moving. See that splash against the left edge of the ball?"

Now I could notice: the water lifted against the left side of the ball in a steady splash that I had disregarded because the contrary waves were so obvious.

"Current's flowing in opposition to the wind right now." He said it so precisely. "Tide's going out." I trusted David's knowledge, but it still looked like the water moved with the waves.

After three days, household rhythms began to settle in. John spent hours snorkeling. David spent too much time working on the Seagull. Alison drew picture after picture of *Hei Tiki*. I wrote in my journal in the morning, then read. I had just begun *Dove*, written by Robin Lee Graham, who at seventeen had sailed around the world.

A fast-paced outboard approached, throttling down as it neared our stern. Here came a couple, about our age, in a gray rubber dinghy. David called out a friendly greeting: "Come aboard."

"You're from Canaveral," said the man, nodding toward the stern, where a boat's name and home port are painted. He let his outboard idle, sculling off our stern. He smiled sweetly.

I leaned out to explain. "The boat's from Canaveral. We're from Virginia."

"We're from Wisconsin, but our boat stays in Canaveral when we're not on it. Ed and Marge on *Windsong*." He offered an outstretched hand. His wife smiled, too, her broad tan face shaded by a canvas hat that matched his. "Where you headed?" Ed asked.

"As far as we can get in the time we've got," David answered.

"And you?" I asked.

"We're meeting friends in Marsh Harbour and then heading to Eleuthera. We spend the winter aboard, then go back to

Wisconsin every summer. Just getting started this year. We'll
keep an eye out for you."

They kicked up a plume and blasted away toward town.
Marge leaned into the acceleration, holding the bow line of the
dinghy with one hand and her hat with the other. All their
moves looked so second nature. Would I ever feel that comfortable? Nice of them to come say hello, but I doubted we would
ever see them again.

"Look, Mommy, what I did." Alison held up her journal.
Every time she drew the sailboat, she added a new detail. Two
days ago, it was the anchor, which she drew like a star at the end
of a line stretching from bow to ocean bottom. Today's new fea-
ture was the binnacle.

"See what I wrote?" She turned the page.

---

the Boat is Fun. And you
have a good time.
And the Boat is ok.
I dond have a tv.
And I have My DaD.
And MoM to.

I gave her a hug. "Good job."

John showed endless patience in scanning the ocean floor. He
would paddle about, only his snorkel tube showing, then dive
and chase after any living thing. Then he blurted back up above
water, calling out names.

"Yellow grunt!"

"Surgeonfish!"

"Blue runners!"

"Alison, come quick, it's a trunkfish!"

"Stoplight parrotfish!"

Then one time he yelled, "Lobster!"

"Pick it up, John," David urged.

He dove down, came spluttering up for air, then dove down
again and came up holding a spiny little creature, green and red

speckles against a sand-colored shell. Only just larger than a crayfish, it was the smallest lobster I had ever seen. Its long antennae waved gracefully. Its fantail futilely pumped the air.

"That's a bug, all right," said David. "Good spotting. Bring it aboard and you can have it for supper."

"Isn't there a size limit?" I whispered.

David answered, "Let him taste success."

It was not easy, learning to work the stove.

They may have looked like gas burners, but they didn't operate like them. I knew that I was supposed to open the valve, release a squirt of alcohol, then close the valve and light that bit of fuel, to heat up the element. In a few minutes I could open the valve again, and the burner would stay lit.

All I needed to do was boil a pot of water. I opened the fuel valve just a second, closed it, and lit a match. Nothing. Tried again; same thing. I opened the valve longer, then shut it. This time, when I lit the match, flames whooshed a foot high, dancing like blue devils around the burner pan and trying to lick the varnish off the wood trim above the stove.

David saw what was happening. "Need any help?" he asked. But I could tell he wasn't worried. He was trying to leave me alone.

"What should I do?" I yelped. It seemed that everywhere I turned, I needed his help. He stood up. "Don't do it," I said. "Tell me how."

"Let the flames go out, then try again," he said. "It just takes a feel for it."

Two more tries. No go. No feel for it. "You do it," I finally insisted.

David opened the valve, closed the valve, lit the match. No go for him, either.

"Needs pumping," he said.

"Pumping?" Something more I had to learn.

He reached into a cupboard and pulled out an old bicycle pump. He opened the space below the stove, and pumped air into a small yellow tank.

"The alcohol is pressurized," he said. "Got to keep up the pressure. Try it now."

The burner lit right up.

I needed lessons on how to work the head, too. Marine toilets use salt water for flushing. On ours, a lever by the side of the toilet opened a valve to let salt water in. Flip that lever up and pump. Soon salt water flowed all around, inside the bowl. Flip the lever down. That closed off the incoming salt water, although you still could pump the toilet dry. The biggest mistake was to leave the lever up. That left salt water flowing into the bowl. It could overflow the toilet. It could fill the floor of the head. It could, theoretically, sink the boat.

I understood all that. I flipped the lever up, filled the bowl with a few inches of salt water, flipped the lever down, and sat down. David and the kids just pooped overboard, but I needed my privacy.

Finished, I pumped and hoped the stuff would quickly disappear. Then I flipped the lever and pumped the bowl dry. Still a little left in there. Lever up, water in. Lever down, water out, washing away the last of my morning dump. Lever down, toilet cover down. Wash my hands and on to the day.

Later that morning, I noticed that the head smelled bad. "You're not flushing," David said.

I felt like a child being taught to use the toilet. Was there anything on the boat I could do without lessons from my husband?

He flipped the lever up and pumped. "The stuff has a long way to go once it leaves the bowl." He flipped the lever down and pumped more. "You can almost feel it leave the system," he said. "There. I guarantee you. It won't smell anymore." Begrudgingly, I accepted his advice. From then on, I pumped at least twenty times after the shit went down.

That evening, we heard the thump of reggae music after dark.

"Friday night!" David hooted.

"Is it Friday?" I had lost track.

"Who cares?" he said. "Let's find the party."

"All of us?" John asked.

"Sure," said Dave. "Family outing." We followed the music to an open-air bar where a dozen other customers drank Kalik beer from the bottle or rum punch from plastic cups. We ordered Cokes and Kaliks. A tall black Bahamian, dressed in slinky purple, worked the buttons of a keyboard and a drum machine and crooned predictable numbers: "Kingston Town," "Red, Red Wine," "No Woman No Cry."

"Let's dance," I said, taking David's hand. He hesitated, then moved toward me. It had been years since we had danced anywhere but the living room, and rarely there.

The singer started up a new song:

> *Abaco people, shake their bodies*
> *Abaco people, love their bodies*
> *Abaco people, shake their bodies*
> *Abaco people, love their music*

I started swinging hips and shoulders. He closed his eyes, smiled, and leaned back, satisfied. Then he reached out and took my hand again. We moved naturally with these rhythms. I spun around and glimpsed the children. Alison gazed at us, mouth wide open, entranced by our rhythm and romance. John looked down, pretending disinterest, but shot curious glances our way.

We all had fun until we returned to the boat and it came to bedtime. "John got to sleep in the cockpit last night," Alison whined. "It's my turn." It was ten o'clock. We were all tired, but who slept where was becoming a family issue.

We had five berths to choose from: the V-berth, the center berth in the galley, the starboard quarterberth, and the two narrow cockpit benches. Every night we pulled sheets out and spread them on our chosen berths; every morning we folded sheets up and put them away. I had assumed, before we started, that David and I would share the V-berth. But from our first night at anchor on, David had slept in the cockpit. "I can hear what's going on, see what the boat's doing better from here," he had told me.

"We're not going to sleep together?" I had asked. I wanted

the comfort of the V-berth. The cockpit benches were too narrow for me. But this plan put us at opposite ends of the boat.

"I'll come visit," he had said. He hadn't yet.

John and Alison had fought every night over the second cockpit bench. Tonight, without a word, John had fallen asleep on it.

"John, move," Alison insisted, shoving his husky eight-year-old body with her six-year-old frame. John kept his eyes closed with a vengeance, knowing that passivity would work.

David intervened. "Why don't you sleep out here tonight, Alison? I'll go up with Mom."

Alison hugged David. He helped her tuck sheets around the cushion while I went to spread sheets across the forward berth.

"That is, if I'm invited," David said into my ear.

"Please do," I answered. I was already under the covers, wearing nothing but a T-shirt. He climbed in behind me, curving his body against my back. His hand cupped my breast, then fingered my nipple under my shirt. I felt him press up against my bottom and grow. I nudged in closer, reached between my legs, and pulled him through and up into me. He was so ready. I wanted to dance slowly, and he had already come. It had happened a lot in my life. "Too fast," he whispered. "Sorry."

"Good to be close," I sighed. I felt him fade away.

I lay awake a long time after. A breeze rustled through the rigging and curled down the hatch onto our faces. Stars shone brightly. Small waves rocked me to sleep.

In that first week in the Abacos, I began to notice the sailor's sky. On land, objects intrude upon the horizon. Trees and buildings, hills and mountains, crowd the edges, so that we look at the weather through only a peephole of sky.

On the water, nothing lies between you and that line where the ocean meets the sky. You see weather that is distant in both space and time. You see vast clouds on an even vaster blue. You see discrete precipitation systems. A faraway rainfall shows as a vertical field of gray, as if an artist had taken charcoal and sketched parallel lines joining cloud and ocean. You can see the edge of new weather coming in. You can feel the wind. By its force, you know how fast the weather is changing. By its direction, you know whether those changes are heading your way.

"Lightning," David said one morning. "Lightning in those clouds over there." The clouds' underbellies loomed ominously black, but they seemed remote, traveling in another direction. "I would feel better if we were over in Black Sound." He pointed toward a protected lagoon.

"What's the advantage?" I asked.

"More boats. Taller masts to draw the fire."

"You sure that storm's moving in our direction?" I just wanted to stay put.

"Lightning worries me," he said.

I capitulated. Once the anchor was up, David said, "I'll drive. You spot." My job was to stand on the bow and look ahead for shallows or coral heads, which threw up telltale hues from underwater. David had sailed these waters many times, and he knew the colors. I was still learning, and nothing was second nature.

David was already driving fast, whipping around into the mouth of Black Sound. I shot a look back. "I don't know how," I stuttered, but the wind whisked my words away. I stared down, trying to glean an answer from the water. Then I squinted and stared ahead. We were coming into the narrow sound entrance. The water looked yellow up ahead. *Yellow?*

A Boston Whaler with big outboards zoomed by us on the left; a motorboat, coming out of Black Sound, passed us on the same side. Both boats seemed to have lined up between a row of motley buoys: red ball to the left, yellow jug to the right, striped bobber to the left, black bobber to the right.

I dashed back so David would hear. "That way. I think they're markers."

"No, those are moorings." He kept on driving.

Then yellow got closer. Then shapes on the bottom. I was in the midst of forming words when the boat lurched. I could hear it: fiberglass hull grinding into coral bottom. Yellow cauliflowers bloomed just beneath us: we were stuck hard on coral in three feet of water.

Guilt, anger, fear, accusations, excuses tumbled through my brain. David sprang into action. "John! Get my mask and fins!" He was already in the water, frantically checking for damage. The boat listed helplessly. I raced up and down the deck, unsure what to do. David sputtered up to the surface, shouting, "Second anchor! Jib halyard! We can kedge off."

"Jib halyard, jib halyard," I said under my breath. I had to think these names through consciously. "This one?" I asked, uncleating a line at the foot of the mast.

"Other end!" David shouted.

Other end. Again I had to think it through consciously. The line ran up the mast, then down the forestay to the bow. I dashed to the bow and unclipped the other end. David attached it to an anchor. "When I signal," he told me, "crank as hard and fast as you can." He swam out two boat-lengths, dove down, and set the anchor.

I was beginning to understand. Anchoring by the halyard, we were pulling on the top of the mast, trying to pry the boat off the hard bottom. I threw my whole body into cranking.

Meanwhile, other boats moved in and out of Black Sound, every one of them inside that line of buoys. Some people waved; others pointed; and some went by without even looking. One midsized Whaler slowed down and approached us. I turned away. I didn't feel like talking. David was swimming around the boat now, examining its ever-more-revealed underside. Then I noticed another body swimming beside him.

"No damage done," said a voice distinctly Bahamian. His wet T-shirt stretched over a ruddy tan, a middle-aged man reached out to shake David's hand. They stood knee-deep in the water. "James Saunders," he introduced himself. "It's noon now. Low tide's at two. You'll be off by four."

The boat was leaning twenty degrees now. The cauliflower coral almost grazed the water's surface. The tide had dropped so that ten feet ahead of us, a crag stuck up out of the water, asserting how wrong we were to try to enter Black Sound this way.

"You've got youngsters aboard, do you?" said James Saunders.

It was the first I had even thought about John and Alison since we went aground. Amidst the panic, they had hidden in the cabin. Between the yelling of their parents and the dizzying angle of the boat and the threat of damage to their home and dreams, the children had been terrified. Now they peered out of the cockeyed quarterberth.

"Why don't they come home with us?" suggested James Saunders. "We have a television."

James signaled to his wife, Marilyn, a tomboy grandmother with gray hair and glasses. She brought their Whaler gently up to our stern and helped John and Alison aboard. The Saunders' house perched above Black Sound, so I could watch as they walked up the dock to the sliding glass door. The children didn't even look back.

By low tide, *Hei Tiki* leaned pathetically. Just trying to stand in the off-plumb galley made my head spin. So I perched on the edge of the cockpit. I wasn't sure what to say to David. A knee-jerk "I'm sorry" started to form, but I held back. It wasn't just my fault. We had run aground together. We were both to blame.

Once assured there was no damage, David used the opportunity. He checked the through-hulls. He scrubbed the bottom. He patched a leak where the centerboard drew up into the keel. Then he turned to the outboard, which was getting harder to start every day. Somehow, at that awkward angle, he dissected it into greasy parts and put them back together again.

By four o'clock *Hei Tiki* had started to right itself, but we were still stuck hard on coral bottom. Time moved so slowly, it felt as if we would never float again. I rowed over to the Saunders' to retrieve the children.

"I don't want to go," Alison said when she saw me. She dove facedown into the sofa where she sat, watching TV.

"They don't have to leave yet," said Marilyn Saunders. An American woman half a generation older than I, she was a look-you-in-the-eye Midwesterner. She and James, a white Bahamian from one of New Plymouth's founding families, had met in Chicago, where he had run a roofing business. Now they lived in the Abacos year-round. "There is so much we do not know about the ocean. It fascinates me," Marilyn said. "James and I spend whole days out on the water. We eat from the ocean every day." She was so quiet and compelling, I could see why Alison didn't want to leave.

But by now the mast of *Hei Tiki* was nearly vertical. I said we really had to go. To top off their generosity, James and Marilyn Saunders gave us lobster tails from their freezer, avocados, limes, and bananas from their trees. I felt overwhelmed, unable to return such a wealth of favors.

The children boarded glumly, much preferring surrogate grandparents, television, and a living room sofa to a cramped little boat still stuck on coral. Their spirits lifted when, at 5:12, the boat rocked gently. We were afloat again.

"What did you do all day?" I asked John and Alison.

"We had lunch. We went to see their neighbors' puppies. And we watched television," Alison answered.

"There wasn't much to watch," John grumbled. "They just got a VCR, but they don't have any videotapes."

A light went on. We had brought a dozen videotapes for barter or for gifts. At dusk we dinghied back over, videotapes in hand. "Thanks for being their home away from home," David said to James and Marilyn. From their dock, we could clearly see the channel we had missed.

"It happens at least once a week," James said. "Those aren't much for channel markers."

"Should have listened to my wife," said David. He chortled with James, man to man.

At least he said it, I thought to myself. I felt quietly vindicated. We never talked about it, not that day and not until several months later, but in his comment to James, I saw that David might be willing to factor my judgment into his sailing plans.

3

Taking the Helm

WE SAILED ON TO MARSH HARBOUR, THE ABA-cos' biggest city. Just one day there made me feel claustropho-bic. It was a protective harbor, with no view out. The sky closed in, too, with low, gray clouds. The harbor water looked black and murky. David and Alison took an evening swim and came back chafed by jellyfish. We were ready to get out of there.

I stood on the bow, poised to pull up the anchor. David sat at the helm, turning the ignition key.

Click.

He turned it again.

Click.

Dead battery. We weren't going anywhere.

Although a sailboat, *Hei Tiki* still needs power. It has a sys-tem like an automobile's. The battery kick-starts the motor, and the motor charges up the battery. Photovoltaics give the battery a boost. We used power for lights, radio, GPS, water pump, bilge pump, refrigerator. Looked like we had used too much.

David heaved the companionway aside, reached deep, and yanked on parts in the engine. "Turn!" he commanded. Click. The motor wouldn't start.

David lit a cigarette and looked out across the harbor.

"What can we do?" I asked.

"Battery's dead."

"How did that happen?"

"Ran the refrigerator too long. Too many lights at night."

"But what can we do?"

He didn't answer.

"What are we going to do, Mommy?" Alison asked in a small voice. I patted her knee.

Looking off, smoking his cigarette, David seemed so far away. He was thinking, but he wouldn't say what.

"Will the photovoltaics build up enough power?" I asked.

"Not without sunshine."

That was obvious.

It was obvious as well that we weren't getting anywhere in the conversation, either.

Gray clouds above dissolved into rain.

When it rained, *Hei Tiki* shrank. The bimini curtains kept us dry through a sprinkle, but a downpour forced us inside. Four of us shared the same little patch of floor.

"I'm sopping wet," Alison said. She sat on the edge of the starboard quarterberth, where a trickle of rain funneled down straight onto her head.

"My ear hurts," John said, his face drawing up with pain. He had been battling swimmer's ear.

David slid down into the quarterberth and cupped a pillow over his head.

The weight of the morning landed on me.

We had been on the boat for almost ten days, but we hadn't done any schooling. Maybe today was the day to begin.

"The books are getting wet," I discovered in horror, pulling books out of the bookcase where rain was puddling. I stuffed a kitchen towel under them.

"I want to play a game, Mommy," Alison said.

"This is school time, Alison."

"No." She stomped the short space forward and hid in the V-berth.

"John, shall we read?"

"Play Scrabble."

"Scrabble later. After school."

"My ear hurts."

"I'll get you some Tylenol."

"No." He stomped forward, too.

I felt the rain closing in on me. Big drops now, pounding hard. It drenched the deck, penetrated the cockpit curtains, drizzled into the cabin. The whole world was wet.

I felt alone and powerless. No one, nothing, was the way I wanted it.

So we waited. Five days of gray skies, occasional rain, occasional spurts of sunshine. Never enough to kick the battery into action. Five days without refrigeration. The cheese started oozing inside its plastic wrapper. The lettuce got limp. The beer was warm, but we drank it anyway. After dark, we read by flashlight. We could hand-pump water in the galley sink, but without the water pump, no showers. It was mid-September, still hot and muggy. My armpits felt sticky and started to stink.

"John! Give me a hand here," David said one of those gray mornings. "Half-inch socket wrench." The Seagull lay in pieces on the lazarette again. Half the time it wouldn't start.

"The what?" John asked, looking at me.

I rummaged through David's tool bucket, handed the wrench up to John, and he handed it to David.

They put the Seagull back together again but it still wasn't running well. "Let's take it ashore," David said. "We can work better on solid ground." He lifted the Seagull and cantilevered it out to John in the dinghy.

"John can't lift that motor," I shouted. Even as I said it, John reached up, caught the outboard with his chest, and dropped it down onto the dinghy seat.

When David stood up, pain flashed across his face. He doubled over. I rushed forward, hands out, ready to catch or embrace him. "No big deal," he muttered, deflecting my gesture.

Eight years before, David had damaged a vertebra while siding our house. He resigned himself to a few chiropractic treatments, but then reverted to clenched-teeth stoicism. Sometimes exertion brought back the pain. The contortions brought on by running aground in Green Turtle must have pinched that nerve again. He hadn't said anything to me about it, but now, as he stepped into the dinghy, I saw him draw up into a tense twist.

He asked John to row. I watched them pull away. Soon it started raining again.

The sun broke back out again by noon, so we tried the engine at three. More clicks. "I suppose it would be possible to tow *Hei Tiki* over to a marina and plug in," David said.

"The Seagull could tow this big boat?" I asked, astonished.

"Sure it could," he said. "But I'll be damned if I'll let the whole anchorage know our battery ran down."

"Who cares what they know?"

"We'll get it going."

For someone so sure of himself, sometimes David surprised me. He was more worried than I was about what other people thought.

That night, John and David fell asleep in the cockpit, Alison and I in the forward berth. A full sky of stars shone above.

I awoke in pitch-darkness to rain stinging my face. I couldn't reach up and close the hatch: the windscoop was in the way. I climbed out of bed and over David in the cockpit, shaking him. "Dave, it's raining. Go inside." I stood on the bow, picking at the rainsoaked knots of the windscoop, rain pelting down hard now, drenching my hair and nightgown. I climbed back down to the V-berth and, now, both children. I shoved their bodies apart and lay back down between them.

Gray skies still hovered the next morning. I told David we needed to start school together. "This is a two-parent thing," I said.

"Right," he answered. "We'll do it. Today. One more cup of coffee."

The children were laughing together in the forward berth. "I've been on the boat for twenty years," John said in a mock-bass voice. He was holding a little teddy bear, nautically dressed, that Granddad had given Alison. He bounced it as he talked. "It has been ver-r-r-y interesting."

"How has it been interesting, Tootles?" Alison was dancing one of her two Barbie dolls around, puppetlike, too.

"Well, you see, honey pie"—here both children erupted into giggles—"you see, my boat is only two feet long, and I didn't bring any food, and I'm crossing the Pacific Ocean, and that's why it has been interesting."

"Un-hunh?"

"And I forgot to bring my clothes."

"I see," said Alison studiously. Then she bent the doll painfully forward at the waist, pulled her short-shorts down, pointed the trim pink plastic butt into the teddy bear's face, and blew a raspberry.

They laughed and tumbled in a hug.

"You start with Alison, I'll take John," David suggested. We had already agreed on the plan: he would teach math, I would teach language. We decided, instead of ordering a home-schooling curriculum, to wing it. We brought dozens of children's books, new readers and old favorites and children's novels I had always meant to read aloud.

"Let's start with *Frog and Toad Together*, Alison," I said.

"I don't want to read that book."

"This will be fun. Look at the pictures."

She turned her face away. John, with David in the cockpit, was writing numbers avidly. I wasn't getting very far.

"Why don't you choose a book, then?" I tried to sound upbeat. We looked in the book tub.

"I want this one." She pulled out her favorite fairy-tale collection.

"That's a wonderful book, Alison, but the words are too hard for you."

She hugged the book to her chest and made a pouty face.

"Let's read one chapter of *Frog and Toad Together*," I suggested, "then I'll read you a fairy tale."

She opened the book ceremoniously. I pointed to the words. She read, "One m-. . . ."

"Good. Go on," I said.

"One m-. . . ." she repeated.

"Do you know that word?" I asked. She shook her head. "Let's sound it out. Do you know these two letters?" I covered all but the "or" in "morning."

"Or," she said, and beamed.

"Good. Now put the sounds together." I uncovered the whole word, and she stared at the page.

"One m-or-. . . ." I modeled. "Now what? Sound it out."

"One m-. . . ." She hadn't even followed me through the first three letters. Her eyes flitted about the page, looking for clues in the illustrations. I patterned out the phonetics, pointing to the letters in the word. "M-O-R-N-ING. What do those sounds say when you put them all together?" She didn't follow. I said it more quickly. "M-O-R-NING. Hear it?" Tears were welling up.

"Morning," I finally said. I closed the book gently. "What fairy tale do you want me to read?"

Around noon, a familiar dinghy pulled up to our stern: Ed from *Windsong*. "Saw Dave on the dock yesterday. Thought we'd bring over a battery." He introduced his friend, Charles, steel jawed but friendly eyed. "Aboard *Alison J*," he said, pointing across the harbor.

"We have an Alison aboard," I said. Alison smiled shyly.

"Charles had this extra battery," Ed continued. He had a friendly, chatty way about him. "We thought we'd just hook it up and see if we can get you going."

"Get the engine going now, and we'll let it run all night," Dave said. All three laughed. Male humor. Three heads bent into the engine compartment. They poked, they jiggled, they discussed. They substituted Charles's battery for ours, and David turned the key.

Click.

More poking, jiggling, discussing.

More clicks.

"Can't you hand-crank this one?" Charles said. David grunted, pushing on something arm-deep in the engine, which ground around and pooted out one tiny explosion.

"Again!" came David's muffled voice.

They tried a dozen times, but the motor never fired more than once per try.

"Pray for sun, and thanks for trying," David said.

If it wasn't one motor, it was the other. "John, get the tool bucket," David said an hour later. "We've got to get back to the Seagull."

John stood in the cockpit, tool bucket in hand. He looked at me. "Where should I put this?"

"The dinghy!" David ordered.

John put the bucket down. He untied the dinghy from the cleat at our stern and fought the wind as he wrangled the little boat up toward *Hei Tiki*.

"Give me that line," David snapped. He pulled the dinghy up short, handed the line back to John, and tried to lift the tool bucket. His back gave way again. He doubled over. I ran toward him. My hand touched his on the bucket handle. We hoisted together, but I lifted most of the weight.

As they rowed away, I watched John, tense and uncomfortable. He repositioned the bucket in the dinghy, then glanced up at Dave to be sure he had done right.

We had two motors down, but David kept on going. He kept finding work to do. We had been flying an Old Glory windsock, a cheap nylon tube with blue stars and red and white streamers. We hoisted it up near the spreaders, but it had quickly frayed and knitted up with the line it hung on, fifteen feet up.

"John, get the bos'n's chair," David said late that afternoon.

"The what?"

"It looks like a swing. In the lazarette."

John rummaged past docklines, buckets, fishing poles, dive gear, and the tackle box, to bring up a wooden seat with a loop of rope strapped through it. "Crank me up," David said to me.

"Me?" I said. The very thought of him dangling that high gave me the creeps. He had already hooked the halyard to the seat. I gulped. He was standing on the boom, his butt on the seat, ready. I cranked down with my right hand, belaying the line with my left. David's feet dangled just above my face. Every turn of the ratchet lifted him another six inches. My right arm quivered. The work wasn't hard—it was the knowledge that if I let go, he would come crashing down. "Keep cranking!" David yelled. I glanced up. He was three feet shy of the spreaders.

"Mommy!" Alison called from inside the cabin. "I can't find my stickers." I framed my attention, deliberately not answering. Her voice rose. "I just had them yesterday. Where are they?" I shielded my eyes and looked up, then cranked.

My silence infuriated her. "Mom!" she cried.

"I can't talk," I panted. "See what we're doing? I can't talk."

"Slow down!" David yelled. "I'm at the spreaders." I squinted up at the sky and saw him unravel the windsock. I dared to cleat the line and let go.

"Mom!" she insisted. "Answer!"

"Coming down," David called. I removed the halyard from the cleat. The halyard squeaked around the winch. I controlled it and gave out more line, inches at a time. Lowering him felt even more risky than raising him, because it was only my muscle that kept the line from slipping free.

Outraged, Alison stood in the cockpit, now yelling right at me. David's feet approached the boom.

"Watch it—slow down," he said testily. He saw the competition, and it was a sore point between us. I always let the children interrupt us, he complained. It began with infant cries, then as they grew older, they found other ways that worked to pull me away from him. We could be in conversation, and I would break off mid-sentence, he pointed out, to answer a child. Then, the issue had been talk, somehow debatable; now it was physical safety. No question here. I had to pay attention to what David and I were doing. I could not turn away.

"You need to notice what's going on before you start demanding attention," I told Alison later. "I can't always stop what I'm doing for you." She stuck her lower lip out, but I could tell by the way she looked at me, she understood.

In the time I had found to be alone, I had been writing my first "Letter to Home." I wanted to describe the Gulf Stream passage—no adventure, just the feeling of sailing and the transition from home to here. I wrote in longhand:

> We seek from this sailing life what we have always sought for ourselves and our children at home: aids to reflection, reminders of why we do what we do, a sort of deliberateness, a chance to examine our lives, make them ever again worth living, in Bahamian waters or on our own mountainside.

Now I had to figure out how to transmit the piece to Virginia.

Alison and I explored the dusty streets of Marsh Harbour. I saw a placard hanging over a window: *Abaco Sun*. I had seen the little weekly tabloid for sale. I opened the squeaky door. No one was inside.

"Hello?" I called. Someone rattled around in the back. He came out and introduced himself: owner, editor, one and only writer of the newspaper. He had moved from the States twenty-two years ago. He and his wife had run the newspaper for almost ten. I asked about faxing. He pointed to Batelco, the phone company. There were two typewriters sitting unused in the front office.

"Could I use one and pay you for my time?" I asked.

"Go right ahead. You don't have to pay." On a rickety electric, without self-correcting ribbon, I copied my piece over one more time.

I thanked our host. "Anytime," he said.

————

That evening, David proposed we buy a new dinghy motor.

"I thought you fixed the Seagull," I said, playing devil's advocate. Secretly I was thrilled. I couldn't stand that loud, greasy motor.

"I fixed it for today. It will always need attention."

"How much would a new one cost?"

"The Yamaha dealer has a four-horse for just under seven."

"Seven hundred?"

"Wouldn't be any less in the States."

"But seven hundred?" Out of $10,000, $700 was a chunk.

"I think it's worth buying on credit," he said, and he started talking numbers. "I figure I've spent twenty-five hours working on that damn motor already. We've been out fifteen days. That's almost two hours a day. Ten hours a week. Too much."

"Not to mention the reduced quality of life," I agreed. "You can't put numbers on it, but it matters. You've got black stripes across every shirt you own. You hit me in the face every other start-up. When the motor's running, it's so noisy, we can't hear ourselves think."

I chattered on in support, but he had already decided.

The sun spread a swash of rose across the sky that night.

The next day I woke up wanting to phone home. I rowed through the still-quiet cluster of sailboats in Marsh Harbour. It was 7:15 A.M., not too early to telephone Kathy.

"Suze! Great to hear your voice. Everybody misses you."

The phrase struck me. I wasn't sure what to say. Was I missing anybody? I hadn't noticed. "How's everything?" I asked.

"One rent check deposited in full," she said. "That's all I have to report. Anybody sunburned yet?" We laughed. "You called just in time for the apple smash." Every year we pressed apple cider together. "Doesn't seem the same without you." The reds and oranges across the landscape, the smell of the first frost, the clank of the grinder, the taste of apples off the tree— memory served me a whiff of autumn.

What a different world. The distance between us seemed enormous.

That day, things happened fast. David bought the outboard. He zipped up to the stern of *Hei Tiki*, showing off the shiny new machine, sashaying around the boat and then slicing up along-side. "Starts right up," he called to me, beaming, and proved it; he pulled the crank rope once and the motor started humming. I gave Dave a thumbs-up.

The sun was baking by ten o'clock, pumping energy into the photovoltaics. By two-thirty, *Hei Tiki*'s engine revved. We left it on till after five to charge the battery. Ed and Charles came over, and we made plans to meet in a day's time and sail together to Eleuthera, further down through the Bahamas.

Bed wars erupted again.

"John got to sleep in the cockpit last night."

"But it rained. I had to come inside."

"That doesn't matter. It's still my turn."

John wrapped himself in a blanket, plotting squatter's rights. Alison grabbed the blanket out from under him. John yanked back.

"Both of you sleep in the cockpit," said David. "Mom and I will sleep inside." Our eyes met.

"But I feel so smelly," I whispered as David climbed in, naked, under the sheets. "I haven't had a shower or a swim all week."

He nuzzled my neck, then my armpit. "I love your smell."

"Even this smell?" I asked.

"Especially this smell." He pushed my T-shirt up over my head. Our hands swept over each other's body. His penis greeted my touch, pulsing and growing. I pulled him in quickly, the full weight of his body on top of mine.

"Is this okay for your back?" I asked.

He nodded, eyes closed, striking more deeply. My hips jabbed back at him, driven by some primal force brought out by the salt and the sweat and the feeling that we were mad and lov-ing, growing into our own.

That night, I dreamt I was pregnant.

The plan was to overnight at a jumping-off spot alongside *Windsong* and *Alison J*. Daylight dwindled as we joined them behind Lynyard Cay, a little lump of scrub and sand. From there, we three boats would take off for Eleuthera at first morning's light. To the east, dense cloud banks mustered over the Northeast Providence Channel, the water we were now set to cross. We were leaving the Abacos, northernmost of the seven hundred Bahama islands, sailing south and east to Spanish Wells, at the north end of Eleuthera.

David studied the yachtsman's guide by flashlight. "From here on down the coast of Great Abaco, there's no place we can put in," he said, handing the book to me. "Look at that coastline. No fallbacks. Once we leave here, we have to keep going until Eleuthera."

"How far is that?"

"Forty-five miles away. A good ten hours. If the weather blew up out of the east, it would be a bitch. We could duck in at Hole in the Wall"—he pointed to the tip of Great Abaco, twenty miles south but ten miles west—"but that's no protection at all."

I tried to sleep that night, but fears tugged at me. I kept thinking of the clouds on the horizon, the length of this sail, the unfamiliar waters. Marge and Ed, on *Windsong*, seemed so nonchalant about it. They had done this sail before. "Sleep tight— see you at first light," Ed had crooned over the radio.

We woke before dawn. The gray hint of daylight backlit black clouds on the horizon. "Looks like weather to me," David said. "Might not be the day." We heard the clank of the windlass on *Windsong*, grinding up anchor. Clouds mushroomed.

David radioed over. "*Windsong, Hei Tiki.*"

"Good morning, Dave." Ed's voice, calm and reassuring.

"Morning from *Alison J*," Charles joined in.

"Are we off?" asked David.

"Ready over here," said Ed.

"You guys lead," said David.

"Roger," said Ed. All three signed off.

"You didn't say anything about the weather," I gasped.

David shrugged my comment off. "Anchor up." Another male thing: in a group of three, don't admit any doubts.

We surged past Lynyard. Third to up anchor, still we quickly gained on *Windsong* and *Alison J*. The water changed from turquoise to deep, cold blue. We raised the mainsail but kept the motor running, charging into four- and five-foot waves. In only twenty minutes, our companions had shrunk far behind us. "Shouldn't we wait for them?" I asked.

"I don't want to run the engine at anything less than twenty-six hundred rpm," David answered. "We'd never make it. We'd get beaten back." I sat at the helm, learning the rhythm of sailing to windward. Beat, beat, beat into the waves.

In an hour, *Windsong* and *Alison J* were specks on the horizon. We could hear voices on the radio but we couldn't make out the words.

"I think Ed must be holding back for Charles," said David. "He could haul out and kick ass harder than we are if he wanted."

"I don't like leaving them behind," I said.

"When it comes down to it," said David, "a skipper has to be responsible for his boat and his boat only."

We sailed on alone.

The midday sun beamed down, the clouds long gone. I drove all morning. After lunch, I had to pee. I could squeeze myself into the head and bounce on the toilet seat, breathing in the aroma of who-knows-what coming back up the valve. Or I could do as my friend, the merchant mariner, showed me: hold onto the rigging and hang over the side. I pulled off my shorts and underpants, grabbed a wad of paper towel, and walked up the deck.

"What are you doing, Mom?" asked John.

"What does it look like?" I said. "I'm peeing." The boat was heeling over, so the leeward rail was only two feet from the water below. I grabbed the shroud tightly and hung over. Sea foam splashed my butt.

"Mom's taking a squit-squat!" John sang.

The waves toned down as the day progressed, but the wind

still blew from out of the east. I took the helm again. "Point up," David said. "Cut as close to the wind as you can."

I was beginning to understand. Slice the wind at just the right angle, and the sail fills well. Drive into the wind, and the sail luffs: it flutters, it flaps. That's when I should fall off. Fall off the wind, that's the expression. Back off. Ease up. Let the wind fill the sail. I was getting the feeling.

Late in the afternoon, we reached Spanish Wells, Eleuthera, an all-white town, proud, wealthy, and industrious. We spent the night and then moved on, rejoining *Windsong* and *Alison J* at Egg Island, one of the hundreds of uninhabited coral isles in the Bahamas.

The men bonded over fishing. Ed became an avuncular spearfishing companion for John, pointing out promising holes in the coral. Charles dove thirty feet down, fearlessly gripping a coral ledge with one hand and a spear with the other.

While they hunted distant reefs, Alison and I joined Marge and Gert, Charles's wife, wading ankle-deep up an estuarial creek on the island. We poked at the chitons, armored invertebrates embedded like living fossils on the salt-splashed rock. We heard goats bleat and tried to penetrate the dense bush to find them. Marge found conchs, which we added to the spearfishing catch of seven lobsters and three groupers for a feast aboard *Windsong*.

"Can I help?" I asked Marge, stepping down the companion-way. A cast-iron fry pan held sizzling fish fillets. A stainless steel stew pot was ready for lobster tails. Gert was scrubbing dishes in a sink full of hot soapy water.

"Just make yourself at home," said Marge.

I looked around. Cushions, upholstery, trim—everything seemed showroom quality. A roomy living area, dining table and banquette for eight. An antique map of the Caribbean framed on the wall. A computer and a printer; radio, stereo, speakers. I poked my head forward. Their berth looked like a real bed, with striped sheets and a puffy comforter. Their head looked like a real bathroom, with soap in a shell-shaped dish.

"Big, isn't it?" Gert said to me.

"How big is *Alison J?*" I asked.

"Thirty-one."

We gave each other knowing looks. At forty-two, *Windsong* felt three times as big and ten times as elegant as *Hei Tiki*.

"That's why we have dinner on *Windsong*," said Gert.

"For dessert, we have something very special," Ed said to Alison. "If you guess, you get double."

Her face lit up. "Ice cream!"

"What a good idea," he said. "Marge, do we have any ice cream?"

Marge joined the game. "No, no ice cream. Guess again."

"Cake!" Alison said.

Ed and Marge shook their heads no.

John guessed. "Cherry pie!"

"Apple pie! Pumpkin pie!" Alison cried.

"I'll just have to reveal the mystery dessert," said Ed. He zipped open a plastic bag.

"Cookies!" the children cheered.

First cookies they had seen in weeks. Ed doled out one Oreo each, playing stingy, then handed the children the bag.

Ed proved equally generous with water. "You need it more than we do," he said. *Windsong* and *Alison J* were sailing back together to Fort Lauderdale, while we were continuing southeast, down through the Bahamas. They would have plenty of places to get water, while we weren't sure where the next source of water might be.

To a sailor, the gift of water is a gift indeed. *Hei Tiki* held 130 gallons. We had started out full, but had no gauges to know how low we were going.

When Ed and Charles arrived the next morning with four five-gallon jugs of water, I was cleaning. At home, I had never been much of a housekeeper. There always seemed to be something better to do. But on the boat, I had time. And it was so easy. I could stand in one place and reach practically everything. I had washed the breakfast dishes, scoured the sink, wiped out the refrigerator, swept the floor, and it wasn't even nine o'clock yet.

"Let's get this water into the tanks," David called out. There was an edge to his voice, as if someone was supposed to be helping him already.

We had to fill the water tanks through a single, frustratingly small opening on the foredeck. A hose fit in, but this time we were pouring from buckets. "Get a funnel," David commanded John. He bent awkwardly, protecting his back, and hoisted each bucket. I was scouring the galley countertop. "Watch for overflow," David shouted down. A portion of the galley floor lifted out to give access to electrical wires, the centerboard cable, and water pipes. If we overfilled the tanks, water coursed through that opening.

I opened the floorboard and went back to work. I could hear David barking at John on deck. I rehearsed the speech that had been building for the past week. How I knew that things had been hard on David, what with the motors and his back, and how so much of the work fell on him, but that he didn't have to take it out on us. He seemed so grumpy and short-tempered. I thought this trip was supposed to be fun.

Then I noticed water streaming under the floor. I flung my sponge into the sink as David burst down the companionway, bumping me aside. "What's the matter with you guys? Doesn't anyone watch what's going on? We're overflowing."

For a moment, I stood speechless.

Then I exploded.

"I can't stand this!" I yelled. "I can't do anything right."

David looked up at me. John stood on the companionway, funnel in hand. Alison was in the cockpit, watching. I kept raging.

"If it's going to be like this," I said, "let's just go home."

I stormed up through the cockpit and left all three of them as far behind as I could—which was only up to the bow. I cried and cried, until crying began to feel good. More feelings revealed themselves to me. About David's impatience. The feeling that he knew everything and I knew nothing. Where was the fun? I was trying hard. But I had my fears. My insecurity. I didn't really know how to sail. Could I trust David? I had no choice. And now we were taking off on our own again. I missed my friends. I cried some more.

John was the first to come sit beside me. "Mommy, why do you want to go home?"

I hugged him and looked east.

"I don't think we should go home," he said.

"You don't?" I asked quietly.

"We saved up all this money. I think we should keep going."

Alison must have been watching, listening. She came and sat by my other side. I drew my children close to me. We all looked east. From beside the boat came the gentle snort of a dolphin, gliding silently, breaking the surface to draw in a breath of air, diving back under, and swimming on.

I chose my words carefully at dinner. "I am sorry for what I said. I don't think we should go home. I do think we need to learn to work together better."

Later David spoke, too. Against long breaths drawn by two sleeping children, he said, "I shouldn't have yelled at you. That water system baffles me, I have to admit it."

"It's not just the water system."

He was silent.

"We're just learning, and we're doing our best," I continued. "You're so hard on us. It feels as if you're not enjoying yourself, and you're taking it out on us."

Again he was silent, looking down.

Then he said, "Maybe it's because I have been worrying too much about things. I'll watch it." He didn't say much, but it mattered, coming from Dave.

Late that night, I roamed the cabin by flashlight, too edgy to sleep. All was silent, save the occasional splash of the dinghy,

tied behind us, and the steady ticking of the clock on the wall. I
fingered through David's log book out of curiosity. What did he
write there? I came upon an entry dated one week into our sail.

> I continue to be concerned for the seaworthiness of *Hei
> Tiki*. The two leaks we experienced during the crossing
> caused mild concern for me. Such concern meant that I
> got little rest during the crossing. Susan, J, & A seemed
> unconcerned by the passage.

"Seaworthiness"—it was a concept I had not even considered. Never had I considered the possibility that *Hei Tiki* was
not ready for this journey. And what of David's crew? Were we
considered seaworthy, too? Never had David spoken these
doubts aloud to me. Or had he spoken, and I just hadn't regis-
tered? No wonder that he sometimes snapped. He was carrying
this burden of seaworthiness silently, inwardly, alone.

We left the anchorage an hour past sunrise. South through Cur-
rent Cut, a slender pass between islands, then into the Bight of
Eleuthera.
　　"There might be some coral heads the first hour," David
said. "You spot and I'll drive."
　　"I'd rather drive," I said.
　　"Okay. I'll spot. You drive."
　　I stayed at the helm all morning. The waves were gentle
and the wind filled the sail. "We can put up the jib once we're
through the cut," said David, and the children hurrahed. They
liked it when we flew two sails.
　　We approached Current Cut by eleven o'clock. David had
been studying the yachtsman's guide. He handed it to me.

> Nearing the eastern entrance to the cut, you will see a line
> of six small, rocky cays. . . . Off the end of these cays is a
> submerged rock with little water over it, and immediately
> beyond is the deep water of the cut itself. Don't allow

yourself to slip too far east of these cays, because the water gets very shallow. Leave the submerged rock to port and, once in the channel, turn to port and run through . . .

I read the passage over and over.

"That's from the east," David said.

"We're coming from the west," I said. He nodded. I had to read the directions backwards. I closed my eyes and twisted my body, trying to enact the passage. There was more: "slack tide," "nasty chop," "sometimes affected by the wind."

"Got it?" he asked.

"No."

"Read it again."

I tried. I squinted ahead, comparing the sketch in the guide to real shoreline features. Six rocky cays?

And still the boat surged on toward the cut, shoreline features coming close too quickly.

"We've got to slow down so I can understand what we're doing," I panicked.

"Rock on your right, hug the shore to your left, follow the channel, and take a sharp right on the other side. That's the gist of it," said David. "I'm going forward to spot. You'll do fine."

"But Dave—" I called out. He was already on the bow, grasping the forestay. With his right arm, he motioned straight ahead. He looked back at me, smiled, and nodded approval.

The tide was rushing out, pouring through the cut with us. I could see the water rippling, churning, swirling ahead. As I swooped the boat into the narrow opening, the current picked us up and carried us faster than we had ever moved before. David jerked his hand to the right. I gripped the wheel and leaned into it. Rocky shore to the left of us, shallows to the right. The boat teetered like a shaky ice skater sliding down an icy slope, no way to stop. We burst through to the other side.

"Right!" David gestured madly.

"I'm turning!"

We made it. The boat sank down like a calm sigh. We passed the six rocky cays, then skirted along the shoreline. David looked back, holding thumb and finger in a circle. Perfect. He motioned a turn. I nudged the wheel and headed *Hei Tiki* out into deeper water.

I had taken the helm, and we were going somewhere.

4

Into the Squall

I SWIM IN CRYSTAL-BLUE WATER WITH MY CHIL-dren on either side. We hold hands. Sometimes one pulls back, so that we seem to make no progress. Then one surges forward, pulling us all through the water. I love the feeling, holding hands as we swim.

Then the moment collapses. Alison's snorkel fills with water. She chokes and struggles and needs my help. John breaks away and dives below the surface by himself. Alison climbs onto my shoulders, clasping tightly around my neck. She weighs me down so, I struggle my mouth above water to gasp a breath. John comes up from behind, grabs one of my flippers, and pulls.

I shake free. I swim hard, two circles around the boat.

By myself.

We sailed down the Bight of Eleuthera under blue skies edged with clouds. Suddenly the trolling rod twanged.

"Fish!" I called out. David reeled in the fish: a speckly, iridescent mackerel, almost two feet long. First edible fish we had landed. David squatted on the lazarette. Rinse, slice, guts overboard. Rinse, slice, fillets in the fridge.

Then he said to the children, "Take a look at this."

David probed the fish head with the knife point.

"Ooh, yuck, that's the eyeball," said Alison.

"Can I smash it, Dad?" said John.

David dissected deeper and brought forth a luminescent pearl, displaying it on the tip of the knife.

"That's the brain?" asked Alison.

"It's smaller than the eyeball," John noticed.

"What does this say about a fish's senses?" said David.

John picked right up on it. "They see more than they think."

That day's destination was Governor's Harbour, Eleuthera's largest town, halfway down the island's seventy miles. The square-shaped bay was created when developers attached nearby Cupid Cay to the mainland with a causeway, now a sandy road-bed lined with windswept casuarina trees.

"I'll anchor," I said, trading places with David. I liked driving, but I let him inch the boat into an anchorage. So many quick decisions had to be made, and he sailed more intuitively than I.

Our forty-pound Danforth-style anchor lay flat upon the foredeck. Twenty feet of chain and then three hundred feet of three-quarter-inch line stowed below, in the anchor locker. I pulled the chain and the first twenty feet of line up on board. I looked back to David.

With the engine out of gear, he was watching the water, waiting for the moment that the boat held still. He looked up and nodded. "Drop it?" I called. He nodded. I let go. I felt the anchor touch bottom and gave it more line. The wind was surging out of the east, and the boat promptly lined up and snapped back on the anchor. Line sped through my hands. I fought, chocking it on a cleat. The loops and twists didn't look right, so I unfastened them. The wind pulled more line from me. I chocked it again—loop around the back and over, loop around the front. It still didn't look right, but it held.

"John, let's put out another anchor," I heard David say. John played out the second line as David rowed out and dropped the anchor. "Great," he said to John. "How about a lesson in driving the dinghy?"

Half an hour later, John was buzzing across the harbor, revving up that new motor, seeing how fast he could drive. David sat in the prow, giving John full control.

Alison watched John enviously. She leaned into my lap. "I want to drive the dinghy."

"You will some day," I said. "Even I don't know how yet."

All day, those clouds built up in the east, thick and dense and ominous. Sharp winds kept blowing. "Wind's shifting," said David that evening. "Clocking around to the west. That's why it's gotten so rocky." When we had anchored, the water was calm. Now it had a chop, and the boat was pitching forward and back, as if bucking the anchor.

"I get to sleep in the cockpit tonight," decided Alison. "So I won't get seasick."

"It's my turn tonight," said John. He left it at that.

"Dad's going to sleep in the cockpit tonight, folks," said David. "I need to be where I can see what's happening with the boat."

"I'll get sick if I have to sleep inside," Alison insisted.

"You slept out here last night," John said. He shoved his sister and strode down into the cabin. He climbed back up the companionway, sheets in hand.

"Mommy, tell John he has to sleep in the cabin," pleaded Alison.

"It's my turn!" John yelled.

David ignored the whole interchange. It occurred to me that I could, too. "I'm going to bed," I said, and went to spread my sheets in the forward berth.

The bed war resolved itself when Alison discovered that she could, with only minor discomfort, angle her body in at the helm. The cushion was short and even more narrow than those on the side benches, but then so was she.

The clouds kept building and finally exploded into a violent thunderstorm just after midnight. I awoke to the sound of thunder and heavy rain. I crawled up into the cockpit, only half awake, and helped two wet children into bed with me.

John and I began doing school together the next morning. He pulled out Garfield. "You're smarter than that," I said. I pulled out *Mrs. Piggle-Wiggle.* "We'll read one chapter today." His face squeezed up into a grimace. "You start."

We read about Dick, who was so selfish that he didn't let anyone play with his toys. Mrs. Piggle-Wiggle's cure was to place signs on everything, his book, his ball, his bat: "This is Dick's—don't touch." We read paragraphs, back and forth, until John grew tired. "Now I want you to write something," I said. He groaned. On a new page in his notebook, I printed two instructions:

"Write down the problem Mrs. P-W helped solve."

and

"Write down Mrs. P-W's solution."

I handed the notebook to him.
"By myself?" John whined.
"That's how you write."
"I can't."
"Oh, you can, too."
"I want you to help me."
"You write something down all by yourself first, then I'll come help you."

He huffed resignedly. I busied myself in the galley and watched out of the corner of my eye.

"Let's see what you wrote," I finally said. He handed me the notebook without speaking.

It starts out about a boy named Dick. Dick is a very selfish boy *[here the "b" and the "y" had great flourishes].* Becuase when someone comes over to play he will say "thats mine" and not let them play with his toys.

"Good," I said, and read on.

Mrs. P-Wiggle gave Dick's Mom the Selfishness Kit, All the signs that say Don't Touch! The *[here he drew an arrow to indicate that the word 'signs' should appear again]* made *[divided over two lines thus: m-/ade]* Dick lonely. It made Dick learn to share his toys

"John, that's great," I said. "That's a real paragraph."

He couldn't care less. "Can I go drive the dinghy now?" he asked.

The weather was repeating its daily cycle: blue sky morning, afternoon clouds banking in the east. The wind still blasted and the waves still rocked the boat. Leaning out of the cockpit, Dave was chatting with a fellow cruiser. Randy—dark beard, faded rock 'n' roll T-shirt—was telling David how he and his wife had saved up for years to cruise the Bahamas. Two weeks into it, Hurricane Andrew intervened.

"Luckily, we had insurance," Randy said. "Actually came out ahead. Bought a few new pieces of equipment."

"Do we have insurance?" I asked David later.

"Couldn't even get it," he said.

"Why not?"

"Not worth enough to insure."

"It's worth plenty," I said.

"Not from the insurance companies' point of view. They want their claws in a hundred thousand dollar boat, not this old clunker. Dad used to carry insurance, but they canceled on him."

Alison's shrill voice cut through our conversation. "Give her back!" she cried. John dashed up onto the deck, dangling Alison's doll by one foot.

"Kelly wants to go swimming," he said, laughing. Alison

wrestled with him, trying to rescue her doll. He stretched out over the water, still dangling the doll. He was in full control and loving it. Alison wasn't tall enough to reach, and the more she pushed, the further John held the doll overboard.

I looked at David. "Your turn," I said.

"John," he scowled. "Give her back the doll."

"But Kelly put on her raincoat," John said mockingly. "She wants to get wet."

"John," David bellowed, and stood up. John shoved the doll into Alison's belly. She wrapped her in her arms.

"Kelly is *my doll,*" she said.

"I want a doll," John said, and I couldn't tell if he was mocking his sister or really meaning it.

Again that night, a storm raged through. I awoke to hear the curtain ties flapping fiercely. The wind was blasting. You could feel the rain coming, and it felt as if we could be blown away. I shook John. He climbed below. David and I shouldered into the wind together, untying the bimini curtains. I struggled to the foredeck, worrying about the anchor. David was already up there, shining a flashlight up the forestay that spans from the bow to the top of the mast.

"What is it?" I shouted at him over the wind.

"Frayed forestay," he shouted. Up near the mast, a strand of wire bent free of the stay. "Nothing we can do now." The storm dissolved into a downpour, and we crowded into the cabin together.

"I just noticed it this afternoon," he said as he toweled his head dry. "The forestay's made of seventeen wires, wound to-gether into one cable. We've got some strands working free."

"What can you do about it?"

"Replace the forestay."

"Sounds like a job."

He shrugged. "No big deal."

Rain pounded the deck. Wind shook the rigging. I fell asleep, listening.

We woke to another blue morning. After school, we took a walk ashore. Alison zipped Kelly into her backpack, with the doll's brunette head sticking out at an angle.

"Can I drive, Dad?" asked John. John jerked the motor on, then drove us smoothly across the harbor.

We walked up a steep cobblestone road, peering through croton and hibiscus hedges to see the houses where people lived. Land snails the size of my thumbnail crawled up stalks and under leaves in all the bushes. We followed a sandy road-bed to the crashing surf on the ocean side.

David lagged behind. He had told me his back was better, but now he was limping. He sat on the beach and took his shoes off. Atop one foot was an oozing wound.

"What's that?" I asked, aghast.

"Those damn flippers are too tight," he said. "They've rubbed a hole in my foot, and the salt water doesn't make it any better."

"It looks infected."

"Probably so. This one isn't, though." His other foot had a smaller sore.

"You should do something about that," I said.

"I took an antibiotic this morning," he said. "No big deal."

We had visited the ocean. We had bought potatoes and carrots at the grocery store. We had even ordered lunch, our first restaurant meal—pork chops, panfried gruntfish, peas and rice. While we ate, we had watched a mother goat and two kids frisk about the trash-strewn back alley. We were ready to move on.

A few thick clouds hovered in the east, but the wind and waves felt gentle. We would sail just to Rock Sound—twenty miles, an easy four-hour sail. To the chime of midday church bells, we drove out of the harbor.

"Nasty cloud," I said, pointing. It had all the signs of a storm. The heavy billow, the anvil shape, the height, that dark underbelly.

"But too far to the west," said David. "It'll miss us." He glanced up the forestay, where it was frayed.

I drove straight on. It all changed so fast. In minutes, the wind pumped up, the waves built, the dark cloud engulfed us. Rain thickened ahead, and I was driving into gray oblivion. The wind blew hard this way, that. Waves shattered across the bow. I kept trying to cut the waves at an angle, scared to meet them head on. But the more I edged it, the more the sail luffed, flapping uselessly.

"You've got to drive straight into it," David shouted. He grabbed the wheel as a wave jolted me sidelong. Lightning lit up the chaos. He jerked the boat right into the waves, slicing down their middle. Thunder exploded all around us. "You three. Down below!" he cried.

We scrambled—as if obeying that order might make the storm subside, as if we could escape the fear. We lurched single file, Alison, John, myself, toward the forward cabin. The forward hatch blew open like a door swung loose on its hinges. A torrent of salt water poured down from above. There below, drenched and helpless, lay Alison's doll.

Another wave doused me. I reached up and fumbled to hold down the hatch. Alison curled into a corner, eyes, mouth, and body shut tight. John stretched stiffly on the other side. I stood between them.

On the deck above the V-berth, the anchor swagged like a pendulum. In our nonchalance this morning, we hadn't bothered to tie it down. All forty pounds now flew with the motion, scraping the deck, banging both side rails relentlessly.

John erupted in words of anger. "You didn't tie the anchor down!" he started yelling. "It's scratching the deck!" He kept on shouting. At me. "Mom! It's all your fault!"

I was shocked and hurt. Maybe if I calmed him, his anger would subside. I rubbed his rigid back.

"Don't touch me!" he writhed. "You're hurting me." Against my instinct, I pulled back. The boat shuddered into a wave. Water rushed in on me. I braced myself, outside and in.

"Everybody be quiet now." I mustered a voice as calm as I could. "Quiet. Quiet." I stroked Alison's hair. She had not moved from her fetal curl. "Everything will be all right," I kept saying, like a mantra.

Time froze us in a snapshot of how each dealt with fear. John blamed. Alison introverted. I summoned some deep reservoir of composure. My calm came, too—I recognized as I braced myself in the cabin—from confidence in our boat and confidence in my husband. He would sail us through this terror.

But then I started worrying. Would it always fall like this, throughout our journey? David on the outside, battling every challenge? Me, the Mom, on the inside, keeping the children calm?

Dave's voice called me through the din. I worked my way, hand over hand, out to the cockpit. "I have to tie things down on deck," he cried into my ear. I grabbed the wheel and steered standing. The rain had slackened; the wind was not gusting so hard. The boat still plunged into the heart of the waves. My eyes flashed back and forth between those waves and David, crouching down on the foredeck, lashing tight the red plastic fuel jug that was thrashing loose.

John had followed me into the cockpit. He sat looking outward, face tight, arms entwined. Left in the cabin, Alison started shrieking—the first noise from her since we had entered the squall.

Wordlessly, we shifted. Dave took the helm and I went below. Churning motion. Being thrown around. Confinement in this tiny cabin. It was too much for me. I ripped open the door to the head and puked into the toilet, three, four times. Dry heaves in the end. Exhausted, I rested my head alongside Alison's trembling, wet body.

Finally we reached the far edge of the weather. It had felt like forever, but only forty minutes had gone by. "That's it," said David. "We can turn around now." I helped Alison back outside. I knew we would both do better in the air of the cockpit.

"Back to Governor's Harbour?" I asked, startled, but then I saw how close we were to the inlet where we had started. All that commotion, and we hadn't sailed anywhere.

Back at anchor, we didn't say much. We all just wanted to feel safe again. Each person quietly picked up: books, pencils, dishes, clothing, toys had flown through the cabin. It was an object lesson in why you stow things tightly before a sail. David went to buy beer and cigarettes. The children opted to go with him. Me, I didn't want to go anywhere. I just asked them to bring me a candy bar.

An hour later, the three of them returned, balancing in our little shell of a dinghy. David had to row hard through the stiff chop. John sat in the stern, his jaw set, toughing it out. Alison sat in the bow, leaning forward, gazing down into the waves. She looked so tiny, so vulnerable, so easily swept away.

"We could just sail the Bahamas," David said quietly that evening, after the children had fallen asleep. I felt my body loosen in relief.

We talked about the trade-off. Sailing the Bahamas for a year would mean short sails, anchorages within easy distance, people speaking our language. And home close by, if it came to that.

Our original plan—Puerto Rico by December, Virgins, Leewards, Windwards, and back—meant over three thousand sailing miles, with overnight passages across bodies of water that might prove to be much wilder than this one. How could we do it when a little squall sent the children into hysterics and me into nauseated convulsions, leaving David alone to drive?

But sailing the Bahamas seemed a compromise. It felt like giving up on the plan.

We talked more, and we agreed. We could move on and still reconsider. From Eleuthera, we could sail down the whole chain of the Exuman islands toward George Town, the next town south, about one hundred miles. In George Town, we would decide whether to sail further down-island.

———

The next day, life settled almost back to normal. Alison resisted reading. "I want to do math with Dad."

"No, I get to do math," John bullied. "You don't even know how to multiply."

"Alison does math first today. Time test on addition," said David. I pulled out *Mrs. Piggle-Wiggle*. John groaned.

"Okay," I said. "Today, instead of reading, we'll write our own chapter. What cure from Mrs. Piggle-Wiggle does our family need?"

John shrugged.

"How about a cure for a big brother who pushes his little sister around?"

John frowned. I let him sit in silence for minutes.

"Well?" he finally asked.

"Well?" I echoed.

"I don't know."

"She would probably figure out some way of showing the brother how much he really cares about his sister," I said. "Got any ideas?"

Of course he didn't.

"Here's one," I said. "Mrs. Piggle-Wiggle has a magic medicine. The mother gives it to the brother while he's asleep. When he wakes up, he's totally paralyzed. He can't move. His sister's the only one around. Is she going to bring him breakfast? Is she going to bring him toys to play with, or turn on the TV to his favorite show? She could ignore him, or she could help him. It's all up to her."

John grunted. It was too much like being lectured.

"Or here's another idea," I continued. "The sister goes to live with Mrs. Piggle-Wiggle for a week. She's not there for the brother to tease and torment. Not there for him to play with. At first he's overjoyed. But after two or three days, he actually begins to miss her. After a week, he's begging his mother to bring her home."

"I want to do math," John said. He never wrote a word, but maybe he learned something.

———

"I don't want to read," Alison grumped at me. I had chosen an easier book this time. She had shouted with glee, doing numbers with David earlier this morning. Why did she turn nasty on me?

"Forget it," I snapped. John had used up my patience. I picked up my journal and started writing furiously.

"Mommy, where are the postcards we bought?" she quietly asked me. I reached up from where I was sitting and handed them over.

"Mommy, where is a pen?" I pointed to the canister where we kept pens and pencils.

"Mommy, how do you spell *Hei Tiki?*"

I called out the letters, then looked to see what she had done. In careful print, across the full width of a postcard. she had written to my mother:

Dear Nonny We are on a Boat. The Boat is Blue. I am good. We are on Hei tiki. How are You love Alison

---

"That's wonderful, Alison," I said. She had written five sentences. "We'll mail it as soon as we can."

"I'm going to write another," she said. "To Kathy."

"This time, only write on this half of the postcard." I showed her. "The stamp and address go over here."

She looked dismayed. "I have to do Nonny's over."

"We can mail it in an envelope."

"No," she insisted. She took another postcard and squeezed the same words onto the left-hand side. Then she began another. "Dear Kathy," and she wrote the same five sentences.

She writes more easily than she reads, I thought to myself, and started reformulating lesson plans.

"Crank 'er up," said David, sitting in the bos'n's chair. He was going up to look more closely at that frayed forestay. I cranked and held, then tied off the halyard. David dangled at the very top of the mast.

Back down again, he said, "Only one strand out of seventeen. I wrapped it with electrical tape. Eventually it will need a better fix, but I'm not worried anymore."

"It's as if I don't know how to drive the car," I said to David. "Time for me to learn to drive the dinghy."

"Get in."

"By myself?"

"How else?"

Well, I could think of other ways. This felt like learning to swim by being thrown into the lake, but I didn't want to look like a wimp. I pulled the dinghy up and climbed in.

"The black dial's the choke. The handle on the left's the gear shift. All you've got is forward, reverse, and neutral," he said. I worked the gear shift through all three positions. "Your accelerator's on the other handle. Just like a motorcycle. Pull the cord and rev it up."

I let go of the boat, turned around, and pulled the cord. Already I was drifting away. "Choke!" David called out. I turned the dial and yanked again. "Half choke!" This time it started, but it revved way too high. "Choke off!" David called, louder now since I was drifting even further away. "Now into gear."

I shifted into forward. The dinghy jerked into high speed. I slowed the motor, then pivoted it around, trying to get a feel for steering. Luckily, it was a large harbor, and there were only four other boats nearby. I zigzagged back and forth, gaining control. Within ten minutes, I was feeling frisky. I buzzed *Hei Tiki*. The kids leaned out and cheered. I banked back around. *How do I stop it?* I wondered. I bumped the motor down into neutral just as I collided with the sailboat's stern.

"Great landing," I panted.

"You'll get it," David said with a smile.

John fell asleep in the cockpit, but Alison seemed happy to sleep with me in the forward berth.

"I'm too tired to read tonight," I said.

"That's okay, Mom." At times she could rise to adult levels of sympathy and understanding.

I pulled the sheet up over us and wrapped my arms around her. "Some nights I say the Lord's Prayer really quietly before I go to bed," I whispered. "Do you want to say it with me?" She nodded. I began.

"Wait a minute, Mommy," her little voice said.

"Wait for what?"

"I need to find the place inside where God is."

I waited silently, then she began, "Our Father . . ." I prayed and listened, and I didn't stop to correct her when she said, "Thy kingdom come, my will be done."

The next day we left Governor's Harbour again. This day's sail was the kind that makes you want to keep going forever—bright blue sky, sweet sunshine, wind abeam, steady surge forward. I drove, David read. John and Alison were playing with Kelly.

"Now Kelly's going swimming," John said. He took off her yellow raincoat and started taking off her gingham dress.

"Kelly doesn't want to go swimming," said Alison. She buttoned up the dress.

"Kelly *loves* to go swimming," John said, pulling the doll toward him.

"Does not," said Alison. She pulled Kelly. John yanked back, then both of them gasped.

Kelly's arm had popped out of the socket.

Alison stared at the dismembered doll, then dissolved into tears. John shoved the arm at her.

"Go forward," David barked. John tramped through the cabin and buried himself in the forward berth.

Alison cried and cried, so loudly she couldn't possibly have heard David when he said, "We can fix it." He removed the doll's clothing and poked a finger into the empty arm socket. "Come on, now. Stop crying and let me see the arm," he said. She sniffled and handed it to him. Her little girl voice spoke. "I want Johnny."

John appeared, eyes red with tears. "I'm sorry," he mumbled. The children hugged each other.

"Looks like we have to take off the head," David said. That

set Alison off again. He held the doll sideways and treated her like an object, not a family friend. "This elastic loop at the end of the arm attaches to a hook at the base of the neck. Can't get to the hook without pulling the head out of the socket."

"Off with her head!" John said magisterially. He slashed at his own neck with one finger and let his tongue loll out of his mouth.

Alison cracked a smile. She started giggling. She and John leaned together, laughing, and then David and I joined in too, all four of us laughing, long and loud and together.

The Bahamas stretch across a corner of the Atlantic like charms dangling from an unseen bracelet. They say the islands number seven hundred. The better-known destinations—Grand Bahama, with Freeport and Lucaya; New Providence, with Nassau—are large enough to support cities, roads, restaurants, and hotels. We steered clear of those, heading for islands large enough to have a name but small enough to offer a glimpse of real life. We had visited the Abacos; we were skirting Eleuthera; we would skip down the Exumas, George Town–bound. At every turn we kept asking: Do we have it in us?

Staniel Cay charmed me even before we set foot on the island. "Happy people, happy people," a voice sang over the VHF radio, hailing sailors and inviting them to visit the Happy People Marina.

Dry coral roadways crisscross the island. Tiny square houses face this way and that, intensely pastel: yellow, orange, lime green, lavender. Up to and around each house twist well-worn paths, outlined with bleached white conch shells. Each yard struggles to be a garden. Spindly cornstalks poke out of chalky, rocky soil. Croton and hibiscus flourish. Limes hang heavy on the trees.

We followed a hand-lettered sign up the street: "The Pink Building is the Supermarket." It was a long, low concrete building, stucco siding painted bright pink. In front sat Hugh Smith, owner of the pink supermarket. He greeted us, brown teeth showing in an ageless smile. His hands kept moving, picking up palm fronds from a pile on his right and plaiting them into a ribbon, six inches wide. "We plait the palm and ship it to Nassau," he said. "They sew it into hats and bags by machine."

The promise of a supermarket turned the children gleeful, but their faces fell when they stepped inside. It was low-ceilinged and dark, about the size of our living room at home. Two bare light bulbs dangled from the ceiling. A few dusty shelves held a few dusty items. John brought me a cereal box, eyes imploring, but I pointed to the year-old sell-by date on top. Alison shoved her hand into a plastic candy jar, coming up with bubble gum and hard candy. I bought a can of Irish butter, five pounds of flour, and a dozen key limes. Purchases in hand, we squinted back out into the bright sunshine.

Just one sail from George Town, we anchored all alone in a nook at the north end of Great Exuma Island. The children and I snorkeled, spotting an occasional sand dollar buried in white ripples of sand. John dove and came up with a fist-sized shell, a partridge tun, ridged with delicate butterscotch whorls.

John and Dave rowed over to the nearby island. They returned after sunset, John at the oars. One side of David's head looked all bloody, as if he had been in a fistfight at school.

"Dad shimmied up this palm tree, and then he fell down and just lay there for five minutes," John said breathlessly.

"It wasn't five minutes," grumped David.

"You really ought to clean that up," I said.

"Scraped up my belly, too." He pulled up his T-shirt to show scratch marks, like some massive paw had clawed him from nipple to navel.

"Your ear looks terrible." Blood was caked inside and out, so thickly I couldn't see where the cut was. I reached out to touch it. He drew away. "You should clean it," I repeated. He just grunted.

David is like that. He wants no mothering when he is hurt. My instinct is to reach out and to comfort. His instinct is to draw back, to refuse and deny. Moments in our past flashed by me. We are working together, moving a boulder out of the yard as we landscape. It falls back on his foot. I jump toward him to help. He lashes out in anger, pushes me away. I learned to quell my hurt and disappointment years ago.

"Did you pass out?" I asked. If I keep the interaction rational, I have learned, he will engage.

"Naw. Just lay there for a while."

"I thought he wasn't ever going to get up," John said, eyes wide.

First his back. Then his feet. And now his ear. By the time both children were asleep and David had drunk a third lukewarm beer, he allowed me to soak the side of his head with a warm washcloth and pour on some hydrogen peroxide.

"We all depend on you," I said in a low voice, daubing his wound.

"I'll be fine," he said. For a few minutes, we just held each other.

5

Discovery Day

"YOU'LL MAKE FRIENDS IN GEORGE TOWN,"
Marge on *Windsong* had promised. "Potluck dinners, Volleyball
Beach—it's a real cruising community."

I had paged ahead to George Town in the yachting guide.
Laundromats, gift shops, restaurants, and a market that held
mail for cruisers. We gave that address to Granddad, who was
forwarding our mail.

I had skipped over the sailing instructions. I was more interested in letters, laundry, and food. But as we coasted Great
Exuma Island that morning, approaching Elizabeth Harbour
and George Town, I went back and read them well.

> Elizabeth Harbour. Caution: The approach described here
> is a dangerous entrance in anything but adequate light
> conditions, when hazards can be seen. . . . It is essential
> that Simon's Point be positively identified, and this is not
> easy to do. . . . The best landmark is a pair of large pink
> houses with white roofs which can be seen in a group of
> palm trees silhouetted against the sky. (Be aware that a
> coat of paint could change the color of these in a day.) . . .
> If you mistakenly take your bearing on a house east of Si-
> mon's Point, the 165° course will take you onto the reef.

I struggled to match the words with the chart. "It's not an easy entrance," David said. "Do you want to spot or drive?"

"Drive."

The Exumas lie low and dry, wrinkles of dead coral and dusty green scrub just above the water's surface. Occasionally soft sand beaches meet the surf, but more often the edges of these islands are pock-filled crags of rock. Waves thrash them constantly, and still they stand sharp and hard and treacherous. The same craggy landscape—murder on a boat hull—lies underwater, too.

From a distance, I have trouble differentiating one island from the next behind it. They pile up one atop another, like a child's shoebox panorama, their color and features not different enough to inform my sense of perspective.

"See the hole?" asked David. I began to see water between brown islands. "See the light?" asked David. He pointed left, to a tall, slender pole atop a chunky little island. It hardly seemed a beacon.

"See Simon's Point?" He squatted behind me on the lazarette.

"No," I said firmly. No reason to prevaricate. I didn't understand where I was going or where I should be.

He talked me over to the right. "Now Simon's Point is at one-sixty-five," he said.

I still didn't see it.

"So turn! Turn!"

I turned and headed 165°. "Like this?" I asked. I sensed him nodding, looking ahead.

A lineup of whitecaps, eight to ten feet apart, rolled through the opening. "Did Dad ever tell you the story of driving the U.S.S. *Chicago* into San Francisco Bay?"

His nonchalance comforted me. I held steady and drove as he talked.

"He was a young man, just learning to drive a destroyer. He made the wrong move and broached. Ship rolled over sideways. Took a wave the wrong way."

We were bow into the outmost waves now.

"When he got the boat back on track, he realized his commanding officer was standing there behind him." By now we were surging, waves amidships. I felt the buffeting force of the waves. This was it. "Officer never said a word," David added.

I shot a glance behind. The white wash of a breaker lifted up above his head. "Square it up!" he cried. The wave broke behind us and we swept on through.

Inside the water flattened fast.

"I've heard that story," I said. "Now I know what it means."

We couldn't relax yet. David moved to the bow, pointing through coral heads to safe water.

Christopher Columbus called Elizabeth Harbour the finest in all Christendom. A tight chain of barrier islands skirts the southern end of Great Exuma for a good five miles, with narrow openings top and bottom and a width of over a mile in the middle, creating a broad, protected harbor in between.

Not far into it, we could see the signs of George Town. Bright pink buildings sat on the water's edge: the government headquarters and, next door, Peace and Plenty Hotel. A three-story satellite transmitter for Batelco, the Bahamas Telephone Company, stood on a hill. A pudgy blimp floated high above, its silver fading into the sky. U.S. tax dollars paid for it, we heard later: part of the DEA's drug surveillance plan.

And sailboats everywhere. Twenty to the right of us, anchored by the pink buildings; thirty to the left of us, across the harbor by the beach. We had already passed a dozen as we entered the harbor. And still more: forty behind a spit of land, toward the Batelco tower; twenty in a cove behind the beach.

So this was George Town. It made me nervous. Who would I say I was, if anyone should ask? I couldn't claim to be part of the cruising community. I had been sailing for less than two months, and I had my doubts about the months to come.

We anchored near the beach. As the sun set, people started gathering.

"Want to go over?" David said.

I shook my head. "Too tired."

"So we made it to 'Chicken Harbor,'" David commented, looking out. "It's easy to get this far. Now comes the hard part."

"Easy?"

"Sure, the Bahamas are easy. You're almost always in sight of land. You've got the sound side or the bank side to choose from, so you can always find protection, no matter which way the wind. There's a reason so many cruisers stay in the Bahamas."

I sighed.

"From here on, you're talking serious sailing. Overnight passages, blue water. Turks and Caicos, Dominican Republic, Puerto Rico, Virgins to St. Maarten. Every one of those could be a bitch."

A rubber dinghy motored past our stern. The driver waved.

"When I first sailed the Bahamas, in the early seventies, there just weren't that many other sailboats," David continued. "Now they're everywhere you look. And half the time, the guys at the helm don't know what they're doing."

"I don't know if I could sail full-time," I mused.

"All the new technology gives them a false sense of security. They read the magazines, they buy all the fancy equipment, they get the big boats, but they really don't know how to sail."

I watched the faces of people on the beach, lit up by a bonfire. "I don't know if I would ever find friends."

"In those days, *Hei Tiki* was big," David said. "Thirty-four feet, and she was one of the biggest. Now look. Forty-five, fifty-foot boats. There's big money floating out here these days."

"It's such a male world."

David looked at me. "We've met women."

"But every one of them seems to be along on her husband's trip."

David didn't have an answer.

"I don't want it to be that way," I said. And yet I didn't know how to make it any different.

———

I dreamt I had moved in at Biscuit Run, with my friend Elizabeth and her husband and five children. It was Wednesday night, time for their weekly open house. The house was full of art, noise, music, and people. I felt comfort and pleasure. Now that I lived at Biscuit Run, I would see my friends every day.

I woke up crying. Sadness pervaded the day. I missed my friends, and I didn't see any new ones in sight.

John didn't want to read *Mrs. Piggle-Wiggle* any more. I pulled out a book about U.S. presidents.

"You read the first paragraph, I'll read the second," I told him. He screwed up his face, but stumbled only twice. We got through all four paragraphs about George Washington. "Now open your notebook."

"I don't know where my notebook is."

"Find it."

He sighed. He looked forward, he looked in the cockpit, and finally found it behind us, on the bookshelf.

"Open it up." Did I have to tell him every move?

He opened it to the middle.

"First blank page." Now he was making me mad. "Write one sentence about George Washington."

He huffed and glared.

"John, you just read four paragraphs about the first president of the United States." Putting the pressure on. "Surely you have some idea. Let's look together."

"I'll do it myself," he said with an edge. The pencil moved, then he showed me the notebook.

---

1 <u>George Washington</u>
He lead the American revolution.

"Great," I said. I requested the spelling correction.

"Mom!" he whined.

"John!" I echoed. "Tomorrow, John Adams." He bounced away. "What an ordeal," I muttered out loud.

"John! Alison!" David's voice reared up from the cockpit. He had lifted the bench cushions to clean under them. He stood there, cushion raised, pointing. Hair, peanuts, raisins, corn kernels, bits of tissue, a mechanical pencil, three Lego blocks, and a Game Boy game cartridge. "Get out here, both of you," David yelled. "There's trash everywhere. I can't make a move without having to clean up after you."

Alison silently started picking up. John stood in the companionway, looking defensive, which made David hone in on him. "Get a paper towel and do something," he crabbed. John struggled to rip a paper towel off the roll. "Wet down that paper towel. It won't do any good dry," said David, giving John a shove.

I couldn't watch any longer. "We all contribute to the mess," I said. I stepped between my son and my husband. David glared at me. I lifted the other cockpit cushion and began cleaning, too. I hoped my actions would say it: *We need to work together.*

"You're always protecting him," David told me that night.

I sighed and looked inward. It was hard to speak.

"You get in the way when I'm trying to discipline him," David continued. "You defuse my efforts. You cripple me."

"Sometimes I think you're hurting him," I said quietly.

"I never mean to."

"He gets that look on his face, as if he's in such pain."

"You know he overreacts."

"He needs support, not criticism."

"He's turning into a Mama's boy."

I did not answer that one.

"I give him support," David added.

"I hope so," I said.

Our conversation dwindled. I felt unsatisfied. David poured himself a lime toddy. I took a sip. He emptied the glass. Soon he was snoring faceup in the cockpit. I slept alone in the forward berth.

———

It had been a month since we last used a laundromat. When I told the children to pull out their dirty laundry, they emptied their cubbies onto the cabin floor, creating a pile of clothes that were not smelly, not dirty, but stiff with salt. Same with the sheets. After six weeks of saltwater spray, frequent swims, and no fresh-water showers, our bedsheets had sucked up so much salt that they were stiff, dingy, and always a bit moist. In all, we had one tall bag plus two pillowcases full of dirty laundry.

David motored Alison and me over to town. You could feel the hustle-bustle of a small town's lunch hour. Four taxi vans parked in front of Peace and Plenty, their drivers leaning up against them. From a lunch wagon nearby, you could smell the hot fat, where a portly woman cooked conch fritters. Across the street, under the umbra of a huge tree, women rearranged their straw market wares. T-shirts hung from flimsy structures and fluttered in the wind. Boxes, baskets, bags, and bowls of woven straw piled all around. Schoolchildren in brown plaid mingled in twos and threes, laughing and talking, pushing and running, not much concerned about the occasional car zooming by. The school bell rang. Children swarmed into a small frame building set on stilts above a bare, rocky yard. Suddenly the street was still, except for a bantam rooster and two hens, pecking for what little they could find in the school yard dirt.

Alison complained that the laundry was too heavy, so we sat down to rest.

"Mommy! Kids!" a voice rang out. Suddenly a child was dancing around us, Little Mermaid sunglasses bouncing on her nose.

"Arielle, slow down now." Her mother was tall, slender, and straightforward. We greeted each other, wordlessly noting our bonds: sailing Americans with children who needed friends. Alison, though, acted standoffish. I wasn't sure this woman was my type, either.

"I'm Pat. We're on *Jim Hawkins*, the white motor-sailer," she said. " The sixty-foot tank," she added, smiling.

"Susan. *Hei Tiki*," I said. "Thirty-four-foot sloop, blue decks." The girls were skirting the park already, Arielle dragging Alison along. Alison glanced back at me, yearning for rescue.

"She's desperate for friends," Pat said. "We've been here a week, and she hasn't met any girls yet. Lots of boys here this year for some reason."

I asked where they were from.

"Marathon. Florida. We live aboard. We came across this time because some Americans on the island hired Jack, my husband, to help build a house. Usually he works on boats, but this time he's getting up every morning and catching a ride ten miles up the road."

"So you're here for a while."

"At least a month, till they get the roof on."

Alison had come back. She pushed laundry at me. "Come on." I wasn't ready to leave yet.

"We'll see each other again," Pat said.

As we walked away, Alison said, "That girl was too young for me. She's only three."

I kidded her a little. "She looked at least three and a half."

The next day in town, again I found Arielle and Pat, this time with Jack. Swarthy and serious, with a thick black beard and a Miami Dolphins cap shading his nose, he asked where we were headed.

"We wanted to go down the islands. Turks and Caicos, the Dominican Republic," I said. Angling for information, I added, "I hear it's kind of risky."

"I sailed the south coast of D.R. You hear about robberies, but we felt safe. Every anchorage has an armed guard on the dock all night."

"You'll like St. Maarten," Pat added. "We lived there five years. Sold our last boat there."

I was warming up to them.

"We sailed through a squall in Eleuthera," I said. "It was a nightmare. Kids got hysterical, I got sick. I don't know if we could take another."

"Remember the Fastnet?" said Jack. I didn't, but I kept listening. "Twenty boats went out into gale weather. And what happened? The boats all made it back. The people didn't. They panicked and jumped. You have to have faith in your boat. Boats are designed to survive. You watch the weather and make your decisions. But finally, you just do it."

I knew Dave would like this guy. When we went back to the boat, I told him so. Later that afternoon, he and Alison dinghied across the harbor, looking for *Jim Hawkins*. An hour and a half later, they returned. David handed over a roll of paper. "Charts of the Turks and Caicos," he said.

I raised my eyebrows. This was a serious step toward sailing on. I started to say something, but Alison interrupted.

"They have a TV on board, Mommy. And lots of toys."

"She's not too young?" I asked.

She shrugged it off. "She's almost four."

David fell asleep early that night, but the children wanted to stay up reading. The twelfth of October was approaching. I rummaged through the books and pulled out the one on Christopher Columbus. I read how three little ships set out in August 1492. How they stopped at the Canary Islands to provision. How from there, they sailed on into uncharted waters.

About three weeks into the voyage, the men began to complain. They were bored, tired, and probably frightened. During the past few weeks they had seen nothing but water, sky, and each other.

"Sound familiar?" I asked. Alison nodded drowsily. John's breathing was already deep and rhythmic.

They wanted to turn back. Columbus refused. For years he had dreamed of this journey and little else.

Alison's body relaxed into mine. I shifted around and kept reading.

By October 6, I read, they had sailed 2,400 miles. On October 7 birds flew overhead. On October 11 branches floated by. On October 12 they saw land by the light of the moon. A watchman called out, *"Tierra!"*

"What does *tierra* mean?" I asked. No answer. Both children were fast asleep. I read on aloud, simply for my own sake.

They saw a small island, one of the Bahamas. They shouted and sang. They prayed and cried for joy.

Five hundred years ago, without charts or navigation, in creaky, leaky little wooden boats, they made it across the Atlantic.

Surely we could sail the Caribbean.

The next day we motored across the harbor to fill up with water and fuel. As we steamed back across Elizabeth Harbour, a red rubber dinghy skidded up alongside, the driver waving us down. Beside him sat a towhead about John's age. I could hardly hear his voice over the engine. "Beach . . . four o'clock . . . kids can play." He waved and shot off in another direction.

When four rolled around, I asked who wanted to go with me. Alison was hesitant. John was eager.

"I'll stay here," David said. "I need to work on the refrigerator." It hadn't been cooling for two weeks.

"Do you want help?" I felt guilty, socializing while he worked.

"No. Take both kids, too."

I tried to ignore the feeling that he was glad to get rid of us.

The three of us drove to the beach. The place invited you. A broad curve of warm white sand, splashed by turquoise water. Weather-worn picnic tables here and there. One ragged rope swing, hanging from a tall casuarina tree. Nearby, a noisy game of volleyball.

Two women sat on the beach, dangling their toes in the water. We exchanged names. Desi was tall, heavy, easygoing. A straw hat shaded her face, an oversized shirt covered her torso.

Tina was petite, angular, intense. Her skin shone nut-brown in a coral-colored two-piece.

Tina was the mother of the towhead in the dinghy. He and his younger brother were already diving the shallow water with John. Desi had a son and daughter, ten and twelve, walking further down the beach. Alison sat for the moment between my knees.

We pointed out our boats. Tina and Peter lived aboard *Scud*. "Steel boat back in the hurricane hole." Desi pointed out her boat, *Manifest,* a large ketch in the distance. I pointed out *Hei Tiki*, anchored close by.

"Four people live on that?" Tina asked, surprised.

I nodded.

"You must get along well. How big?"

"Thirty-four," I said.

"*Scud*'s forty-one, and we're bursting at the seams. Of course, *Scud*'s the only home we have," Tina said. "We've lived aboard for twelve years. We spend winters here, then New England in the summer."

Desi said they would sail home before Christmas.

"Where's home?" I asked.

"Massachusetts. We can't afford to stay all winter."

We talked about school aboard. Both families were following the Calvert curriculum. Tina and Peter divided the work, each teaching one child. Desi's husband didn't teach at all. She did fine with her son, she said, but she and her daughter struggled through four or five hours every day.

I said I was a writer. "I keep a journal," Desi commented. "It keeps me sane. Daytime feelings, nighttime dreams. When I'm on the boat, I dream in the colors of the coral reef."

"I've been dreaming a lot about life back home," I said. "I haven't found many people to talk with. Sailing seems such a man's world."

"I could take it or leave it," Desi said. "I come sailing because this is the only time my husband is really happy."

As she spoke, that same red rubber dinghy drove up the

beach not twenty feet away. Peter stepped out, dangling a massive lobster by an antenna. His companion—Desi's husband, Tom—stretched a fleshy, brown grouper across two hands.

Without a word, Tina sprang into action. She took the grouper and, kneeling at the water's edge, sliced its belly, scooped out the organs, trimmed off two thick fillets, rinsed them in salt water, and ziplocked them in plastic. Fish head and spine in hand, she hopped into the dinghy.

"I'm going out to the trap," she yelled, yanking the motor on. She zoomed away, kicking up an outboard plume.

"Tina catches sharks," Desi explained. "She baits huge hooks with fish heads on a mooring outside the harbor."

"What for?" I asked, amazed.

"Cleans the jaws and vertebrae. Collects them, sells them. Makes jewelry. Sometimes eats the meat."

I watched the dinghy speed away, headed for deep water. Finally, a woman who made this cruising life her own.

When we got back to the boat, Dave was mad. "I wanted to go to the post office, but it's too late now," he grumbled.

"What's the rush?"

"Dad sent a single-sideband receiver."

"He bought one for us?" This was good news. Months before, when I had suggested a weather radio, David had scoffed, saying we could get news everywhere by VHF.

Not true. In the Abacos, yes, we heard Florida weather. But as we traveled south, those broadcasts had grown faint, then disappeared.

"When did he tell you he sent it?" I asked David.

"The other day."

"So why are you just now checking the mail?"

He didn't answer, turning the question rhetorical.

The children were absorbed in the forward cabin. I could hear their voices, creating Lego fictions. I decided to address David's state of mind.

"What's making you so grumpy?"

"Hunh?"

"Every time I turn around, you're mad about something. Nobody seems to be doing anything right."

"You don't know why?"

I stared at him.

"Isn't it obvious?" he continued.

"No, it's not obvious," I said righteously.

"You don't know why I'm so testy?" He paused. "We haven't made love for two weeks."

"We what?"

"You heard what I said."

"What does that have to do with it?"

"I get grumpy."

"You never told me that before."

"You never asked."

"It has that much effect on you?"

"All men," he said.

"How do you know?"

"We talk about it together."

"You do?"

"Don't women?"

"No," I said. "At least I don't."

He didn't say anything more.

Alison and John slept in the cockpit that night.

David's hands slid under my nightgown. His lips teased my nipple. I felt desire brewing in my belly. It wasn't just obligation. I realized I wanted union, too. I pulled him over and into me. I gripped the tight flesh of his buttocks. I felt him arch, shoot up inside of me. He let out a muffled sound. We lay together, coupled. I hummed a deep sigh. "Thank you," he whispered.

We celebrated Discovery Day in George Town. It was the five hundredth anniversary of Columbus's landing. There was politically correct skepticism in the States, but here in the Bahamas, it was a holiday to be proud of, pure and simple. Signs posted all over announced Quincentennial Celebrations at two o'clock. The children and I—and at least a dozen other Americans—were there at the park ten minutes early. We were the only ones around.

Slowly, Bahamians began to assemble. Someone tapped and blew into the microphone, and by a quarter to three, a good hundred sat in folding chairs before the makeshift stage.

John had wandered toward the waterfront, where three dark-skinned boys were showing him how to smash snails to bait tiny fishhooks. Alison had befriended an elfin little girl. Cocoa skin, winsome smile, wiry little body, she wore Alison's hot pink sunglasses and got the boys to chase her.

"Five hundred years ago, a great thing happened, here in these beautiful islands of ours," spoke Isadora Lloyd, M.P. from the Exumas. "We in the Bahamas feel the inspiration of Discovery Day every day." She paused, and everyone applauded.

Schoolchildren trooped onto the stage, dressed in blue or green or brown plaid. One group Bahamianized Pete Seeger: "from the fields of Abacos, to Nassau city, this land is made for you and me." Another chanted a poem with a populist refrain:

> *Columbus wasn't a big shot mon,*
> *He was common mon like you and me.*

For a grand finale, twenty children danced around a maypole, weaving ribbons of turquoise, yellow, and black, the Bahamian national colors. Then to a scratchy recording of a drum roll, a color guard of two, spitting clean in military dress, raised a flag created for the Quincentennial. Halfway up, they realized the flag was flying upside down. They pulled it down. The drum roll started again. They raised it again, and everybody cheered.

Alison kept a stream of postcards going home. She was writing them three, four, five at a time. For each batch, she would compose a series of sentences. Then she would write that message over and over, to schoolmates, friends, and relatives.

Dear Cindy,
We are in Georgetown. That
is in the BaHaMas.
I like the
BaHaMas. I, am
OK. Are you OK.
Love Alison

But reading still frustrated her. She seemed to have no sense of sounding out letters. She was shaky even on vowel sounds.

I made a chart of the vowels and tongued the short *a* sound at her. "What words *can* you think of *that have that* sound in them?"

This one came easily. "Alison . . . Dad . . . apple," she said. I wrote them down.

Short *e* was more difficult. She couldn't hear it.

"*The,*" she said. She knew it had an *e* in it.

"But does *the* have the sound of *eh*?" I asked. Her face tensed up. I tried short *i*. "What word has that sound *in* the *middle* of *it*?"

"Alison," she said quickly.

I wrote down *Alison* again. "Another?"

She paused and frowned, then up and shouted, "I can't do this." She tore out the notebook page, crumpled and threw it. It just fell to the table, which made her even more mad. "I hate this!" she yelled. So did I, but I bit my lip.

At the same moment, in the cockpit, John and David whooped it up over math. "Another, Dad," I heard John say.

I felt jealous. I felt trapped. In a low voice I said, "I'm going to stretch my legs while you calm down."

Standing on the bow, I filled my nostrils with fresh salt air, my eyes with the serene turquoise blue of the harbor. Three minutes later, I had a new plan.

"All right, Alison, *you* do the writing." I dictated a familiar sentence, one from a book I had read her since infancy.

She wrote without hesitation:

The Cat Sat on the Mat.

"Hear how the three words rhyme?" She nodded. "Now tell me a word you know how to write." She chose "in." We listed words that rhymed. *Rin . . . fin . . . tin . . . min . . . sin . . .* I had her write them down, then make a sentence of them.

The pin is in the Bin.

She smiled. "Another!"

From the cockpit we heard John cry out, "No!" I glanced up to see David bop his head with a magazine, then point vehemently at the notebook. John held back the tears and scribbled.

I kept my focus on Alison's lesson. "What's another word you can write?"

"And," she said. We thought up rhymes. She wrote a sentence:

I Love Bands And Sand.

She bounced up and down. I glanced again at John and David. They were sitting close together, David's arm around John's shoulder, John's chin stuck on his fist.

Alison couldn't be stopped. She scribbled fast.

Bad Dad is Mad.

She showed me the notebook. I pointed to the words and read out loud. We giggled nervously.

Then it was John's turn for school with me.

"I don't want to read about presidents."

"You can't quit now. You've done Washington and Adams. Jefferson is one of the interesting ones."

He harrumphed and crossed his arms.

"Okay," I compromised. "I'll give you a break from the

presidents, but not from writing." He loosened up a little. "Write a list of every fish you've seen."

Begrudgingly he began. Soon he was writing energetically. Ten minutes later, he showed me his notebook.

A list of all animal
we've seen: 1 Barracuda   2 Nurse Shark
3 Grouper   4 Lobster   5 Sea Turtle   6 Yellowtail
Snapper   7 Rock hind   8 Remora   9 Yellow stingray
10 spotted eagle ray   11 Atlantic manta ray
12 Balao   13 Redfin Needlefish   14 Bigeye
15 Yellow Jack   16 Peacock flounder   17 Queen
Angelfish   18 Gray Angelfish   19 French Angelfish
20 Sergent major   21 Neon goby
22 Cleaning goby   23 Sharknose goby
24 Queen triggerfish   25 Blue tang
26 Scawled filefish   27 Ballon fish
28 Lesser erlectric ray   29 Flying fish
30 Dophlin

"Impressive," I said. "That last one—do you mean the fish or the mammal?"

He took the book back and added:

---

31 Dolphin fish

"Great job," I told him. "You can add more along the way."

He carefully put his notebook and pencil away. "Now can I go swimming?"

David and John went across the harbor to town. On their list: motor oil, dinghy fuel, hose clamp, electric tape, and a post office visit to look for the radio.

Alison wanted to make afternoon plans with Arielle. "Call them on the radio, Mom."

The VHF radio intimidated me, but I didn't want to admit that to my six-year-old daughter—especially since here in George

Town, it seemed second nature to everyone else. Sometimes we just left the radio on, listening to traffic on channel 16, the general hailing channel.

At other times we switched channels and eavesdropped on other people's conversations about dinner, diving, and beach rendezvous.

Listening was easy. Speaking was different.

"Come on, Mom," repeated Alison. "Call and make plans."

I took a deep breath, held the microphone to my mouth, and pushed the transmit button. *"Jim Hawkins, Jim Hawkins. This is Hei Tiki."* Everyone in the whole anchorage listened in and instantly knew I had never used a VHF before.

We stood by. Silence. One, then another conversation started up on channel 16, as if our call for *Jim Hawkins* had been bumped from the roster.

I breathed in deeply and lowered my voice. *"Jim Hawkins, Jim Hawkins. This is Hei Tiki."*

A voice said briskly, *"This is Jim Hawkins."*

"Pat? This is Susan. How're you doing? I was calling to ask—"

"Let's switch to channel twelve."

Radio protocol. I forgot. Fumbling, I switched the dial.

"Jim Hawkins," I heard her voice declare.

I sighed and started talking. My first VHF conversation. We made plans to meet and climb Stocking Island that afternoon.

"See you then," I said. "Bye."

"Jim Hawkins back to sixteen," Pat said nonchalantly.

"Hei Tiki back to sixteen," I modeled after her. It felt odd, but I could get used to it.

While David and John went spearfishing with Jack, Alison and I climbed Stocking Island with Pat and Arielle. My feet gripped the chalky white rock; I protected Alison from the barbs of palmetto. We reached the top and leaned against the ten-foot-tall stone beacon. The wind blew, strong and steady, from the east. To windward, whitecaps churned the water as far as the eye could see.

"Looks rough," I said.

"When are you guys moving on?" Pat asked.

"When we get up the guts to do it." We laughed. "Dave's father shipped us a single-sideband receiver. We won't leave until it arrives." I kept staring out at the ocean.

"You get used to the passages after a while," Pat said. She knew what I was thinking. "But it's hard with kids."

I nodded. "Alison gets seasick."

"Do you give her pills?"

"So far, no. She just sleeps."

"That's best." We stared out at the whitecaps. "Worst one's the oh-my-God-a-passage." We laughed again. She meant the Anegada Passage, the northeast corner of the Caribbean, the stretch of open water between the Virgin Islands and St. Maarten. "That's the roughest. But it's also the shortest. You'll like it down-island."

"It's all worth it?"

She nodded. "Definitely."

Our hunters brought home dinner: five lobsters, two grouper, and one triggerfish. We gathered on *Jim Hawkins*.

"You eat triggerfish?" I asked Jack.

"They have tough skin and a bitter organ you have to remove," he said. "Then they're delicious." He handed me a fried chunk of flaky white meat. Pat came up the companionway with a plate full of fish debris: heads, spines, tails, and lobster shells. "Come and get it," she called, dumping it overboard. "Got to keep the harbor sharks happy." John watched the water, hoping to see something snap up those bones.

As the evening wore on, Pat and Jack showed us their photo album. Pictures from their Pacific crossing, before Arielle was born: Papua New Guinea, Fiji, Singapore. Pictures of *Wave Dancer*, their sloop in St. Maarten. They turned another page. Landscapes changed abruptly. Red clay dirt, dense forest greens. We seemed to be looking at pictures from home.

"Twenty years ago, Jack bought fifteen acres in the hills of

Tennessee," Pat explained. "Some day, we'll sell the boat and build a house there."

I stared into her life as if I were looking into a mirror. They had been living for years on the water, building a mountain home in their dreams. We had built that home, and now our dreams were taking us sailing.

Both exhausted, John and Alison fell asleep as soon as we got back to *Hei Tiki*. The wind was picking up, and we felt rain in the air. Aboard *Jim Hawkins*, we had heard the marine weather report: low pressure system moving off the southeast United States. David and I worked silently together, snapping up the cockpit curtains.

Inside that canvas shelter, we opened a bottle of wine. "You get to a place like this, you start thinking about long-term cruising," said David.

I took a sip.

"No reason I couldn't find work along the way like Jack does," he continued. "I'd have to bring along more tools, but if we're having refrigeration problems, so is everyone in this anchorage."

"I can write anywhere," I slowly said. "Especially if I had a computer. Or at least a typewriter."

"No reason why not."

"But I would miss the garden." At home, we owned sixteen acres. We grew flowers and vegetables, and our little orchard was just starting to produce. So much of my writing before had been inspired by the land—trees, flowers, rocks, snakes, ladybugs, weeds, the compost pile. At home now, I would be harvesting fall salad greens, canning applesauce, raking leaves. The seasons had always seemed so essential to life. Now here we were, moving to different rhythms.

"I never knew how good it would feel to be with the children," David said softly. Outside, the wind piped up more loudly.

"I wondered how you would feel without work," I said.

Five years ago, when he ran his own business, he had said: "My work is my identity."

"This is work," he answered. His hands testified: grease under the fingernails, knuckles that wouldn't come clean, a gash in one thumb.

"So I guess we're sailing on," I said. We hadn't talked about it for a week. But David had gotten those charts, and I had bought a book in town: *The Gentleman's Guide to Passages South* by Bruce Van Sant. The title was a joke on the expression, "Gentlemen never sail to windward."

That was what we faced now: a massive sail to windward. At George Town, we sat on the twenty-third parallel. We were crossing the Tropic of Cancer, into the realm where the trade winds reign. From here on down the islands, we could expect a steady easterly wind, into which we would have to point in order to move from longitude 76°, George Town, to longitude 61°, Martinique—furthest point east in the string of islands we planned to visit. We faced eight hundred miles of easting, long ago dubbed "the thorny path."

"I'm ready," said David.

I felt ready, too. What an irony: new friends had helped me discover the courage to leave them.

"All we need now is the damn radio," said David.

And then we got socked in by a week of raging weather. Winds pumped through from the northeast at a steady twenty-five knots. Waves coursed through the anchorage so stiffly that no one left a sailboat for three days. Hard rain pounded down, then gray clouds hung over, dense, low, cold, and threatening. The children and I read all of *Black Beauty*, huddling in the forward berth for hours every day.

When the weather broke, David checked the post office one more time. "Bureaucrats with an attitude," he said. "I had to force them to look at a carton high on the top shelf." Postmarked October 9, it had been in George Town almost as long as we had.

With the radio came a package of mail. Alison flipped

through it. "Mom. Mom. Mom." She kept flipping. "Mom. John. *John?* Nothing for me?" She sank with disappointment. "Nothing for *me*?" she repeated.

"You have written more postcards than the rest of us put together," I said, commiserating. She ran forward into the cabin to hide her tears.

John ripped open the large manila envelope addressed to him. Soon he was laughing out loud.

Each child in the third-grade class he would have attended in Virginia had written him a note.

Dear John. is the Sea Fun. Brandon

Dear John, Have you got seasick yat? Have you seen a light house? How are the island? Latoya

Dear John do you have to cacht fish. Lov Kacy

Dear John Hav you Bin Swimn? Hav you sen an ilun? Amy

That last question sent John into hysterics. "Alison, you've got to see these letters."

Alison reappeared, clutching the new radio. "Dad and I decided that since we didn't get any letters, the radio belongs to us," she sniffled.

John read the letters out loud to her. She sat beside him, radio in her lap. Soon they were snickering together. "I can write better than that," she said, "and I'm in first grade."

David had already awakened when I climbed up into the cockpit, book and journal in hand. He was smoking a cigarette, mug of coffee by his hand. The rising sun shone behind Stocking Island.

"Soon go," he said.

There was so much packed into those two short words. We had been eighteen days in George Town. We had made friends. We knew our way around town. It felt as if life here was just beginning.

"Wind's shifting," David said.

At the same time, it felt time to sail on. Staying in George Town would be too easy. We had a goal: to sail down the Caribbean islands. Others had done it; so could we.

"One more day here?" I asked.

David nodded. "Got to get ready to sail."

I glanced into the cabin. The boat looked lived in. Books and papers piled on the galley table. Pencils and clothespins loose on the counter. Bread and fruit out in the open air. Time for cleaning, stowing, picking up, packing down.

In a satisfying burst of activity, the four of us made the boat ready to sail by noon. That left the afternoon to go diving with Tina. "Just inside the harbor," she had suggested. "Nothing hard. Bring the kids." Alison and I accepted. One more glimpse underwater seemed a good way to say goodbye.

At first, I glided over pure white ridges, a sand bottom as blank as morning snow. All I could hear was my own hollow breath through the snorkel, like that of an astronaut walking on the moon. A dozen blue runners streaked by with effortless tweaks of their tail fins. We approached a coral cluster. Life began to accumulate.

Purple and yellow sea fans waved in the underwater currents. Corky sea fingers wagged toward the water surface. Feathery Gorgonians stretched above a foundation piled high with coral structures. The current shoved me into the coral. I thrashed, trying to escape. I kicked backwards to the periphery of this little universe. A three-foot barracuda appeared. It hung in the water, staring, sharp teeth bared. I gasped and backed away further. The barracuda disappeared.

Tina's head broke the surface near me. "How can you see anything?" she said. She dove at the coral forest, her lithe body stretching upside down. She spoke in mutters and bubbles, pointing at something I couldn't see. I moved closer. Shadows, light, shapes, colors. She muttered again, then we came up for air together.

"Did you see the lobster?" she gasped at me.

I hadn't.

"Hey, Pete," she yelled, and motioned.

I hung on the surface and watched the two of them hunt in synchrony. Peter drew his spear taut and teased the animal from behind. Tina hung in the water, ready. They glanced at each other. Their eyes met in an all but imperceptible nod. Now I could see the lobster. Antennae waved madly. Beady eyes peered out. Tina aimed and shot. Then the water went chaotic and she surfaced, a writhing crustacean on her spear.

"You've got to get your face right down in it," Tina said to me.

No longer linger on the edges. Let these waters engulf me instead. The closer I pulled down into this world, the more I could see. Better to dive deep, discover this vast other world, and make it my own.

We left George Town at dawn. Clear skies, light wind, promising clouds. It was time. We slow-motored around *Jim Hawkins*, David at the helm. I stretched out from the bow and handed over a book Pat had lent us. Arielle stood in her nightgown in the cockpit. Alison cried and refused to wave.

Circling back out the harbor, we passed *Scud*. There was Tina, waving goodbye. Alison's crying intensified. David took her on his lap and spoke gently. "It's good that you're crying." That got her attention. She gulped. "It means you made good friends."

Tears warmed my eyes, too. They were not, like Alison's, tears of apprehension. She feared leaving the certainty of these friends for an unknown in which she might never find others. My tears sprang from other feelings. Sadness, yes, in saying goodbye to comfortable people and places. But I also felt a surge of joy, pride, fear, excitement. These George Town friends were cheering us on down the islands. Meeting them was our initiation into the league of those who cruise. Saying goodbye, sailing on, was consummation of that rite.

The trolling line zinged. "Fish!" John shouted. We knew

what to do. I slipped the motor into neutral and let the sails take control. David gripped the stern with his feet and fought the fish in.

"This guy's diving way down," he said. "It's not a barracuda. They just slither along the surface."

"It's a dolphin!" cried John. Glancing back, I saw that aquamarine shimmer in the water.

In a matter of minutes, we had landed a two-and-a-half foot dolphin, finest fish we had caught so far. Fat fillets went into the refrigerator. "Good thing I got it running," David grinned.

Half an hour out of the harbor, we could see the sail we were in for. If the weather had been too bad out there, we could have turned around. It was time to commit to a long day of sailing. "Family vote," David announced. "Go or no go?"

It all felt right. A brilliant blue day, winds well off the bow. We were leaving satisfying times behind. We had supper in the fridge, smooth waters ahead.

"Go," I voted.

"Go," said John.

"No go," said Alison. "I don't want to leave George Town."

We all looked at David. He nodded. "We go."

Far Out

WE FLEW OUT OF GEORGE TOWN. THAT DAY'S sail was so magnificent, David and I considered sailing through the night, all the way to West Plana. Then Alison moaned. Seasick again.

"If we keep going, we'll get to where the hutia lives," said John to encourage her.

"The what?" she asked glumly.

"Remember those bunnies with short ears? We saw pictures of them. Hutias. They still live in the Plana Cays."

"Bunnies?" Alison heard.

"The wind's in our favor, less than twenty out of the east," said David. He opened up a chart entitled "Far Out Islands." That was the term used for the area that now stretched south and east before us. Long, Crooked, Acklins, Mayaguana— several big islands, many small ones, few towns, and no tourist cities. The map showed George Town in the northwest, Turks and Caicos in the southeast, and an arrow pointing to the Dominican Republic off the map. In the middle, East and West Plana Cays were two little dots, hardly dimensional. We took a chance on the weather and kept on going.

Alison moaned. John put his arm around her. "Don't worry.

We'll find you a hutia. A cute little fuzzy hutia. You can keep it on the boat as a pet. What will you name it?"

"Stupidhead," she said. She grinned. Sometimes John had a way of turning the world around for his sister.

Ten at night. Everyone else is sleeping. I am sailing, mainsail only, wind well off the port bow. I am soaring. There's a romp in the wave. I drive the boat as I would ride a horse: move with it, anticipate the rhythm. I set my sight on a star just starboard of the mast, one that grows brighter as the night blackens. A hazy crescent moon hangs at the horizon. I stand at the wheel. I dance to the surge of *Hei Tiki* slicing through the water.

Now I climb higher. I stand on the lazarette hatch, leaning up against the bimini frame. I steer with my right foot. I sing whatever song comes to mind—shape note hymns, Broadway hits, campfire rounds. One sweet little folk song feels so good, I sing it over and over.

> *I see the moon, the moon sees me.*
> *God bless the moon and God bless me.*
> *There is grace in the cabin and grace in the hall,*
> *And the grace of God is over us all.*

My mind slips. I sing about "the grace of love," and that feels right, too.

David and I had agreed on two-hour watches through the night, but when midnight came around I let him sleep another hour. Then he did the same for me. I fell into a dreamless sleep, and when his voice woke me, it was almost four.

I climbed up into the cockpit. "I need to check our position," David said. "I've been dodging lightning all night."

We kept dodging into the morning. At sunrise, violet clouds striped a disk of brilliant orange. John woke up and set the trolling line. Alison got up, looked around without a word, then clenched back into a corner of the cockpit as if denying it all. At times, her arms would drop limp and her face would relax. At other times, more conscious of her misery, she clutched her knees and looked grimly out at the moving horizon.

She must have been fast asleep when we noticed the tiny songbird, a nondescript warbler. No land in view, it pumped hard just to stay above the water's surface. It dipped, almost touching the water, then flitted under our bimini. It perched on Alison's shoulder, preened, looked around, and flew away.

The three of us watched in silence. After the bird flew, John burst out, "Alison! Wake up! A bird just landed on you!" She half-opened her drowsy eyes, smiled meekly, shifted position, and settled back into oblivion.

We anchored just before noon, dodging coral heads and snugging up close to the beach of West Plana. Blue arched overhead, but clouds congested the eastern horizon. To the north, waves washed over ancient coral washboard. To the south, white sand stretched a quarter of a mile. Back behind us, to the west, we could just see Acklins, nothing but a brown line above the watery horizon. We had seen East Plana as we came in, but now West Plana blocked it from view. We were the only boat in sight.

David took Alison out to teach her to drive the dinghy. In minutes, she was zooming out and back, bringing it gently up to *Hei Tiki*, then turning around and jetting out into open water again. The wind blew her hair high, and she was glowing.

John was hours in the water. First he brought up a moss-encrusted conch shell.

"It's dead," I said.

"It has a fish in it," he said. We filled a bucket with water, dropped the shell inside, and watched. In a few minutes, a tiny Spanish hogfish—brilliant purple above, yellow beneath—nosed its way out.

Then John saw a flounder. "Come watch me spear it," he said. He pointed. All I could see was white sand. He writhed downward, spear poised. He shot at the bottom. Wings arched, throwing sand, the fish slid away.

Then he saw the triggerfish. A queen triggerfish, drab gray shot through with neon blue. It wasn't much bigger than my spread hand. It meandered through the water. John aimed the spear and let go. It bounced off the triggerfish. Aimed again. Bounced off. Either stunned or stupid, the fish just hung in the water, looking. John shot one more time, and he had a fish thrashing at the end of his spear.

He broke the surface of the water, panting desperately. He had been spearfishing many times, but this was the first fish he had speared on his own. He knew the rule about holding the catch well above the water, so as not to attract sharks or barracudas. He jerked around like someone learning to swim. "Mom, take the spear," he gasped. I swam away. A deliberate move. If he was going to spearfish, he had to carry through.

He struggled the fish aboard. David helped him clean it. We had two bites each that night. "Just call me 'Mighty Hunter' from now on," John remarked, bringing his voice into its lowest register. He was only half-kidding, and very proud.

The next afternoon, the children and I walked the island. We ventured inland, up to the edge of a shoulder-high stand of cactus. Songbirds flitted in the sea grapes. We turned the corner and traipsed along the beach facing south, a long gentle span of bright white sand sloping down to water, uninterrupted by rock or coral. From water's edge up to the bush, picking up shells and chasing the foam behind the waves, we added human footprints to the lizard tail tracks and the seabird hatch marks already etched in the sand.

Alison, tired of walking, sat down on the beach while John and I ambled on. The further we walked toward the southeast point, facing out into open ocean, the better the shells we found. I expected a sad and whiney Alison when we doubled back, but instead she was quite satisfied, playing by herself, and had found some treasures of her own.

How rarely, I realized, had I spent such simple, empty time with my children. At home, we were always rushing to get somewhere on time, always busy, always late. If there ever were time to spare, my mind would race to think of what else I could get done on my list. Even on a weekend, I felt pressed and busy. If the children asked to take a walk or play a game, it threatened my productivity.

Did we have to come this far, to an island with no one, no jobs, no telephone, no house to clean, no garden to weed, no homework, no team sports, no lessons, no appointments, in order for me to realize how important just doing nothing with my children could be?

We were circling back to *Hei Tiki* when another boat sailed into view. The closer it sailed, the more clearly it headed for West Plana, tacking all the way. Short tacks, south, east, south, east, shifting all three sails to one side then the other. Show-offs, I thought to myself. Why not just motor in? Must be real sailing purists. They sailed a broad white ketch, a bit longer and considerably tubbier than our boat, with carved wooden scrollwork along the sides.

"What's that guy doing?" John asked a half hour later. A snorkel was moving slowly from the ketch toward the beach, floating over shallow reef. Every now and then the swimmer's head jerked up, then he looked back down and fluttered further.

"I think he's fishing," Dave said. "Look now." All four of us watched the swimmer jerk a hooked fish above the water and hold it high as he swam back to his boat.

"That's a parrotfish," said John. "He eats parrotfish?"

"It takes all kinds," said David.

Blam. I wake up. Lightning smashes, thunder crashes, rain drives into the forward hatch above my bed. I bound awake. The clock says 1 A.M. David tramps across the deck above me, tying things down. The boat champs at the anchor line like a dog worrying a tether. Snarling winds have whipped up waves more than two feet tall. Out the galley porthole, I can sight on the anchor light atop our neighbors' main mast, shining through the commotion.

David jumps down into the cabin, his rain jacket dripping, his hair plastered down. I pull the companionway hatch shut as far as it will go, but still rain drives down into the galley. Noise and motion surround us, and now I glimpse the anchor light out the porthole on the other side. The storm has swung our boat around 180°, and now we're feeling the wind on its backside. I steady my eyes on that anchor light, the only thing that is holding firm. I'm terrified that we'll break anchor and slide right into the rocks or the shore.

Kaboom! A crack of lightning, a ball of fire. An explosion inside my head, it's that close. An explosion out there, on that other boat's deck.

"Did you see that?" I blurt out. "It struck them." I see the worry in David's eyes, but he says nothing. We stand close in the galley, knuckling the handrails. I fully expect to see the other boat burst into flames.

Lights inside the other boat's cabin. Storm noises move further away. Dull thunder without lightning. The howling dies down. The world calms. Amazingly, both children sleep on through it.

"That was terrifying," I say.

"I think it's past," says David. He stretches out on the galley settee, pulls a sheet over his face, and falls asleep fast. I wedge myself into the forward berth between the children. I open the hatch above us, now that the rain is gone. I lie there and listen to faraway thunder.

We woke up early to listen to the 6 A.M. weather from NOAA on the single-sideband radio. We needed to decide whether to keep on sailing. From Plana, we had a long run to Provo—short for Providenciales—our one projected landfall in the Turks and Caicos Islands. There were a few spots where we could hitch up for the night, but nowhere with solid protection, nowhere with food or fuel, for the next 120 miles.

David telescoped out the antenna, resting it gingerly on a lifeline, then adjusted the dial, seeking amidst the static that robotic voice that sailors dub November Mike.

"Sa-tur-day, Oc-to-ber twen-ty-eight," the synthesized voice said in machine monotone. Words, numbers, latitude and longitude, flew right by me. I caught "Seas, ten to twelve feet" and shot David a glance of horror.

"Off the coast of Carolina," he said. He was understanding

more of the report, traveling with his mind's eye down the East Coast, region by region. "Won't affect us, but they're feeling it at home," he said. "First frost in Virginia."

More words and numbers. Fronts, troughs, and systems, wind speed and direction, height of waves.

"Southwest North Atlantic," we heard the passionless voice say. David leaned in toward the radio. "No sig-ni-fi-cant features. I-so-la-ted thun-der-storms."

"At least when we're sailing, we can dodge them," said David. "I say it's a go."

"All the way to Provo," I voted. We had been averaging a speed of five knots—just over five miles an hour. That meant twenty-four hours of sailing before we reached Turks and Caicos. If we wanted to get there in the midday sun, to see our way through the reef, we could leave no later than noon. It was time to get ready.

David went through his customary presail routine of setting lat and long coordinates on the GPS. He kept pressing buttons. No lights, no numbers. It wouldn't even turn on. He reached behind and checked all the connections, then checked the antenna on the stern.

"Something wrong?" I asked.

"Lost it," he said. "Can't go anywhere."

At times like this, I wanted him to talk more. Tell me what he had found, what he suspected, what we could do about it. "What do you think happened?" I probed.

"It'll take weeks to repair. Might have to scrap the whole trip."

"Was it the lightning?" I asked.

He brushed by me, ignoring my question.

"Wasn't there a marine supply in George Town?" I continued to ask. He didn't respond.

"What's the matter, Mommy?" Alison asked, now by my side.

"The GPS got blown out by lightning," I said quietly.

"What'll we do?" she asked.

"I don't know."

Once David had checked every connection, wired the unit back up, and pressed all the buttons one more time, he declared our navigational equipment dead. That ball of lightning I watched strike the boat beside us must have fried our own electronics. The equipment carried a one-year warranty, but we had to send it back to the U.S. for repair. "There's a month or more of waiting," said David, intensely glum.

"I wonder what happened to them," I ventured, nodding toward the other boat. The couple on that boat seemed to know how to sail. Maybe help was not so far away.

David poured himself a rum and lime juice. Half a glass of rum, a splash of lime.

"David," I chastised. "It's not even noon."

"We're not going anywhere."

The day dragged on in muffled tones. David soon was snoring. Alison drew pictures, then refolded the clothes in her cubby. John snorkeled every coral head in sight. I wrote in my journal, glancing often at our neighbors. He was deeply tanned, a head of thick brown curls. She was fair, light orange hair pulled in under a turquoise bandana. A stout yellow cat prowled their deck.

By midafternoon, David had slept off his dark mood. "We're here tonight, no question about that. Might as well make the most of West Plana," he joked. "Then we'll decide what the hell we're doing."

He and John set out spearfishing. It surprised me, fifteen minutes later, to notice that David was standing up in our dinghy, holding on to the boarding ladder of the nearby boat, talking to the curly-haired man. When he came back an hour later, I asked him about the neighbors next door.

"They're going to Mayaguana tomorrow. Turks and Caicos, too, hopping their way down. He says we can sail along."

"What about the GPS?"

"We'll figure it out in Provo."

I liked the idea of sailing partners.

"What are they like?"

"He's into electronics."

"Did they lose anything last night?"

"They unplugged."

"Where are they from?"

"Massachusetts. Left home about the same time we did."

"Where are they going?"

"Don't know. Down-island. Same way we are."

"What's their boat's name?"

"Aerial."

Dave dinghied to *Aerial*, charts in hand. Half an hour later, I swam over, too. "Come aboard," a voice said. She stretched out a hand. She wore no more than a halter top and underpants over her slender body. Freckles bloomed all over her face and shoulders. The sun had bleached her eyelashes. "Becca," she introduced herself, "and Willie the cat," who was already doing a serpentine purr between my feet.

It didn't take long to start talking about things that mattered. "We sold our house, paid off the loan on this boat, and took off. We're looking for home," Becca said. "Our island is out there somewhere."

I told her about home in Virginia, about our year away. I told her about the children. John was still snorkeling between our boat and theirs. Alison was on the foredeck of *Hei Tiki*, washing dishes.

"She likes housework?" asked Becca. "We'll adopt her."

"This is a new thing," I said. "It will last about as long as my visit over here."

Male voices bantered below in the cabin. "They're talking about a course to Mayaguana," said Becca. They climbed up the companionway and I met Michael. An amused elfin face, a strong, solid body, tanned darker than most white skin can manage. He wore a small red bathing suit with a white shirt, unbuttoned, slipped over.

"Tough luck on your electronics," he said.

"I thought the lightning hit you for sure."

"Just an illusion," he said. He aimed his fingertips at *Hei Tiki* and hissed an imaginary charge.

"Felt real to me," I said.

Mayaguana stretches twenty-four miles, west to east. Abraham's Bay takes a bite out of the southern coast, yet the memory of the unbitten coastline persists as a near-solid fringe of coral. Underwater elkhorn forests grow so tall and dense that even at high tide, they break the water's surface. From a distance, you can trace the five-mile-long line of disturbance. We sighted, poked, poled, inched our way through the reef and into the bay.

The next day we sat at anchor—Michael and Becca's call. It was October 31, and that made Alison homesick.

"You mean they don't have Halloween here?" she asked.

"We can have Halloween, even if they don't," I told her.

"It's not the same," she said. She sank into a funk.

"You have a neighborhood," I said. "We've got *Aerial*. Let's have a party."

She looked up.

"We'll invite them to our boat for supper."

She almost smiled.

"You can dress up if you want to."

"I don't have a costume." Her spirits slid again.

"I do," said John, one-upping her. He grabbed his mask from the lazarette, pulled it on, and uttered some word through his snorkel. Snorkel out, he said it again: "Fishbuster."

"I have an idea," I said.

"What?" she asked glumly.

We had been using a dozen cotton bandanas for dinner napkins. I found the most colorful ones—turquoise patched with leopard skin, yellow-and-pink paisley, and purple Southwest print. "Stand here in front of me," I said. I tied one around her chest and the other two into an ankle-length skirt.

"There," I said. "Bahama Mama."

"What's a Bahama mama?" John asked. I shot a frown his

way. No literalist questions allowed. I took Alison's hands and danced with her, singing the words "Bahama Mama" over and over in an island rhythm. Whatever a Bahama Mama is, Alison was one of them.

She had to exchange the purple print for an orange, and she had to look in a mirror, then change to a bathing suit rather than panties underneath. But with John's encouragement and David's praise, she finally counted it as a Halloween costume.

We set out that afternoon to snorkel the reef. Becca and Michael dinghied out to the breakers ahead of us. Alison balked. "I don't want to snorkel in the deep water."

"See those whitecaps out there?" David said to her. "That's where the coral touches the water. We'll stay close by. You don't have to be afraid."

She finally agreed, but when we dinghied out and dropped anchor, she got scared again. David and John had already finned far away. Here I was again, stuck with a child who needed comforting.

"I'm going in," I said, feeling mad and guilty both. It seemed as if I was always giving up my snorkeling time when she was too scared to go under.

She probably said something, but I lowered myself out of earshot, tightened my mask, blew out my snorkel, and looked down at the most amazing underwater world I had yet seen. The shapes, the colors, the life-forms were familiar, but everything had tripled in size.

Great arms of elkhorn reached up from the ocean floor. Fallen stalks littered the sea floor like ancient ruins. Fish darted and skidded, clustered and hid. Schools of sleek striped yellow snappers. Bermuda chub, flat, round, and gray, with shoe button eyes. Triggerfish, electric blue arabesques, stared imperiously at me. This was their world, not mine. I felt tiny, and outnumbered.

I wanted Alison to see this world, too. I looked back at her. There was our new friend, Michael, hanging onto our dinghy by his elbows, helping Alison on with her mask.

I dipped back down, relieved and thankful. I came face-to-face with a sluggish fish, mottled and striped a muddy brown. Its grumpy lips recalled a grouper. I pinwheeled around, looking for John to help with identification. As I spinned, I caught a glimpse of that archetypal shape, twice as long, four times as wide in girth as I. I panicked, quelled my panic, looked again, and the shark was gone.

There comes a time when the afternoon light slants so that the sun, which has been highlighting the coral, instead throws into relief all the bits of dust and life suspended in the water. High noon crystal becomes afternoon haze. When that happened, we retreated to our sailboats.

As the sun teased the horizon, Michael and Becca arrived for Halloween dinner. Alison, in costume, played hostess all evening. She served up drinks from the galley, passed out hand-written menus, and wrote down orders painstakingly.

"Beans and rice, yum," said Becca. "I'll take that." She played along—there was no other choice offered.

John had refused to costume up, but he didn't mind being disk jockey. He chose *Planet Africa*. Senegalese Ismael Lo, Gabanese Pierre Akendengue set the beat. Pulsing drums, brash trumpetry, voices singing out in the fine, open vowelry of African French.

"I have this album," said Michael. "One of my favorites."

These people already felt like friends.

We left Mayaguana at midday, spent half a night on the island's southeast corner, then woke at 3 A.M., ready to sail to Provo. David started *Hei Tiki*'s engine. A cloud of diesel smoke soaked into the darkness. Stars speckled the universe. A meteor skidded across the sky. I uncleated the anchor line and held it taut, leaning like a water skier on a tow line. I glanced back. Lit by the dim red light of the compass, David's face gave a silent nod.

Slowly, methodically, I hauled in. I pulled until the boat

stood tight above the anchor. A strong jerk dislodged the hook, and I pulled the anchor up through the water. I shot a thumbs-up to Dave. Anchor up. I manhandled all forty pounds under the railing and onto the deck, tied it down with knots now second nature. Our boat turned slowly southward. A dimly lit *Aerial* was moving, too.

The children sensed the noise and motion. They both straggled out into the cockpit to say goodbye to the Bahamas. We had been almost two months in this nation of islands, and it felt as if we were leaving a friend.

Our next landfall took us to a new country: Turks and Caicos. Part of the Bahamian archipelago, they remained in the British Commonwealth when the Bahamas gained their independence in 1973. Provo was a tourist town, with telephones, airport, and shipping service—all of which we would need to fix the GPS.

We sailed out of the night, and by daybreak were crossing the Caicos Channel, a wild, wide stretch of water. We were heading almost due south; wind pressed hard from the east. Waves attacked from the side, curling far above then tumbling under us, tossing the boat from side to side. I gripped the wheel and tried to keep the boat in line.

"Don't oversteer," said David. "When they're this big off the beam, head right in, then roll back over. The boat will right itself. It's different from sailing to windward."

I started to get the feel of it, less a victim, more a vanquisher. I tempered the turn of the wheel. Now and then a wave smacked us broadside, drenching me. My body stayed stiff, my attention focused, up a twelve-foot wave, down a twelve-foot trough, trying to steer a steady course.

Aerial kept the same course a short distance away. Longer and stouter than *Hei Tiki*, she still seemed a floating toy. Michael caught my glance and waved.

By 8 A.M we could see the freighter mentioned on the chart. Such an eerie feeling—using a wreck to guide us. It ran aground decades ago and stands there, battered by the elements, crumbling imperceptibly, a reminder of how predatory the reef can be. We

tacked down the Sandbore Channel, into Sapodilla Bay by noon:
murky water beneath us, but a pretty crescent beach ashore. To
the east stretched the Caicos Bank, our next sail. At the first opportunity, David went looking for a telephone, GPS on his mind.

A new boat slid into Sapodilla Bay: a long, sleek luxury yacht,
four times the length of *Hei Tiki*. Glistening white, not a trace
of algae at the waterline. Smoky glass doors and windows, not a
glimpse of life inside. On its stern, a huge French flag. Below, in
golden calligraphy, *L'Aquasition*. I watched crew members hus-
tling about, dressed in spotless white. They anchored, then they
disappeared inside.

Alison had other things on her mind. "Let's play restaurant," she proposed. "You be at home. I'm going to call you.
Brrring."

I answered.

"Hello, Tina? This is Arielle," she said.

We chitchatted.

"Let's meet for tea at that restaurant," she said. "Do you
know the one I mean?"

Of course I did. We met in the cockpit.

"Well, yes, I came on my boat." She sat cross-legged,
hands folded, lips pursed, the perfect picture of a six-year-old
sophisticate.

"The boat's name?" she continued. "*L'Aquasition*. It's one
hundred feet long. Yes, we have seven crew members. They
cook dinner and make our beds. My boyfriend is a fisherman.
He might bring us enough grouper so you could come over to
dinner. And we wouldn't even charge you for dinner, even
though it would cost at least twelve dollars."

I reveled in her imagination. Fancifully weaving details she
had been collecting along the way, blithely mingling class dis-
tinctions, she spoke so earnestly that I dared not even smile.

The patter continued all afternoon. I could see her mind
and spirit at work. It was Alison's way of taking the helm and
navigating this new life crashing in on her.

Granddad offered to purchase another GPS for *Hei Tiki*, since repair of our blown equipment would take three weeks, and he knew we wanted to keep sailing. He would ship it to Provo right away. A few days' wait at the most.

"You think Becca and Michael will wait it out with us?" I asked David.

"Up to them."

I imagined the same conversation going on aboard *Aerial*. We had solved our immediate problem, the initial reason to sail together. But I liked these people, and I liked the feeling of friends nearby, a light out there in the darkness, someone listening for our radio call.

Despite fair weather, *Aerial* stayed. No one said so, but it seemed as if they were waiting to sail with us.

It certainly wasn't because of the charm of Provo. Town was ten miles from Sapodilla Bay. You hiked a dusty half mile from the beach, then you hitchhiked. Becca and I caught a ride to a supermarket, where we bought a few high-priced provisions. Michael and David worked together on our VHF antenna, also obliterated by lightning. The new GPS equipment arrived in a tidy three days, but by then, the easterly winds had cranked up again. "Come over this evening for dinner," Michael radioed. "We'll listen to Herb together."

We had heard about Herb in George Town. A seasoned sailor who lived in Bermuda, he helped cruisers with weather. He collected information from every source he could, then answered single-sideband calls from Newfoundland to Grenada, advising on whether to sail and what course to follow. If November Mike was a weather robot, Herb was a weather wizard. Sailors seemed to trust his predictions more than any others.

"*Aerial, Aerial. Southbound Two.*" It was the call we were waiting for. We sat together in *Aerial*'s comfortable cabin. Michael swiveled around to the navigating table, put on half-glasses and headphones, and adjusted the dials.

"*Southbound Two,* this is *Aerial*. How are you, Herb?"

"Good to hear from you, Michael."

Michael knew the routine. He read off numbers. "We're in Providenciales. Latitude 21°47′ north, longitude 72°17′ west. Winds today were twenty to twenty-four knots from the east-southeast. Waves three to four feet outside the anchorage. Barometer reading 30.4 and steady. Over."

"Very good, Mike. Over." Herb collected numbers from every sailor who called, too, finetuning his picture of weather systems.

"So we're here in Provo waiting to cross the Caicos Bank to Luperón, in the D.R.," said Michael. "But things are kicking up a little more than we like them out there. How does it look to you, Herb? Over."

There was a trough to the northwest of us and a high pressure ridge along Puerto Rico, said Herb. "My sense is that over the next two days you will see even stiffer winds. I would wait," he said. "Over."

Michael thanked Herb, signed off, and turned back to us, finger lassoing the air. "Whoopee. More fun in the sun in Provo."

Two days became two weeks. We kept trying to leave Provo.

First, straight out across the bank. We needed visibility, but the water was so stirred up there was no way to see shallow reefs ahead. *Aerial* led the way. They rammed into coral twenty minutes out and turned around.

Next day we tried again. We banged into three-foot waves for about five minutes and turned back again. It would have been slow torture.

Day after day, those easterlies kept pumping.

Michael and David came up with a new plan. Sail down the shipping channel, heading almost west, then turn and sail the far edge of the Caicos Bank. "We get into deeper water, there won't be this chop," they hypothesized.

The shipping channel was eighteen miles long—a morning of quartering seas, a swift, smooth sail. We came about onto our true course toward Luperón, and it was as if the weather gods turned the tempest on. The sky turned slate gray, the water pitch-black. Twelve-foot waves vaulted over us. Angry winds thrashed the sail. The boat lurched and shuddered.

"*Hei Tiki, Aerial.*" Becca's voice on the radio. "We're turning around, guys. This is too much for us."

David looked at me.

"Me, too," I gasped, already turning the wheel. "Coming about."

Exhausted, we took shelter behind West Caicos, an uninhabited island just north. We hunkered in the lee, but waves still rocked the boat frantically. "We have to sleep through this?" I asked David.

"Better than driving into it," he answered. He dinghied over to *Aerial* to plot our next move.

As long as we stayed in the fresh air of the cockpit, the children and I did okay. I couldn't read for fear of seasickness, and game pieces would slide all around. We started singing.

"How about this one?" I asked, belting it out.

> *What shall we do with the drunken sailor?*
> *What shall we do with the drunken sailor?*
> *What shall we do with the drunken sailor,*
> *Ear-lie in the morning?*

Alison sang with me. John watched, too shy to sing.

> *Drag him off the stern and use him for shark bait,*
> *Drag him off the stern and use him for shark bait,*
> *Drag him off the stern and use him for shark bait,*
> *Ear-lie in the morning.*

I couldn't remember the verses, but I didn't care. I made them up.

> *Make him scrub the deck with a dirty washrag,*
> *Make him scrub the deck with a dirty washrag,*
> *Make him scrub the deck with a dirty washrag,*
> *Ear-lie in the morning.*

"I've got one!" John cried. He spoke the words, and I re-shaped the rhythm to fit the song.

Make him drink the dirty bilgewater,
Make him drink the dirty bilgewater,
Make him drink the dirty bilgewater,
Ear-lie in the morning.

Alison made up another, rhythm nowhere near what the song required, but we didn't care.

Make him eat fish guts,
Make him eat fish guts,
Make him eat fish guts,
Ear-lie in the morning.

We laughed and laughed, and even John started singing. Alison clapped and called out, "More!" We sang every verse we could remember all over again.

The sun had set—a magnificent landscape of violet, coral, amber, and mauve—by the time David dinghied home again. It was too rocky to cook. We sliced white bread from a Provo bakery and spread it with peanut butter and guava jam.

Both children insisted they would puke if they slept in the cabin. Dave climbed into the forward berth alongside me. His hand caressed my butt. An invitation.

"What took so long over on *Aerial?*" I asked.

"Just talking." He turned his body toward mine. The boat rocked, back and forth, back and forth. I wedged my back up against the slanting sidewall and pulled him closer.

"About what?"

He answered by pressing his lips against mine. The rhythm of the boat rocked him toward me and back. I felt my body pick up the rhythm. My tongue roamed his. His mouth moved down my body, seeking my nipple. My neck arched back. I guided his search.

"We had a great time here, singing," I murmured.

"Mmm-hmm," he said. Then language disappeared.

And that sweet little space of a cabin became a cradle for our loving, and the rocking, like the loving, grew more and more intense. My left leg stretched out long and straight, my right leg lifted up in invitation. I found a foothold on the ceiling, so close in above us. He kissed and caressed me until I exploded, and then he plunged inside me and he gasped and exploded too, and we lay there, close enough to feel each other's heart beating, and then we parted and then we slept, rocking, rocking.

Next day, back to Provo. The landscape had changed at Sapodilla Bay. *L'Aquasition* had departed, and in its place, tied up near the gas dock, was a boat unlike any we had yet seen. An unpainted wooden hull, shorter than *Hei Tiki*, low to the water. A twisted tree trunk for a mast, a roughhewn rudder. A coarse patchwork sail, tied down with bits of twine. A three-foot barracuda, split down the belly and spread-eagled, teeth still vicious, hung from a spar to dry.

"It looks like a Haitian boat," I said at a glance. Not that I had ever seen one, but the news was full of rickety sailboats, overflowing with people, foundering between Haiti and neighboring isles. This one had made it, with produce to sell. A dozen adults with skin the color of eggplant milled around on the deck and the dock nearby, shouting French at each other. The smells of overripe citrus, unwashed clothing, and salted fish mingled in the air.

Oranges, grapefruit, limes, mangoes, papayas, avocadoes, tomatoes, little tiny peppers. Some huge orange tuber I had never seen before. I hung back, taking it all in. Alison gripped my thigh. John inspected the barracuda. David was already offering cigarettes to one of the men. The Haitian grinned, showing a half set of teeth. He put one Camel in his mouth and another in his pocket. David gave him a light, then gave him the pack of matches. They were talking together, even though David knew little French.

A woman of about thirty sat on the cabin roof, holding a rusty coffee can. Dressed in a tight green polka-dot dress, she barked out orders in a creole twang. I saw shallots in the can. *"Échalotes?"* I called out to her. She scowled and showed me a handful. *"Combien pour les échalotes?"* I asked. She squawked something at me. *"Combien?"* I asked again. It just made her scowl more. Others joined in with chatter, but I couldn't understand.

Finally I pulled a dollar out of my pocket. *"Pour un dollar américain. Combien?"* I asked. She poured out half a cup. *"Pas beaucoup,"* I said, and scowled. I held up three dollars. She gave me a pint of shallots.

We spent twelve dollars. We went back to the boat with a dozen grapefruit, two dozen oranges, twenty limes, six avocadoes, four mangoes, ten tomatoes, the shallots, and a hint of landscapes to come.

The waves were down, the wind had shifted. Finally we left Provo, sailing south-southeast to Luperón, 150 miles away, on the north coast of the Dominican Republic, not forty miles from Haiti.

It seemed impossible, after all those days of waiting, that the ocean could be so velvety calm. Great swells, the remnants of storms that brewed days ago and hundreds of miles away, lifted and let us down again in a giant oozing motion. The sail flapped uselessly, there was so little wind. Our engine pressed on.

"Nice ride," Michael radioed, an hour and a half into it. "Tune your radio dial to 81.7. I'm going to shoot some music your way."

"How can he do that?" John asked David.

"He's got a transmitter."

"He's got an aerial," I added.

We turned on the radio. Salsa rhythm. Upbeat trumpets. Sweet, soulful Spanish.

We sang on through the night.

7

The Smells of Luperón

WE SMELL THE LAND BEFORE WE SEE IT. SOIL, mold, rot mingle together in a smell of earth. It reminds me of home, of wet leaf mulch in our forest. Yet here and now it strikes me as new and rich and different.

The dry coral islands never smelled this way.

Soon after the smell of earth engulfed us, shapes of land began to emerge. Black space began to separate into a perspective of grays. Jagged shoreline, hills and mountains. Beyond them, even taller mountains, silhouetted against the predawn sky.

"Incredible," said David.

"It goes on and on," I said.

For months, landfall had meant low brown islands, just wrinkles above the water. Here, we were three miles offshore, and the mountains towered.

"See the opening?" said David. I didn't yet, but he guided me. "Straight for the buoy." We glided, sails down, by engine only, past foam-tossed rocks into a still lagoon.

"Far side of the buoy, then cut a sharp angle to the right. There should be markers," said David. "I'm going up to spot."

We headed down a narrow inlet, edged on either side by

dense mangrove marsh. Ahead, a crooked stick stuck up in the middle.

"Is that the marker?" I called anxiously. David nodded. "Which side?"

"Right!" he called back.

"I go right of the marker? Or I put the marker on the right?" My voice rose in pitch.

He shot back an impatient look. *We have had this conversation before,* I knew he was thinking. I tried desperately to remember. "Sailors speak as if the boat is at the still center of the universe," he had told me. "The rest of the world moves around it." The concept still wasn't second nature. I pointed the boat to the left of the stick.

"Not so far!" David yelled. "Straight at it until you're almost on top of it." The boat slowed, as if lurching into molasses.

"Reverse! Reverse!" David yelled as he slid the sounding pole straight into the water.

I revved it in reverse, and the boat eased out of the mire. "Let's try the other side of the marker," I called up to David.

Right of the marker, we slid through.

The mangrove avenue curved around and opened out into a picture-perfect harbor, round and flat and nestled in among gentle hills, green with pastures and palm trees. A white blur of hundreds of egrets dominated a mangrove thicket. They squawked and chattered, restlessly exchanging branches, perching, balancing, flying away.

A tall concrete jetty projected into the center of the harbor, boats tied up on either side. Another two dozen boats at anchor scattered the harbor. One couple sat in their cockpit, watching *Hei Tiki* motor by. Another fellow actually stood on the bow and watched us anchor.

David took the helm and I stood on the bow. I unfastened the anchor and glanced back for signals. He worked the throttle, watched the water, nodded silently.

Let the guy watch our every move. We had it down.

Luperón's water was so murky I could not see the anchor fall, but I felt the line give as the anchor hit bottom. I pulled back, seeing in my mind's eye the two points of the anchor scrape, then dig in. David chucked the motor into reverse, pulling the boat back, then spun his finger in the air: a signal to cleat the line.

"Got enough line out?" he asked cheerily, joining me on the foredeck.

Without a word, he loosened the anchor line and gave out another ten feet.

Without a word, I frowned, hands on hips. *Does he have to check everything I do? I've been anchoring for almost three months now. I can make some judgment calls.*

It's no longer a matter of David the sailor and Susan the novice.

This is feeling more like David the husband bossing Susan the wife around.

"We'd better clean up below," he said, brushing past me. *Clean up below?* What was he talking about? Everything was stowed two days ago for sailing. We had just sailed through the night. No mess could have accumulated in the cabin.

"Can I have my Coke now?" Alison pleaded. It was 7:30 in the morning, hardly time for a soda. But David had promised Alison a treat when we got to Luperón.

"Not until we're cleaned up." David assigned Alison the task of hoisting the yellow flag, signal that we had not cleared customs. We had heard how officious the Dominicans could be. David wanted to follow every rule.

I was stowing charts when John called down from the deck, "Here come some men dressed like soldiers."

I ducked my head up out of the companionway. A ramshackle rowboat, any paint long faded, carried five men our way. Four wore shorts and shirt sleeves. One wore camouflage fatigues and a black beret.

"False alarm," I told David. "Just locals, gawking." I went back to folding up charts.

The Spanish voices came closer. Something bumped up against the hull. Shiny black combat boots were boarding *Hei Tiki*. The man wearing them reached toward the photovoltaic panel to steady himself.

"No! no!" I came out yelling. I patted my hand on the railing. "Hold on here."

The other men from the boat clambered aboard, slipping off their sandals, chattering knowingly, laughing among themselves.

The children had disappeared into the cabin. David was in the head, shaving. What little Spanish I knew had vanished. I was supposed to be polite. I fumbled for words. Only when David appeared, blotting his chin with a towel, did one of the men speak English. "This is customs immigration officials. He is *commandante*," he said, pointing to Camo-Man.

The *commandante* struck an intimidating figure: skin like a dark-roasted coffee bean, a majestic eagle-nose, a muscle-bound physique cinched in with a belt. First David, then I, shook his hand. He stayed seated, never cracking a smile.

"My name Feli," the interpreter said. "We come to help with the English."

David played the gracious host. *"Café?"* he said. The word bounced among the five men, three of whom looked at me and said, *"Si."* I retreated into the galley and started making coffee.

"You have your pass-e-port-es, please," Feli said. David opened the leather case in which we carried our papers. The *commandante* pointed into the galley, chattering in Spanish. The others laughed. I felt vaguely victimized by their good humor.

David handed over passports. The assistant copied names, letter by letter, onto his printed form.

"Nombre de barco?" he said, looking at David.

"Name of boat," Feli translated.

"Hei Tiki," David answered.

"Ediki?" the assistant echoed. It didn't translate well.

"Hei Tiki," David repeated, offering the boat registration. All five passed it around, consulting on pronunciation. The assistant copied it, letter by letter. *"Tonelajes neto?"*

"What is it weigh, the boat?" Feli translated.

"Eleven." David held up ten, then one, fingers.

"Pasajeros?" asked the assistant.

"Passengers," said Feli. "How many, what their names."

"He already wrote everybody's name," David said.

"He need the name on these card also," said Feli.

David spelled our names, struggling to translate the alphabet. Finally he gave up and displayed our passports again, one by one. *"Dah-veed Wah-een-ay,"* the assistant spoke out loud, spelling it wrong and dropping David's last name altogether.

He looked more closely at the next one. *"Chon?"* he read for John. *"E muchacho o muchacha?"*

"Juan. Muchacho," I said. The officials chattered.

"Alisón?" he read. *"Muchacha, si?"*

I nodded. I knew the children were right behind the bulkhead, listening to every move. I herded them into view. Clucks of approval made them smile shyly. John clung behind me and Alison nestled into David's lap.

The water finally boiled, but by then it was too hot for coffee. I made up some Spanish. *"Prefero café caldo o soda fresco?"* I asked. They understood when I opened the refrigerator. The *commandante*'s face lit up. He nudged his assistant, pointed, and chattered.

One by one I pulled out every cold drink we had. Two Coca-Colas. *Commandante* and assistant popped them open right away. Grape soda and apple juice went fast. A can of V-8 juice was rejected. One juice left: some sweet concoction in a ghastly green box decorated with the cartoon creep from *Ghostbusters.*

Ghostbuster Green got passed around. The *commandante* pointed and laughed, then he pocketed the box. He patted his bulging breast pocket and smiled.

Cold drinks loosened everyone up. Feli looked straight at David. "Now you are expect to give the *commandante* something for his trouble."

"How much?" asked David.

"You choose, you choose," Feli said, shrugging his shoulders, looking away. The officials sat, waiting.

David was prepared. He pulled out a ten dollar bill. He

handed it, folded in half, to Feli, who simply handed it to the *commandante*, who slipped it into his pocket, right behind Ghost-buster Green. No words were spoken.

Then David reached back into his pocket, pulling out an aluminum tube. He opened it, and the fragrance of cigar tobacco made all eyes widen. The *commandante* snatched it. Business complete.

Camo-Man left feeling good. He stretched, stood, booted up, and climbed into the rowboat with his motley entourage. Feli manned the oars. As he turned loose of *Hei Tiki*, he gave a last friendly smile. "You need anything, you remember Feli. Gas, diesel, water. Anything. Adios. Goodbye."

David and I breathed a sigh together. We had made it into the Dominican Republic and, what's more, we were official.

"Time to take down the yellow flag, Alison."

She didn't answer. We looked over at our little girl, hanging onto the companionway, her face contorted by holding back tears.

"What's wrong?" I asked. She burst. It took a minute to understand the words through the sobbing.

We had given away her soda.

I read, wrote, rested into the afternoon. Something inside me needed quiet. But when the plan arose for a girls' trip to town— Alison, Becca, and me—I agreed.

We could walk the narrow, crumbling, concrete sidewalks or we could walk the clay-gray puddled road itself. Tiny wooden houses toed up to the sidewalks, houses made of roughhewn siding, scavenged plywood, corrugated roofing. Barely six feet tall and wide, some had doors, all had windows. The air smelled of ripe mud and deep-fat frying.

A chestnut-skinned girl in dingy underpants hung from a doorjamb, silently watching us with wet brown eyes. Behind her, the table was set with faded plastic flowers; a faded Virgin Mary gazed toward heaven from the wall.

The road split into a boulevard. In the center, trees shaded a concrete table. Five men sat on crates and buckets, intent on a domino match. They cackled, laughed, jogged each other playfully. A motorcycle droned in the distance. We had to sidestep a stream trickling out from behind a house. Smells everywhere: manure, wood smoke, salted fish, fermented citrus.

From between two houses, three little mud-caked pigs snorted across our path. A matted gray burro, loosely bridled to a doorknob, stood with head bowed down. An auburn rooster pecked the neck of a small black hen, preparing to mount her. She squawked and flapped free.

A woman shuffled past us, wrinkles framed in a kerchief. I looked into her basket: tomatoes, peppers, eggs. I looked into her eyes, and at the same time, Becca said to her, *"Ola."* She smiled a sweet, silent smile and shuffled on.

We found a grocery store. Our mission: to buy Alison a cold soda, to make up for morning losses.

The man at the counter nodded toward me, ready to help. *"Hay Coca-Cola?"* I hazarded.

"Si, si. Cuanto?"

I ordered three. He pulled three thick green bottles out of the vintage cooler.

"Abiertos?" he asked, pantomiming with a can opener.

"Si, gracias."

He named the price of three Coca-Colas. The sounds tumbled into my brain.

"Trente-seis. Teertee sees."

Now to pay. David had given me some Dominican currency. I pulled out of my pocket three grimy bills and loose change.

The grocer placed coins one by one on the counter as if teaching a toddler. *"Diez, diez, diez, cinquo, uno. Trente-seis."* His friendliness dissolved my embarrassment.

Walking out, we stepped over a mangey mother dog, leathery teats depleted, puppies crawling over her. I ran my hand through salt-caked curls. "Know what I just realized? I never combed my hair today."

Becca grinned. "You fit right in."

———

I woke up the next morning grumbling that we hadn't done lessons for a week.

"The kids don't need it in a place like this," David said. "Just watch them as they walk down the street. They're absorbing so much. They learn by being here." So David took the children into town by midmorning. I just wanted to hole up on the boat.

"Hey, hon, can you give me a hand?"

It was hot, dank, steamy. After noon. The air was so still, and I was almost asleep. I had written two letters, then worked at finishing Michener's *Caribbean*. Thick and dense, it was taking me weeks to read.

"Help me with these cartons," he said. Under the railing came a case of Presidente beer and a case of soda.

"What's in here?" I asked as David heaved up our canvas go-bag. A dozen soft yellow rolls. Hard white cheese and coarse red salami, each wrapped in butcher paper. Squares of chocolate, wrapped in red foil. Two cartons of Marlboros. Four bottles of rum.

"Great prices," he said.

"I hope," I muttered. "Where are the kids?"

"Back in town." He opened a beer and sat down.

"You left them in town?"

"It's perfectly safe here." He was lighting a cigarette. "These are such loving people. They wouldn't think of harming a child. Want a beer?"

"Are they by themselves?" I was freaking out.

"Michael stayed in town, too."

"Is Michael with them?"

"I guess so."

"David!" He seemed oblivious. I moved toward the dinghy. "I can't belive you left them in town alone."

"I thought you wanted to stay on the boat."

"I do!" I was almost shouting. "But now I'm worried about the children."

He tossed his cigarette in the water and took the dinghy line from my hand. "I told them I would come get them," he said in a low, slow voice. He rowed off without another word.

An hour and a half later, I watched David and the children row Michael over to *Aerial*. Another hour later, David and the children returned, instantly replacing my quiet with noise.

"You should see the fish store," John was saying. "It's just a little shed. All they have in it is a freezer, and you open up the freezer and there are all these fish, frozen solid, lying one on top of the other. I saw a barracuda, and a parrotfish, and a triggerfish, and a dolphin, and a bunch of grunts."

"Mommy, Daddy wants to buy me a dress," Alison interrupted.

"They were stiff and covered with frost and all piled up together."

"It fit fine, Mom," Alison said, pulling on me, "but he wants you to see it."

"He doesn't have to ask my permission," I said, voice dark with bitterness—I wasn't sure why.

"I met this girl and we played together," Alison kept bubbling. "We made friends."

"It was sweet," said David. "You should have seen them." I smiled insincerely, avoiding his eyes. "One little girl who knows nothing but English. Another who knows nothing but Spanish. They spent an hour in the park together."

"What did you do all that time?" I asked Alison.

The answer came trippingly. "Oh, we chatted."

For the moment, the darkness gave way. I reached out to her for a hug.

David proposed dinner out with Michael and Becca. The thought of being served, rather than cooking canned food in the galley, sounded great, but here? There was mud, filth, smells.

"We found a place. Michael and I had a beer there," said David.

"You have to come see my dress," said Alison.

For her, I agreed.

In among fancy pastel crinolines and too-too pretty lace and bows, Alison had found a beauty: bold tropic print of red, blue, and yellow; dropped waist and gathered skirt; short puff sleeves and clean white collar. It fit her perfectly.

"Do you want to wear it right now?" asked David.

Alison bounced up and down. She ducked behind the cash register then came out pirouetting. We adults oohed and ahed.

"Guess we should dress up for dinner, eh, Juan?" Michael joked.

White linen napkins fanned out from crystal glasses. Six tables were set, but we were the only customers. Our hostess greeted David and Michael like old friends. We chose chicken, steak, fish—familiar fare, but with a Dominican twist: fried plantains instead of french fries.

By the time we left the restaurant, the streets of Luperón were beginning to throb. People everywhere—doorways, sidewalks, street corners. Middle-aged women sat in threes and fours, chatting, gesturing, watching. A naked baby toddled and fell, picked herself up and this time made it from one woman's arms to another's. Radios played merengue mixed with static.

Rounding a corner, we passed an elderly woman, eyes sunk into a weathered face, white hair knotted at her neck. She sat alone, rocking. Becca murmured, *"Ola."*

The woman held out a sinewy hand toward John. She lifted her face, taking in his youth. He held her hand. She spoke words none of us understood. He nodded slightly and answered her eyes. She smiled and spoke, I am sure, some final blessing. John listened. *"Gracias,"* he spoke quietly. She went back to rocking.

I felt proud of how he paused, how he heard her human kindness and, by listening, returned his own.

I awoke dreamless and grumpy again the next day, feeling as if I did not want to go back into Luperón. There was a fascination, yet a horror, about the place. The filth repelled me: those rivers of mud running between the houses, the smell.

David couldn't get enough of it. The life-spirit thrilled him. He could walk down the street and engage any Dominican in conversation, even though he didn't know Spanish. He and the children, dinghy piled high with dirty clothes, went to town again, following signs to a "Lavanderia." Alison held her nose as they walked past a pig pen. John looked in: a mother pig nestled down in mud, nursing six babies.

They followed a path between the pig pen and a tumble-down house. Signs pointed to a little shed set back from the sidewalk. They looked inside. No one there. *"Ola!"* David called. A little woman shuffled in from the back, clucking in Spanish and motioning to put the laundry down. She led them to the back room, where she proudly showed them two huge cast-iron kettles, one lined with smooth, gray rocks.

David used gestures, English, and a few words of Spanish to come to an understanding. He would return for the clothing at four that afternoon. She smiled and nodded, then started talking under her breath again as she hoisted two buckets and went behind the house to fetch water.

David and John returned to town at a little after four. A breezy, blue-sky afternoon had freshened the air. As they walked down the street, John noticed rags strung all around the pig pen. Then he noticed his tie-dyed shorts among the rags. Then he noticed that it was our family's laundry, hanging on the pig pen's barbed wire fence.

The laundry woman was already bustling out her door. *"Oh, señor,"* she said. Her hands worked precisely, picking the clothing off the fence without a tear. When David tried to help, he snagged a T-shirt. She gestured, showing him that some of the clothing was still damp.

"No problema," David said, almost bowing. He and John brought the clothes back and told the story to Alison and me. "We're lucky the pigs didn't eat our laundry," John said overseriously.

I sniffed a T-shirt: smelled clean. This is what David meant, making lessons out of life in Luperón.

David and Michael had been gone since five-thirty. They were supposed to just go and check us out. We were planning to sail out of Luperón at dawn tomorrow. Now they had decided to have a night on the town, leaving me with the children. This felt too familiar.

I was about to burst with anger. I finally decided to radio Becca. "Have you heard from Michael?"

"Probably decided to have a few beers. You know them."

Just what I didn't want to hear. She seemed indifferent. I wasn't, but I didn't feel like pouring it out.

"Give me a call if you hear," I said, and signed off.

Year in, year out, I would sit at home and watch the evening go by. And here it was happening again. Finding friends was one thing. But forgetting our own partnership, just as it was growing stronger?

I was jealous. David had a better friend in Michael than I had in Becca, and all three of them spent more time together than they did with me. I was the designated parent. I stayed home with the kids.

It made me furious. It made me cry.

"What's the matter, Mom?" asked John, climbing down into the galley.

"I guess I'm just feeling sad." I tried to be honest, not hateful. "I feel like Dad has decided to spend tonight with Michael rather than us, and it makes me sad."

"Me, too," he said quietly.

Both children had fallen asleep by eight-thirty, when Michael and David dinghied up to our boat. They were laughing, punchy. I was solemn, but no longer crying.

"So six-thirty?" David called out as Michael revved his dinghy motor.

"Daylight hour, six-thirty." He roared away.

"Where were you?" I choked.

"What a night." He peed over the lifelines. "What a place."

"Where were you?" I bit my lower lip to steel myself.

He still didn't answer. *Is he trying to annoy me, or is he just oblivious?*

He laughed, remembering something that happened. *Oblivious.*

"That *commandante* is some guy."

"Where were you?" I asked, my voice chilly. *Now he must be ignoring me. Or he's too drunk to notice.* "Why did it take you three hours to check out?"

"We couldn't find the *commandante.*" He had heard me; his voice took on an edge. "We had an appointment at five-thirty. We got there a little late, but he wasn't there anyway. His assistant kept saying '*Mas tarde,*' but he wouldn't name a time. So all we could do was stay in town and check back, hoping to find him."

His story sounded plausible, but I didn't warm up any.

"So we go back at eight o'clock. By that time, the whole town has lost power. Totally dark. No radios, nothing. We knock on the door and the assistant says yes, he is in, but he's taking a shower. He wanted us to come back later, but we just stood there.

"So in comes the *commandante* with nothing but a towel wrapped around his waist. Grinning, talking up a storm, saying something about going out to shoot his gun. But I think he was out with his girlfriend, shooting off another gun. He was certainly pleased with himself."

He lit a cigarette. I clenched my jaw.

"So his assistant holds a candle, and the *commandante* holds his towel around his waist, takes a pen, and signs our papers with a grand flourish."

He took a long drag on his cigarette. "So that's what took so long," he said.

I could feel the stillness. My turn.

"I've been having a hard time this evening, Dave." I had to eke out the words.

"What's the matter?" Oblivious.

"All those feelings from years gone by, that you got to stay out as long as you wanted and that you're doing what you want while I'm back home, just taking care of children and being a nothing." That last word ground out of my mouth, gristly with self-loathing. "I'm glad we have people to sail with, but it feels like you and Michael are the partners on this sail, not you and me anymore."

His face turned down.

"I'm not even part of the sailing decisions anymore. You are always going over to *Aerial*, talking with Michael and Becca about where and when we are going. I'm never included. I'm always back here taking care of children. You go off and get to have adult conversations, and I'm sitting here alone all the time." My voice was rising. "It's making me really mad."

He sat still, listening. It was always his way when I confronted him. He would never engage. We never had a good, healthy argument.

Finally, tensely, I asked, "Will you please say something?"

"I'm sorry you are upset." Not very satisfying. "We did what we had to do."

The air was chilly. We weren't connecting. He lit another cigarette. I looked out over the water.

He ducked down into the galley. Even that made me mad. I hated cigarette smoke inside the cabin.

He came back up with a flashlight, a chart, and the Van Sant book. "We did check out of Luperón," he said. He spread the chart across our knees. "See what you think about this plan." He pointed. "We leave in the morning, rest an afternoon at Sosúa, then sail the coast all night. We'll make Samaná in two days."

I looked at the chart, but my mind was in turmoil. I couldn't concentrate.

"Well?" he asked.

"If that's what you planned," I said.

He was trying to make me happy. I wasn't going to make it that easy.

Coasting

The North Coast of the Dominican Republic is the roughest passage for yachts island-hopping from North America to the Virgin Islands. But one of the oldest ploys in sailing can make it quite a pleasant trip.

For almost five hundred years sailing vessels have navigated the North Coast of Hispaniola, against the very strong winds and seas, by hiding behind the headlands and capes during the day and proceeding close to shore at night where the more moderate conditions permit a slow progress against the wind.

—BRUCE VAN SANT,
The Gentleman's Guide to Passages South (1989 edition)

Hispaniola, the island shared by Haiti and the Dominican Republic, earns distinction throughout the Caribbean by being tallest of all the islands and second in land mass only to Cuba. In the Bahamas, the biggest islands we had seen—Great Abaco, Great Exuma—seemed whiskers of land compared to this one. Now our task was not to sail from island to island, but to move two hundred miles east along a coast shaped with utter disregard for human need, where rock and forest shot straight up from the water's edge. There were few of those fall-back positions

David always scanned the charts for, few harbors at all between Luperón and Samaná.

"It's one cape after another," David said at midday. "Cabo Macoris, Cabo Frances Viejo, Cabo Cabrón, Cabo Samaná. Let me tell you, the rough part's going to be out there at the end of the capes. They stick out there with nothing between them and Africa."

Heading east-southeast, we were charging nose into the prevailing trades. If they kicked up, waves could beat us down to the speed of only a knot or two. Then all we could do would be to keep on sailing or to turn back. Three hours into it, though, the sailing was not hard. Four boats had slipped out of Luperón at dawn. We had radioed back and forth and agreed to sail together: *Seascape* and *Second Vow* joined *Hei Tiki* and *Aerial*. We had met *Seascape*'s owner, Bill, in Luperón. All he could talk about was how much better the bars were in Samaná. We hadn't met Patrick and Catherine, driving a motor yacht, *Second Vow*. We knew where our allegiances were, if pressed.

We tacked far off the coast, around Puerto Plata, D.R.'s biggest northern city. A jumbo jet screamed overhead at midday. We were approaching Sosúa: tourist territory. Our plan was to rest up in Sosúa, then head out as night fell and sail twenty-four hours straight to Samaná.

We angled toward the land. The water bustled with activity: bathers dabbling, speedboats cruising, jet skis slicing through the scene.

Aerial had already anchored. I drove straight for them. David motioned violently from the bow. I spun the boat around. He rushed back. "Watch me, not the jet skis, will you?" he spat out. "Reefs everywhere—this is treacherous. You almost took us right over a coral head."

"Yes, sir," I said with an edge.

"Let's try it again." He sounded like a worn-out parent.

We nudged in more slowly, David at the wheel, and anchored without incident. A low-slung motorboat had come up to *Second Vow*. "Customs?" I suggested.

David shrugged indifferently. He had already opened a bottle of beer, mind set on a nap and nothing else. The drone of jet skis was going to make sleeping hard for me. I started a soporific lunch: chicken soup, extra rice.

"Seascape, Seascape, Second Vow," Patrick radioed Bill. We listened in. "They say we can't anchor here. I offered a bottle of rum. Ten bucks. They say no way."

"Those shits. Who are they?"

"Nobody showed I.D. They came off like they mean it, though."

I broke in. *"Second Vow,* the *commandante* in Luperón said we could stop in Sosúa. I asked specifically."

"Doesn't seem to matter. They say there's another anchorage up the coast, a public beach."

"Let's not do anything too fast," Michael chimed in. David, sipping on his Presidente, just listened.

But in another ten minutes, the low-slung boat was bumping up against our white fiberglass with its heavy wooden gunwales. In the boat were seven men, only one wearing a shirt, and one woman, her hair punked red.

"You cannot remain here," said the man in shirtsleeves.

"The *commandante* in Luperón said we could," I argued. The man spoke to his cohorts in Spanish then repeated, "You may not remain."

David simply insisted, "We will leave tonight."

"Your boat cannot be here. If you do not go, the police from Puerto Plata will put you in jail." All eight looked straight at us. "You go now." He revved his outboard and pushed off our bow.

Michael called on the VHF. "What do you think, Dave?"

"I say we cool it. I'm taking a nap."

Michael was agreeing, but then a jet ski sliced through the water not three feet from the bow. It swerved and bore down across our anchor line again. An attack.

"Aerial, we're out of here," Dave said abruptly into the microphone. "Pull up the anchor," he ordered.

I heaved up on the anchor line. David jerked the boat into gear. The anchor line snapped straight, but it wouldn't pull any further. The bow lurched forward; the anchor wouldn't let go.

"Pull it up!" David yelled.

"I'm trying!" I yelled back, yanking. He stormed up on the bow with me, shoving me aside.

"It's hooked on a coral head, goddammit." He handed the line back to me. "I'm going to drive up on it. Let the line out, then pull up hard." The orders tumbled out of his mouth. I tried to ask a question. He wasn't listening. He threw her into reverse, jerked back, threw her into forward. Still stuck.

"I told you to let go!" David yelled. Again: reverse, jerk back, throw forward. Still stuck.

"Can't you understand what we're doing?" He stormed up toward the bow.

"I don't understand because you don't explain anything!" I yelled.

The nasty jet ski buzzed our bow.

"Get back there and point the boat the way I tell you." I did what he said, but I felt like a child. "More power! More power!" he yelled. I rev the motor. He jerked back. Anchor line freed. I turn the boat sharply, out toward open water.

David returned to the cockpit, face pinched. "Bent the anchor," he said. He looked out over the water, not at me. "A two hundred dollar anchor." My throat filled with guilt. We had two other anchors, but only half the size and a third the weight. I felt incompetent, at fault.

We sailed grimly to the next beach: a brown sand spit. The bottom shallowed up enough to hold an anchor, but there was no protection. Waves washed around the corner almost as tall as out at sea.

I broke the silence. "Should I get out the other anchors?"

"The big one will do."

"I thought it got bent."

"We'll watch it."

Suspicion and anger tangled with guilt. Was it a crisis? Or was David just making a crisis out of it?

According to theory, the waves would diminish after sundown. Our four boats pulled out at six o'clock for an all-night sail. But the trade winds kept pumping relentlessly, kicking up even taller waves than in the morning. *Hei Tiki* bucked up one wave, plunged down the next. I held tight to the wheel. Just moving through these waves took energy and concentration. One hour out, we had only traveled two and a half miles, and the waves were growing steeper.

"No good," David said. "We've got to turn around."

"Good," I grunted. That was all I had the energy to say. The work was too hard, and both children were looking blue.

We radioed *Aerial*, then the others. No one argued with our plan: duck back into Sosúa and leave again before daylight.

We skied back down those steep, sharp waves. John read numbers off the GPS. "Seven-five! Seven-eight! Eight knots!" Never had *Hei Tiki* traveled so fast.

It was a moonless night. Pitch-black silence blanketed the harbor. An eerie light loomed underwater. Becca radioed: "Watch out. Night divers." David swept a flashlight beam ahead, spotting an unlit dive boat. I jerked us around. We anchored by whisper, slept soundly, and motored out again before five.

The sea can change so quickly. Last night's trade winds had dwindled to nothing. The ocean swelled and lifted, a vast, featureless desert. The wind was so impotent, the boom swung lackadaisically and the mainsail flapped all morning long. The sun glinted off the water. I could taste the sweat dripping down my face. *Hei Tiki*'s motor droned on. I hung limply over the wheel. Our progress seemed slow-motion, but David said the GPS read four knots. Each time we crested a swell, my stomach heaved.

"I need a break," I said. David took the wheel. All I wanted was to lie flat on my back and do nothing.

"Mommy, I don't feel good," Alison said, inching in next to me.

"Too hot to cuddle," I muttered. "I don't feel good either." I made room for her by my knees.

When I tried to sit up, I felt queasy. I couldn't imagine taking the helm. Alison kept asking me to do things—read her a book, tell her a story. "A story about your animals," she asked.

"Maybe later." I just wanted oblivion.

I lay there for hours. The sun passed overhead. The boat almost drove itself. Every half hour, David left the helm, plotted our position, checked the engine. Every time he lifted the companionway steps to check the engine, the spin and clank of the moving parts, the smell of diesel drove me further inward.

"No way we'll make it to Samaná," he said at two. "We'll have to put in at Escondido."

I only nodded. The motor droned on. I spoke an obligatory apology: "Sorry I feel so terrible." He acted as if it was no big deal. I kept my eyes closed, just squinting toward David. I did feel bad, but there was more going on. Some voice deep inside was saying, *Let him see how it feels when I'm not a part of the team.*

As the heat retreated, I came to. Mauve sunset faded behind us as we spotted Escondido, a hidden anchorage sliced into this rocky coast. One by one, four boats turned into the shadowy fjord.

Sheer rock and jungle shot up from the water. On a bit of pristine beach, a few perfect palm trees clustered. *This belongs in* National Geographic, I thought, *but what kind of lens could capture it?*

"Drive right up to the beach," said David. "The bottom's as steep as the cliffs. It'll be a bitch getting an anchor to hold."

Seascape and *Aerial* had already anchored, well off to starboard. I was worried about *Second Vow*, just off our stern. I could hear Catherine and Patrick yelling. He worked the helm, she worked the anchor. He kept motioning violently. She kept jerking on the anchor line. "Show me, goddammit!" I heard him yell.

"Pay attention!" David yelled at me from the bow. He grappled with the anchor line.

Second Vow revved their motor and came even closer.

"Hey!" David yelled. He was motioning for me to back up. *Back up much further and we'll ram into them,* I told myself.

I popped into reverse, gave it a little gas, then dropped into neutral.

David shot me an angry glare. He pushed his hand back impatiently. He wanted me to back up even further.

I chugged another quick reverse. He kept on glaring and waving. *Second Vow's* white hull hovered at our stern. I started calling out to David to explain what was going on when he dropped the anchor line and stormed back toward the cockpit.

"What are you doing?" he raged.

"What are *you* doing?" I yelled back. "We're going to run into them!"

"I can see what I'm doing," he hissed. "We are anchoring in the dark in a difficult anchorage. We are not going to run into *Second Vow.*" He reached past me, rammed the gear shift into reverse, and jerked the wheel around.

I was outraged. He was pushing me out of the way. He thought I was dispensible. *All right then,* I thought. *Do it your way. Do it by yourself. I'm sick of being ordered around. Sick of my opinions not counting.* I fled into the cabin.

I disappeared, but my senses stayed tuned. I could feel the boat lurching, hear David running up and down, bow to stern. He drove the boat backwards for a good ten seconds, then jammed it out of gear and ran up to the anchor line. He ran back to the helm, jerked backward, rushed forward. He managed to anchor alone, and we never hit *Second Vow.*

I tried to act busy down below, but I was a bundle of confusion. I wanted to matter on the boat. I wanted to make decisions, too. I wanted to be an equal. All day I had been trying to prove that David needed me, by feeling ill and refusing to sail. But my plan hadn't worked. He sailed us here. He anchored, in the dark, in a squeeze, all alone. As much as I had learned in three months on the boat, as sweetly as he might say I had become the better helmsman, he had years of experience over me. Always would.

It made me even madder.

A radio call interrupted my silent ranting. *"Aerial, Aerial. Seascape."* We listened in.

"Hey, Bill. How you holding?" Michael asked.

"Hell of a rocky anchorage," said Bill on *Seascape*. "What time we heading out?"

"Dave, you there?" said Michael. David picked up the microphone.

"I'm here."

"What do you say, Dave?" asked Michael. "Six?"

"Might make it even earlier," Bill interrupted. "Patrick had a little run-in with customs before the rest of us got here."

"Five-thirty," Dave said.

I wanted to hear more. I took the microphone and asked what happened.

"Patrick pulled in half an hour earlier than me and customs just appeared," Bill said. "Said we weren't allowed to anchor here. Patrick invited him aboard and gave him a bottle of rum. That made the guy happy. But when Patrick told him three more boats were coming, the guy got upset. Said he'd be back in the morning. Wanted to see all our papers."

I spoke for our boat. "Five o'clock."

"Five it is," Michael said. "We're turning in. *Aerial* back to sixteen. Signing off."

"Back to channel sixteen," I said. I paused. I still needed to connect. "Good night, Michael."

"Good night, Susan." Michael's quiet voice comforted me.

We ate without saying much. The children soon fell asleep. Waves ricocheted off the beach and pitched us up and down on the anchor line. David braced himself at the galley sink, mixing rum, lime juice, and sugar.

"Want one?" he asked.

"Sure," I answered.

He sat down beside me. "We can't have scenes like that during anchoring," he said quietly. My heart started to pound.

"I was doing my best," I said, defensive already. "I was afraid we were going to run into *Second Vow*."

"I was watching. I knew what was happening."

I shifted the playing field. "I should be able to make some decisions sometimes."

"In the middle of a maneuver like anchoring in a place like this, there can only be one skipper. In a situation like this—"

I interrupted, raging. "So you're telling me you're the only one who gets to make decisions on the boat."

"I didn't say that." His voice stayed slow and quiet. "I said that when we need quick decisions and concerted action, one person has to call the shots." He paused. "It's not me lording over you," David continued. "It's a practical matter. It's the way things get done on a boat."

I sat quietly. Inside, I could feel it begin to make sense. Feelings sorted themselves out, repositioning and resettling. I did not have to give up my strength, my independence, my opinions, my importance, in order to agree that a boat needs one skipper.

"I couldn't do this without you," David said quietly.

And even though the boat rocked disarmingly, even though I had languished, half-conscious, most of the day, even though we had laid a bent anchor down into this steep bottom, I slept deeply all night long.

Just the hint of daybreak lit our way out of Escondido. The weather was mild, the waters gentle. We plied through vast woven mats of golden sargasso weed. Less than twenty miles away was the tip of Cabo Samaná, where we would turn and head southwest into the bay, toward the next place we could settle, rest, provision, and explore: the city of Samaná, Dominican Republic.

The sun rose to illuminate the steep rock cliffs of Cabo Samaná, spectacular precipices shooting straight up from the sea. Words from some hymn or poem echoed through my mind. *A landscape not made by human hands.*

That was the cliché. This was different. This landscape was bigger, wilder, fiercer, sterner, more terrible, more magnificent than any human being could contemplate. Untouched, untouchable, by human hands or feet.

Aerial flew ahead of us, all three sails unfurled, gracefully heeling into the broad, inviting waters of Samaná Bay. "We can sail this," David cried. "Turn off the engine! Get out the jib!" The children cheered. It was like a party whenever we raised our second sail. So many miles of sailing east, when only the mainsail could sheer some power out of a wind blowing in our faces. Now, heading west into the mouth of the bay, a sweet twelve-knot wind flew from our stern quarter.

David and John worked together on the bow, pulling the jib out of its sail bag, clipping it to the forestay, knotting the sheets to its feet, and running them the length of the boat, through the blocks to the cockpit winches.

Then David squatted amid-deck while John and Alison wrapped the leeside sheet on the winch. David nodded to me. I pointed *Hei Tiki* into the wind. With all his muscle, David pulled down on the jib halyard, raising the sail. It flapped a raucous moment, then John pulled the sheet up short. Alison heaved on the winch crank. I edged the boat back off the wind. The jib sail billowed in a pregnant curve.

We gloried in the sounds of sailing. The deep-throated clicks of a ratchet. The squeak of the jib sheet as it wrapped around the winch. The rhythmic surge of bow breaking water. The crisp snap of a lax sail filled.

We had coasted the Dominican Republic's rough northern shoreline. We were sailing into Samaná. It felt like a victory. *I am not a passenger on this journey,* I was feeling. *I am driving. We are partners.*

Progress under sail.

Samaná Thanksgiving

ON OUR FIRST MORNING IN SAMANÁ, ALISON noticed something different. No one was pulling up anchor. No one was reading numbers off the GPS. "You mean we're not sailing anywhere?" she asked. "We get to stay here today?"

David smiled. "A few days," he said.

"Yay! Johnny! We don't have to move the boat!" She was overjoyed. It had only been three days of sailing from Luperón, but to her, that was too much.

Her question made David think calendar. "When are the Moores arriving?" he asked me. Neighbors from home were flying to Puerto Rico for a week with us. For the first time in months, we had a deadline.

"You're the one who made those plans," I chided. "Third of December."

"What's today?"

"November twentieth. A little less than two weeks."

"We'll stay here a *long* time, Alison." That was John's interpretation. David went back to his reading. I knew what he was thinking: not long enough. Between Samaná and Puerto Rico, we had the Mona Passage to navigate, the longest passage of the whole trip. Less than two weeks didn't give a lot of time to wait for weather.

"When can we go to town, Daddy?" asked Alison.
"Today," he said. "After school."

All morning it kept raining, so hard it drove us all inside. *Hei Tiki* could barely hold us. David and John did math in the quarterberth, dodging rain blowing in through the hatch. Alison and I played word bingo on the galley table. An annoying drip landed right on my head. I checked the source and discovered a tiny stream of water eking through the porthole trim, running down the wall, troughing up in the bookshelf. This was the reason that our books got wet. This morning they were sitting in a half inch of water, most with a sopping lower-right-hand corner.

It kept raining. Alison organized us into a water collection brigade. Other cruising sailboats have clever systems by which the rain funnels directly into water tanks. All we did was to collect it in pitchers and buckets. Rainwater puddled in the cockpit awning, which John diverted to a plastic tub.

With all this fresh water, I set to work washing laundry. By the time I was finished, wet clothing ran the full length of the life lines. "Fresh water rinse!" I said, and the rain kept beating down.

John resisted reading. I made him do one chapter in the presidents book—he was up to Van Buren—and then I suggested he begin another task. "I want you to make a list of state capitals," I said. "Look them up in this atlas. Plus, write the year that state joined the union."

He finished seventeen, then complained he was bored. "I want to do the Caribbean capitals instead," he said.

"That will be next."

"You know, Mom, after we do this sail, we could go around the world," John mused. He had thumbed through the atlas to a map of the Pacific. "We could go through the Panama Canal, then sail to New Zealand, then sail up to Japan. How long do you think that would take us, Mommy?"

"Years," I moaned.

"No, really, Mom. How long?"

"Ask Dad," I said. "I'm only interested in getting from to-day to tomorrow."

Gray clouds scudded across the sky the next morning. We still hadn't made it to town. After a perfunctory attempt at school, six of us, Michael and Becca included, crowded into *Aerial*'s red rubber dinghy to visit Samaná.

The city concentrated at the waterside, but commercial buildings and houses spilled uphill from the public dock. The closer we got to the city, the more trash we had to dodge— plastic shopping bags, coconut husks, stray lengths of plastic line floated in the bay. Slowly we puttered through the confusion of boats tied up at the pier. We worked our way to the rebar ladder where dinghies could tie up and unload. A rotting scow claimed most of the space between us and the ladder. As soon as we bounced up against the scow, a gaggle of preteen boys greeted us from the dock, calling to us in Spanish and English. "Watch-a yo dinghy?" one yelled above the rest.

Before we knew it, two boys stood in the scow, scraping our dinghy up tight toward the ladder. Michael tried to keep control. The kids up streetside cackled. One put out a gentlemanly hand, guiding John and Alison, then me and Becca, across the nasty scow and up the ladder.

We stepped into a street scene of noise and commotion. Along the waterfront boulevard, the world buzzed by. Motorcycles zipped in and out. Two steps toward the street, more voices clamored for our business. *"Motoconcho! Aqui! Aqui!"* they shouted. Drivers perched on small motorcycles, chrome glistening. They motioned us to climb into the rickety, black six-seater carts attached behind: Samaná's "motoconchos," motorcycle rickshaws.

"Tooreests! A-may-ree-can tooreests!" a teenager taunted. He leaned against a building, wearing a Chicago Bulls T-shirt.

A ragtag boy, shorter than Alison but bulky in chest, stepped up to us. He held out a rusty tin can, looking at us with hungry eyes. He reached his empty hand out, palm up. David gave him a thick Dominican coin. Emotionlessly, the boy handed David something from inside the can.

"What is it, Dad?" John whispered.

Six small peanuts in the shell, wrapped in a scrap of brown paper.

We hailed a motoconcho. All I could think to say was, *"Al mercado."*

It worked. *"Sí. No problema."* We climbed in, Michael and Becca on one seat, Alison between them; David, John, and me opposite. The driver turned around and grinned at us, then we roared away. We sped by shops and houses, outdoor café patios, a tiny downtown pasture where a swaybacked horse and a burro grazed. The motorcycle engine strained as we started up a hill. The driver shifted into lower gear and gunned it. The children squealed as if they were riding a roller coaster.

Samaná's market building is a modern concrete structure in the middle of a concrete park. Activity swarms beyond its walls all around. People standing, sitting, walking, talking, calling out with things for sale. A woman sold clothing, wrinkled and colorful, out of a four-foot heap on the sidewalk. A man brushed by, carrying a basket of fragrant, fresh-baked bread. At every turn, men peeling oranges and offering them to us.

A toothless man smiled and displayed a colorful array of syrup bottles. David nodded with interest, and in a flash the man was planing a block of ice. He caught the shavings in a paper cup. The fear of local water shot through me, but David had already initiated the sale, and by now the ice man and the children were counting on it. I swallowed my fears and let it happen. The vendor looked straight at Alison and, speaking in Spanish, pointed toward the dozen tall bottles.

"He's asking you what flavor," said David. Alison chose red. "Juan?" David asked. John chose *mentha*, an emerald green.

We squeezed through the narrow opening into the market building. Tall, crude tables piled high with produce. Tomatoes, green to bursting red. Peppers, green, orange, red, and purple, some long and slender, some squat. Bunches of plantains, green, yellow, and black. Tiny pineapples, more leaf than spiny fruit. Burlap bags full of oranges, some small and smooth, others huge and warty. Burlap bags full of grapefruit. Piles of potatoes, small, red, and dusty.

The six of us had scattered, absorbed into this fascinating commotion. I wondered where the children were, but I did not worry. The market hummed with vitality, with a sense of what was real and important. Here people came to buy and sell the good things in life. David had said so in Luperón, and I was learning to accept that he was right: no one would hurt my children, and in the meantime, they were soaking in this life.

Behind and around the building, vendors had spread produce on lengths of burlap or bright blue plastic tarps. One woman sat on a stool, minding mounds of tubers, half a dozen varieties, each a different shade of dirt-brown. An ancient woman with wrinkled, dusky skin and wise, green eyes sold string-tied bouquets of oregano and thyme. Atop the rubbish pile yawned a bovine jaw, butcher's refuse.

I found Michael and David, chugging Presidente beers at a shop on the edge of the marketplace.

"Seen the children?" I asked.

"Who, *Juan y Alisón?*" Michael said with a grin. "They went inside."

I soon spotted them but stood at a distance so as not to intrude upon their business negotiation.

"Cuanto cuesta?" John said with worldly gusto, pointing to a pineapple.

"Doce pesos." The merchant lady, white hair wrapped in a purple bandana, stood barely taller than John. She smiled with grandmotherly amusement.

"It costs twelve pesos, Alison. Do we have that much?" They pooled coins and proudly bought the pineapple.

Past the vegetables and through the crowd, we peered into the truckbed of a beat-up pickup. *"Pollos!"* John said, pointing to cages in the truckbed stacked four high. Each cage held a snow-white chicken with beady, red eyes.

His interest attracted the attention of a boy, not much

older than himself, who spoke in fast Spanish. I struggled to say we were just looking, not buying chickens. I didn't even have money in my pocket. The boy kept talking. He pulled out a chicken and presented it for inspection, talking away. I nodded and smiled, stuttering something like *"No tengo pollo."*

That must have been the wrong thing to say, because the boy went running through the crowd, chicken under his arm.

"Where's he going, Mom?" asked John.

I gulped. "I think he's going to dress the chicken." The children looked at me.

"Dress the chicken?" repeated Alison quizzically. I didn't have time to explain.

"You stay right here. I've got to find Dad. I'm going to need some money."

I ran haywire into the crowd. Finally found him, fingering passion fruit.

"David," I said breathlessly. "I think I've just bought a chicken." He gave me a funny look. "We were just looking. The guy kept on talking. I didn't know how to stop him. Then he ran off with the chicken. So I need money. Now."

I ran back, gripping bills, just as the boy returned with a naked, headless chicken.

"Oooh, yuck," Alison said.

The boy slid the chicken into a plastic bag and handed it, feet up, to me. We struggled through a conversation about money. The price came to just over three dollars. No different from what I would pay in the States. But you couldn't beat this one for freshness.

By the time I had paid, the children were fighting over who got to carry the chicken. Alison won, and she walked through the Samaná marketplace, proudly gripping dinner by its scaly, yellow ankles.

We walked around the square and found Dave still eyeing the passion fruit, which these people called *chinolas*. We bought two pesos' worth—half a dozen. And three chayotes—yellow, pear-shaped gourds. One breadfruit—a warty, green globe the size of a melon. We filled up our go-bag with grapefruits, oranges, cabbages, onions, potatoes, carrots, peppers, eggplants. For under fifteen dollars, we had fruits and vegetables to last us weeks.

Sated, we walked back down the boulevard, leaving the marketplace behind. A party atmosphere seemed to ring all through town. We schlepped our bags into a nearby restaurant. Four or five tables, stone floors, a fountain dribbling down potted plants in the back. From behind the bar, a stocky, round-faced man with tired eyes called out, "Hey, there. What'll it be?" Very American. By the time David brought back our order, he was buddies with Wally, the owner of the bar.

"Hi, beautiful," Wally said, pinching Alison's cheek. He pulled a chair up from another table and straddled it backwards. "Just get into Samaná?" He knew we were Americans, knew we were cruisers. The deep tans, the salt-encrusted eyelashes, the beach-bleached sandals, the mildewed canvas bag— something tipped him off. Wally was crude and outspoken, a breath of fresh American air. He had lived in Samaná for twenty years. His wife was Puerto Rican.

"Do you like Barbies?" he said to Alison. Her eyes gleamed. "I know someone else who likes Barbies." He took her by the hand and hobbled toward a back room. "Morgan!" he yelled. We heard footsteps.

Morgan was the strikingly beautiful product of her American and Latin parents, with olive skin, golden curls, and chameleon-green eyes. She wore a frou-frou party frock, yellow organdy puffed up with lace.

"Morgan is going to a birthday party," Wally said. "Maybe you want to come along." Alison drew back, clinging. But when Morgan brought out a tricycle and started wheeling in and out between the restaurant tables, she couldn't resist. Soon they were giggling over Barbie dolls. When the time came to drive to the birthday party, the two girls were fast friends.

"Can I go, Mom?"

"Where is this party?" I asked Wally.

"At the Buccaneer, right above the public dock. Where you left your dinghy."

David and I looked at each other. Right on the way home. "Sure," he said. "Go ahead. Have fun." Morgan gave Alison a hug, and the two girls climbed into the back seat of Wally's open-air Jeep.

Half an hour later, we were still at Wally's bar, talking to a Canadian couple. The telephone at the bar rang, and the waitress Wally had left in charge answered it in Spanish. She beckoned to me.

"*Tu muchacha,*" she said to me. She traced tears running down her cheeks. "She not happy."

I couldn't pry David from his beer and conversation. "She'll be fine," he responded. Becca and I walked on ahead.

It had started drizzling again as we neared the public dock. Trumpet music blared from the Buccaneer. I glimpsed balloons and streamers. I could sense the energy of a crowd.

Alison hung watchfully on the doorjamb. She was looking out, her face in agony, and when she saw me, she let loose her sobs. I hugged her tightly.

A matronly woman, dark in complexion, smiling in spirit, appeared. "Your little girl she is not happy," she said. "She cry and cry. I try to talk with her."

"*Gracias,*" I said. I wanted to say more, but had no Spanish words for it. I pushed into the loud crowd of people, Alison glued to me. People of every age were there, from infants crawling on the floor to white-haired matrons, canes in hand. Children ran around in a raucous game of tag, girls in crinolines, boys in shirts and ties. I couldn't tell whose birthday they were celebrating. For every child there were two adults, amounting to fifty or sixty people. The music was loud, the talking and laughter louder.

"This sure isn't like the birthday parties we know, is it?" I spoke into Alison's ear. She sniffled and shook her head. "Where's Morgan?" I asked her.

She shrugged her shoulders, then her face drew up again. "Once we got here, Morgan acted like she didn't even know me," she sputtered.

My diminutive six-year-old daughter, alone in this crowd, surrounded by loud music and a language she didn't understand. I admired her bravery. "Come on," I said, helping her off the bar stool. "Becca's waiting outside. Let's go home."

Michael, John, and David were outside, too. It was raining again. By the time we got back to our boats, we were drenched.

Only eight-thirty, and both children fast asleep. David mixed us lime grogs.

I sipped and sighed. "I don't know, Dave," I said. I felt tears well up. This was unexpected.

"Don't know what, hon?"

"You seem to be so happy."

"I could keep going another year like this. I wish we could afford it."

"You could?"

"This is the life, as far as I'm concerned."

"I can't say that I agree."

My tears surprised him as much as they surprised me. "What's the matter?" he asked quietly, touching my knee. I didn't know the answer, but I tried to find it by talking.

"I feel dirty half the time," I began. "My body, my hair, my clothes. The sheets on the bed. They're so salt-soaked, they're stiff like starch."

"Yeah, isn't it great?" He was only half-joking. It didn't bother him at all. There he sat, wearing the same shorts he had worn all week. His hair, which the sun had turned from gray to white to yellow, stuck up like funny, windblown fuzz. He probably did like salty sheets. They signified the cruising life.

Tears blurred my vision. I wished I could feel as carefree as the street music in the distance.

There were things I couldn't say to him. How I felt dependent. How I felt unsure. How easy it was to do things for him and for the children, but then how that made me forget who I was. Always following, always fitting in, always serving, never quite knowing what I wanted myself. Then, when I finally started gaining my own, I ran smack up against him. A boat can have only one skipper. Well, how about a marriage? How about me?

Finally I found something I could say out loud. "I'm afraid I'm not getting anything done," I said. "I write in my journal now and then, but who knows what that will come to?" I heard myself wallow in self-criticism. In fact, most days I felt proud of how diligently I was keeping my journal. Three notebooks filled already. Many pages, almost every day. What would it all amount to? That was up to me.

"I need to figure out how to find time for myself now and then," I said. I felt as if I were caving in. Tears kept coming, and a little sob. "I don't know what's wrong."

"I think you're doing just great," David said. He hugged me, then started spreading sheets in the cockpit, making his single bed.

I swallowed back into myself, my mind still spinning. Doing great at what? Taking care of the children? Being a cheerful wife and first mate? Cooking edible food out of cans in a cramped little galley? Right now none of it made me feel any better.

And I started to worry: how will it be to grow old with David? How will we share a life over years to come, if he just wants to keep sailing? What do I get out of it?

I spread sheets in the forward cabin and decided to indulge myself. On top of the salt-soaked bottom sheet, I spread another, unused, only slightly musty from storage. It felt soft and clean beneath me. I opened the hatch and stared up into the stars. A rain-washed breeze caressed my face. The boat rocked gently, pulling back on the anchor line.

Light rain, falling through the hatch onto my face, awoke me. Outside, darkness, silence. I sensed David stirring in the cockpit. Wrapping his sheet around himself like a cocoon, he descended the companionway, eyes barely open, and rolled into the quarterberth, out of the rain.

He left the children behind. Groggily, I moved out to the cockpit and shepherded them down into the forward berth, tucking them into sheets still warm from my own body. They sprawled askew in the V-shaped space, never quite awakening.

The rain intensified. The rest kept sleeping. Now the faintest hint of dawn. Early light so slight, rain so dense, it felt as if we were all alone, even though another dozen boats shared the anchorage. I tiptoed around. I liked being the only one awake. I stood naked on the lazarette hatch, spreading my arms, raising my face to the soft, clean rain.

I could taste the salt dripping out of my curls. I opened my mouth to drink the rain. I lathered thriftily, worried that it might slow down before I rinsed. But it kept on, a slow, steady downpour. Clean felt so good. Scrubbing out salt, sweat, dirt, time, trouble, discord, confusion. Rinsed clean. I wrapped myself in a towel, freshest one I could find. The rain beat down, still so dense I could barely see the other boats around us, even as dawn's light turned the day soft gray.

It rained all that day and the next day too. Clothespin stains were beginning to show on the clothing I had hung out days ago. Rain flattened the anchorage, and its water turned the color of coffee ice cream.

During a break in the rain, the children and I explored the nearby island. Once built as a tourist casino, according to Wally, the island was now a crumbling treasure, taken over by salt, graffiti, and vines. You could still climb down the far side of the island and look out Samaná Bay toward the Mona Passage. Eighty more miles of coasting with nowhere to put in, then eighty miles of open water, some of the Caribbean's most treacherous.

I could feel it in my belly. My period would soon come. I hugged a pillow and plunged back under. I wanted more sleep.

Voices woke me: David scolding the children about a mess in the cabin, the children trying to explain. "How can we possibly fit another three people on this boat with this mess?" David ranted. The impending visit of the Moores, Walter and Polly and their fifteen-year-old son, Jeremy, was making every tense moment tenser.

I wasn't ready for the melee. I moved silently through the galley. I sat on the lazarette and sipped hot coffee. The sun was bright, the wind brisk. It felt as if the weather had finally broken. I gazed over at *Aerial*, two boats away. Michael and Becca both sat in the cockpit, reading. I envied their childless calm.

"Why are the Moores even coming?" David said abruptly. "I don't remember inviting them. Whose idea was this, anyway?"

I took a deep breath. "David," I said, modulating. "You were the one on the phone with Walter from Florida, even before we sailed. You were the one who called him from the Bahamas. You could have called off their visit."

"Who invited them, anyway?"

"I guess I did." I resigned myself to his line of questioning. "Walter told me six months ago he really wanted to feel what it was like, living on a boat, and he wanted Polly and Jeremy to find out, too. I guess in my overly generous way, I said, 'Sure, no problem,' and that started everything. I was inviting everybody before we left home, and he was the one person who took me up on it."

"Well, it's not a good idea."

"Well, it's not negotiable. They're coming, and we're going to have to make room for them."

He flicked his cigarette butt in the water. "When do they arrive?"

"I've told you over and over," I said, losing patience. "The third of December."

"What's today?"

"November twenty-fifth," John piped up. He had been hanging out in the companionway, eavesdropping nervously.

"Tomorrow is Thanksgiving," I added.

"That means we have to make Puerto Rico in less than a week," David said. "Fucking schedule. You should never sail on a schedule."

"What's your problem?" His foul humor and foul language were pushing me over the edge.

He never answered. Up drove Michael. "Come on aboard," David called out to him, instantly magnanimous.

Michael shook his head. "Just came over to invite you guys on a little adventure," he said. "Short motoconcho ride, spectacular waterfall. Interested?"

I said sure. In an hour, Michael said.

David plummeted again once he left. "That's the end of our sail with *Aerial*, of course," he said to me. "Michael and Becca aren't going to wait around while our friends tour Puerto Rico."

"David." I felt like taking his shoulders and shaking him like a child. "The Moores are coming. We are going to welcome them aboard. It's a done deal, and it doesn't help to complain about it."

Motoconchos swooped in on us as soon as we climbed up onto the dock. We negotiated with gestures and rudimentary Spanish: thirty pesos to the waterfall. Riding the unmuffled drone of a 125-cc Honda up the boulevard, we passed Wally's, passed the market, passed flimsy houses by the side of the road. Higher and higher we went, out of the city. At one turn we caught a glimpse of the ocean, far below.

The landscape turned densely green. Here and there an unpainted shack perched on stilts above the jungle. We banked around a curve, sped down one hill and up the next, the motorcycle spitting as it struggled upward. Then the driver stopped and pointed. A footpath led into the underbrush.

"Here?" said David. *"Aquí?"* We piled out, paid our thirty pesos, and stood there, wondering what next. A young man materialized. No taller than me, he had a long face, brown trousers, and bare feet. He said nothing. He simply gestured with his eyes for us to follow, then started along the rocky path. The children followed. We adults held back.

"We don't need a guide, do you think?" I said under my breath. "This path looks pretty obvious."

"We didn't hire him. We don't owe anything," Michael muttered back.

The path climbed up and down, in and out among knobby tree roots. A shallow, rock-strewn stream gurgled alongside. It reminded me of home. Dappled light, forest ferns, soft green moss, scattered rock. I smelled the mold of the forest floor, felt mud ooze around my feet. But then a banana plant declared itself, or a bold jungle philodendron, and I remembered that this was the tropics.

Our guide, still unsmiling, stepped onto flat rocks in the middle of the stream. He reached his hand out, helping each of us across. He paused at a tree, waiting. He jerked off a pod, split it open, and held it out without a word. Inside, white custard cradled auburn beans. He dipped his finger in and tasted the custard.

"Cocoa," he said, passing the pod around. It was the first word he had said. We each tasted: a whisper of sweetness.

We walked on, cutting the corner of a little homestead. Red hibiscus bloomed gloriously. An elderly man poked his head out to see us. Beyond, I caught the first sight of the waterfall, a sheer cascade down rocks and vinery.

The white noise of water plunging into water grew louder as we approached. Falls slid down from the mountain cliffs above. One tumbled over rocks like a staircase. One shot out at an angle. One dripped down through hanging vines into a churning pool. The ceaseless sound of falling water pounded all around us. I could barely hear the children, but I could see them shriek delight to each other.

We tossed off our shorts and T-shirts, stripping down to bathing suits underneath. John skidded down the face of a rock into a pool at the foot of the falls. David squatted under a veil of water. Alison held Becca's hand and ventured in. Michael sat with his back straight up against the rock cliff, a target for the two-hundred-foot plunge. He lifted his face and basked in the falling water as if it was sunshine. Sun-dazzled water sliced down, searing, pounding, pelleting, stinging, insistent, never ending.

Our guide came alive. He waded hip-deep beneath the

waterfall, mouth wide open with laughter. He grabbed a coconut as it bounced by and heaved it against a flat rock, shatter-
ing the husk. With another heave, he had cracked open the
shell. He passed out sweet nut meat for us to eat.

Our guide leapt up onto rocks above and beckoned to
John to follow. They scrabbled up ten feet above us, then disappeared behind thick drapes of green.

A primeval yodel from far, far away pierced through the
oblivion. I looked around. Then I looked up. Fifty feet up.
John's face smiled down at me through the veil of falling water.

I quashed the worrying mother in me, banished the image
of John tumbling down. So much more important was the ela-
tion, the sense of conquest, that this eight-year-old boy must
have been feeling, his memory now filled with the sounds, the
smells, the power that come from within the waterfall.

One of Alison's new entertainments was to stage an art gallery.
"You stay in the cockpit until I tell you," she would say. Then
she would call me to the forward berth.

There, laid before me, were a dozen drawings, some done
weeks before and some that very morning. Two of the boat, one
with people on it, labeled Mom, Alison, John, and Dad, with
five flags of different designs flying above their heads. One island
scene, with one-window houses set on a steep, green hillside
and an electric-red sun shining above. A market scene, including a woman selling vegetables and a smiling man selling one big
blue fish. A pencil sketch of a beach scene: palm trees, pineapple on the ground, woman in a two-piece and, beside her, a radio.
Most of the drawings had prices on them: twenty cents.

"So hard to decide," I said. "Are they all for sale?" She
nodded. "Even this one?"

I picked up a drawing, done in marker, of a man and a
woman. Her hair was brown, shoulder length, her eyelashes
pronounced, her lips full and red. She wore a dress striped
purple, with earrings to match, red high heel shoes, and red
fingernails.

Her hand almost touched the hand of the man standing

next to her. He wore a formal suit, dark pants, white jacket, ruffled shirt, all touched off with a red bow tie. His thin mouth smiled. Red hearts bubbled up above each figure. Red arrows pointed from one person's heart to the other's. It was a portrait of the romantic ideal, emanating from my six-year-old daughter's imagination.

"Is this for sale?" I asked.

"Oh, no," she said seriously. "This is for my private collection."

I bought a boat, an island, and the beach scene. I paid her in Dominican pesos. "And if you ever decide to sell that one," I said, pointing to the couple in love, "let me know."

Twenty-one of us cruisers gathered at Wally's for Thanksgiving dinner. The six of us from *Hei Tiki* and *Aerial*, Catherine and Patrick from *Second Vow*, others—mostly couples older than ourselves. No other children. We pulled five tables together. It wasn't hard to get conversation going. Anyone who had made it by sailboat to Samaná had some good stories to tell.

Before each of us, Wally placed a hybrid plate, blending American tradition and Dominican cuisine. Slices of turkey, a dollop of stuffing, a tiny mound of cranberry sauce. Sliced steamed carrots, sliced steamed chayote, fried plantain strips, and eggplant ragout.

We said no grace, but still there was a sense of something sacred. We had come together to celebrate being Americans in this foreign land. I bowed my head inconspicuously. This is the time when, no matter what the storms within, you recognize reasons for gratitude.

Thank you for our boat, which carries us safely. Thank you for my children, through whose eyes I see this whole new world. Thank you for my husband, who dared us into this journey, and whose courage and knowledge carries us through. Thank you for friends, those so close they feel like family and those whom I meet for the first time today, bonded by a Samaná Thanksgiving.

The Sunday after Thanksgiving, we set out to cross the Mona Passage.

I had worried about the Mona Passage long before we even set sail. As we crossed this body of water separating Hispaniola and Puerto Rico, we sailed the edge of the Puerto Rico Trench, the deepest ocean in the Western Hemisphere. Combine a depth of twenty thousand feet, shoaling up quickly to just a few hundred, with the unbroken sweep across the Atlantic, and you had the potential for the fiercest of marine conditions.

From Samaná to Boquerón, Puerto Rico, David calculated 150 miles. Once we left the Bay of Samaná, there was no place to put in. At our average windward speed of five knots, it would take us all day to get to the Mona, then all night to get across. By morning we would make it into the wind shadow of Puerto Rico. Even then, no harbors opened up until well south. We planned to pass by Mayagüez, a big port city, and anchor at Boquerón, on Puerto Rico's southwest corner.

It could take thirty hours. We had to reach Boquerón with enough light to pick our way through the coral reef that fringed the harbor opening. Working backward, we had agreed with Michael and Becca to leave Samaná at 6 A.M.

At the first beep of the alarm clock, I sat bolt upright. "David," I said, shaking him gently. "Five-fifteen." I flicked on the light in the head to put in my contact lenses. I wouldn't take them out until late the next day.

I made coffee and looked around. Everything was stowed tightly. Limeade in the fridge. Snack foods in the cupboard—sardines, crackers, Mas-Mas, Dominican chocolate bars.

The crank of a chain came across the water. Becca was working the windlass, pulling up an anchor. At the top of *Aerial*'s mast, the green running light came on.

"Ready?" I asked David.

He sat behind the wheel. "Let's do it," he said, and turned the ignition key. I strode to the bow. Up anchoring had become a dance we both did well. By the light of our running lights, I brought both anchors aboard. I looked back and nodded. David swung us around and we headed out.

By flashlight, David wrote the passage's first entry in the log book:

Mona Passage—Samaná, D.R. → Boquerón, P.R. 0600. Up anchor. Calm, light air, some swell. 2200 rpm/no sail.

The day's sail was hard. Cross-swells confused the seas and the winds kept shifting. Four other sailboats had headed east out of Samaná at daylight, too, but by noon, they had disappeared below the horizon. Only *Aerial*, leaning with all three sails into the wind, remained within sight ahead of us. "We're a good match," David reflected. "If Michael wanted to, he could outrun us. But he likes to sail. He likes a fifteen-knot breeze. He'd just as soon stay at anchor over twenty."

"Seventeen knots. His idea of the perfect wind," I said.

David nodded. "Michael and Becca are good sailors. I trust them."

Alison's face lost color not two hours into the sail. She curled up into herself and wouldn't budge from the cockpit. I finally got her to sip some limeade, but ten minutes later she threw it up. She looked at me, imploring for relief. All I could offer was love and time. She huddled up against me as I sat at the helm.

"Tell me a story, Mommy," she said. "A story about one of your animals." I told her about the rabbit who gave birth without my expecting it, how the tiny, hairless newborn seemed so weak it would not live, and so I placed it twenty feet from the mother, under an apple tree to die, and how the next morning the little thing had made its way back to the mother's cage. She had heard that story before.

"Tell me another, Mommy," she said. By now John was listening, too. I told of the time when David brought home twenty chickens, and how they didn't lay any eggs until I cut off the head of one and cooked her for dinner, and then the others started laying the very next day.

"Tell us another, Mommy," the children said together.

"Enough animal stories," I said. My narratives had taken their minds off rough seas, but I didn't have the energy to spin yarns and drive for hours.

By midafternoon, the winds had picked up and the waves had steadied. Now our problem was lightning storms. Straight ahead loomed a giant thunderhead. A flash lit it up from inside.

"Let's cut in closer to shore," said David.

"Coming about," I responded. He and John worked the mainsail as I made the turn.

We sailed into the night. The storms dissipated. The seas developed muscle and the wind blew even stronger, but with a regularity that made for easier work at the helm. The boat settled into the steady surge through waves to windward that had become so second nature to me. Plunge, plunge, plunge into the waves, with the motor a steady undertone, the mainsail tight-hauled and taut with wind.

Both children had been sleeping since dark. David and I traded watches twice before midnight, but neither of us had really relaxed. Now, though, I could tell by the way he lay on his back with his mouth wide open, David had finally fallen asleep. I looked back and saw the lights of three vessels. Each one could be the boat of our friends. I reached for the VHF radio microphone.

"*Aerial, Hei Tiki,*" I called.

Becca responded. "Michael's fast asleep," she said.

"David, too."

"Roger that. It's just you and me then, baby." In my mind I could see her smile.

"Becca, I can't tell which boat is yours back there. Turn on your spreaders."

Silence. Bright lights halfway up the mast on the boat closest to us blinked on and off.

Her voice came back over the radio. "Did you see that? Over."

"Saw it," I answered. "You are who I thought you were. Just wanted to make sure."

"We could start a business, Susan," Becca said. "Psychological counseling in the middle of the Mona. Come sailing with us. Find out if you really are who you think you are."

We laughed, and sailed on into the night.

In another hour, ready to sleep, I was glad to see David stirring. He was sipping on a cup of lukewarm coffee when Michael's voice hailed us on the VHF.

"I've got a problem, Dave," he said. "Engine's stalling. I'm dead in the water."

"We'll be right there," David said, instantly alert. "I'll take the helm." I willingly moved over. "Coming about," he said. I pulled in the main sheet, worked the boom over, felt the sail snap and fill on the other side. David pointed the boat toward *Aerial*, just a pinpoint of light against the watery horizon.

Disappointment hovered in my mind. We were finally making good time. Now we had to backtrack and hold fast in the water while David helped fix their engine, or maybe tow them. But it wasn't only the time we would lose. I was afraid of the maneuvers we would have to accomplish out here in this pitch-black ocean. Would I have to drive *Hei Tiki* up close enough to let David step across onto *Aerial*? Would he take the dinghy into the night? Leave us aboard by ourselves? Could I hold the boat steady?

"Are you sure this is what we should do?" I asked David.

"No question," he said. "They would do it for me."

Michael's voice on the radio again. "*Hei Tiki, Aerial. It was air in the gas lines, Dave. I bled it out. We're back in business.*" The lights in the distance shifted. The boat was coming around, moving forward.

"Great," said David. "Back to course."

"Hey, Dave," Michael said. "Thanks a lot." He paused. "It meant a lot to see you coming back to help."

"*No problema.*"

By daybreak, the winds died to almost nothing, the waters to a gentle toss of waves. The sun peeked over the horizon then, in a matter of minutes, dissolved into atmospheric haze. I had slept a total of four hours: one fitful hour between twelve and one, and then three hours of oblivion between three and six.

Footsteps rumbled up and down the deck. "Land, Dad!" Alison called out. "Puerto Rico!"

"Can't be yet," David said. "John, look on the chart. Tell me the name of that island west of Puerto Rico."

"Desecheo," John read.

"Thirty more miles," said David.

Both children draped themselves from the forestay, looking out across the dimpled, dawn-orange water. "Dolphins! Look, Alison," John cried, pointing.

It had been a long time since we had seen dolphins. Not since the shallower waters of the Bahamas had those friendly faces smiled up out of the water, those slick, gray bodies arcing up, diving down, riding our currents. Like angels from the deep, they always felt like a blessing.

"Look, Johnny! More dolphins!" Alison pointed. There must have been thirty, large and small, lifting and snorting and poking down under. One dolphin matched our speed, swimming right alongside us, banking and gazing up at us with one wise eye. A pair danced through our bubbles, weaving back and forth just inches before the bow. They danced with *Hei Tiki* for a good half hour, then moved on.

By ten in the morning, we could see the mainland. We made slow progress into the afternoon. Storms hovered over the island. One dark cloud moved toward us, then disbursed sheets of blue-gray rain at the shoreline. Further out, we stayed sweaty and sultry hot.

When we rounded the green bell buoy, we could see the bay that earned the town its name: *Boquerón* means "big mouth." "Sticks!" David called out. There they were, a mile away, clustered in the harbor: dozens of sailboat masts, like toothpicks in a plate of hors d'oeuvres. It was a welcome sight. A cruising community. The children cheered.

"Hold your applause," David said. "We're not there till the

anchor's down. Watch the markers, would you?" I corrected course, sighting on the next channel marker. We were in American waters, charted for safety. Red on right returning.

From out of the hills swept another storm cloud. First it misted our view of the anchorage, then it rained at a distance, then it pelted down warm, soft, insistent drops on us, wrapping us in a shower so dense we could no longer see boats in the anchorage.

"Hei Tiki, Aerial." They were ahead of us, already at anchor.

David answered the call. "We're right outside, but we can't see six feet."

"Come on in when you can," said Michael. "Anchoring's fine."

The rain dropped sheer and straight. No sign of a letup. "Shower time!" David yelled. He yanked off his shorts and stood naked on the lazarette, arms and legs spread wide, welcoming fresh water. Alison giggled, pulled off her clothes, and joined him, dancing with glee, bowing her head then tilting it back, mouth wide open.

"What about the motor?" I called to David through the rain.

"Just turn it off! We won't go anywhere."

Then John joined them, scampering up and down the deck like an animal. I couldn't resist. I pulled off the clothes I had been wearing for two days and stretched my arms above my naked body. The salt of our passage dripped down my face, cleansed by sweet, soft rainfall. I twirled, tasting the salt, tasting the rain. There may have been an island, people, a hundred boats just a mile away, but we didn't know it. Our world was contained within this space and moment. We were four happy human beings, a family.

Hooting to be heard above the din of the pounding rain, John called out for everyone to hear, "This is the most fun we've had on this whole trip."

We had crossed the dread Mona Passage. We were dancing in the rain. Whatever doubts I had had in the week before about myself or my marriage dissolved, at least for the moment.

10

Absence and Intimacies

I WAS FEELING SENTIMENTAL. SECOND NIGHT in Boquerón, last night before our guests arrived. Last night for intimacy in the forward berth. Starting tomorrow we would be seven. For ten days we would squeeze three more people on board—Walter, Polly, and fifteen-year-old Jeremy. No more privacy. No more family rhythms. No more unspoken sailing maneuvers. We would be hosts, teachers, guides. Our next ten days would revolve around our visitors.

I looked for ways to celebrate the evening. I cooked up something indigenous: spicy annatto sausage with peppers and onions over rice. I settled in early for a bedtime read, not even sure that we could carry on that practice once the Moores arrived.

We had just started *Little House in the Big Woods*. On the one hand, the house it described felt so familiar, mirroring our own spartan sailing life, and on the other hand, so distant, bringing back images of Virginia, where our house sits at the edge of the forest and we can look out the window and see deer and turkey.

I read two short chapters by flashlight. Alison leaned up against me, already breathing deeply. I slipped out from under her, tucking covers over her, stretching out her body along the cockpit bench. John would sleep across from her, and David and I would sleep together tonight.

"Alison." David shook her gently. "Time to climb into the forward cabin."

I was stunned. This was our last chance to make love for over a week. I just assumed—I didn't think we would even have to talk about it.

"I want to sleep out here tonight," Alison complained drowsily.

"My turn," whined John, half-asleep. I had heard it all before. It was going to be harder with seven, figuring out where everyone would sleep. I thought we would avoid the conflict, tonight of all nights.

"Into the forward cabin, Alison," David commanded. "Get up." He lifted her by the armpits. She stayed as limp as a rag doll.

"Wait a minute, Dave," I said. "I thought you and I would—"

"I'm sleeping in the cockpit," he snapped.

"But I thought—"

"Daa-aad!" Alison thrashed in protest.

"Our last night together, Dave." I cut to the quick. "You and me. I thought we would take the forward berth."

"Whatever you say," he shot back.

A bright beam of light swept across my face, right into my eyes, then moved on to other boats.

"What's with those creeps?" I asked. It was a rule of cruising etiquette: reserve the Q-beam, the most powerful flashlight anyone carried, for emergencies.

The light swept back through our cockpit and off in another direction.

A noisy dinghy motor sputtered past. In the dark, we could just make out an overloaded inflatable, heading further out in the anchorage. Its wake stirred up a phosphorescent glow.

"Whoa," John said. "Did you see how far down in the water that dinghy sat?"

My mind was back on the sleeping arrangements. For his ears only, I murmured to Dave, "I was looking forward to a night together."

"Have it your way," he chucked back, making it sound as if we were fighting.

"Sleep wherever you want," I said, rebuffed and retreating.

The Q-beam glared at us from another angle. The dinghy motor grew louder, then we heard a voice from behind the beam. "Dave? That you? It's Walter. A day early."

Walter, Polly, and Jeremy climbed aboard, heaving travel bags, duffels, backpacks, and parcels, nine in all. "I know it looks like we're moving in forever, but half of this is yours," Polly laughed. We had telephoned a list of things we couldn't find in these islands. Contact lens fluid, cigarette lighters, cheese crackers, granola, children's books, waterproof caulk, spiral-bound graph paper, and more. I hadn't thought about the bulk that list represented. How would we store it all? We just left it in a huge mound on the deck for now.

"Want a beer?" David asked.

"Sure, I'll have a beer," Walter said obligingly.

"Maybe a glass of water," said Polly.

"It won't taste like Virginia spring water," I said, pumping from the tap. "Jeremy, all I can offer is Gatorade or water."

"Okay," he mumbled.

It was hard to think straight. People everywhere. Walter was eagerly talking with David, poring over a chart of Puerto Rico. Jeremy and John bent over the Nintendo Gameboy, which John hadn't brought out for six weeks. Polly told Alison she had brought books from her favorite teacher.

"Can I see them?" she asked.

"Sure," said Polly, starting to unzip a backpack.

I jumped in. "It's dark, and it's late," I said. "Not until tomorrow." I assigned sleeping quarters: David and Walter in the cockpit, Polly on the galley settee, Jeremy in the starboard quarterberth, the children with me in the forward berth. "We'll unpack everything tomorrow."

But the next day, before we could get to it, David said he needed to be on the boat alone. "They have no idea how to stow things," he grumbled.

"Of course they don't. They've never lived on a boat, Dave."

"I've got too much to do to deal with them right now," he said. "I need to patch the exhaust pipe and change the oil. I was going to waterproof the canvas again so that if it rains on us, we can still sleep in the cockpit. Why the hell did they come early?"

Walter and Polly chose not to notice that David banished us from the boat, instead politely welcoming an outing into Boquerón. Since three adults and three children would overload our little dinghy, John drove the Moores to town, then returned for me and Alison. "What time are we allowed back?" I said with a sarcastic edge. Unaffected, David grunted, "When I'm done."

Even in midmorning, Boquerón had a party atmosphere. It's a holiday spot for Puerto Ricans, with a palm-lined stretch of beach and a green park dotted with picnic tables. Near the waterfront, vendors sell oysters with a squeeze of lime, *pinchos*— grilled meat on a skewer, and *empanadillas*—meat turnovers, deep-fried.

American culture proclaimed itself in Boquerón more loudly than anywhere we had visited so far. Marlboro cowboys rode the range on window posters. Shiny American luxury sedans crept down the street, lording over tiny, rusted-out compacts. Rear license plates read Puerto Rico, but front ones, a few years out of date, read New York or New Jersey.

The whirs and dings of video machines enticed the boys into the back room of the restaurant. Walter and Alison followed them, freeing Polly and me to walk together into quieter neighborhoods. "I can't get anyone to speak Spanish," she chuckled. "I ask a question in Spanish, and they answer in English."

Just two blocks from the waterfront, Boquerón blossomed with pretty single-family houses. Flowers lined the walks, plants cascaded from front porches. Ferns and orchids, begonias and hibiscus, drank in the winter sun. Croton plants glistened, some leaves ovate, some slim and fingered, others speckled, others striped. Reds and pinks, yellows and greens. James Michener says the plant embodies the Caribbean: many colors, many shapes, all thriving together.

Finally I asked Polly why they had arrived early. After flying into San Juan, at the opposite corner of the island, they found that a hired car to Boquerón would cost less than a night in a hotel and a bus trip the next morning.

"So how did you find us?" I asked.

"We drove into Boquerón. You had written that we should meet you at the dinghy dock, but none of us had any idea what that was," she said. "So we got out at that corner restaurant. Some Americans asked if we needed help. We told them your name, and your boat's name. Somebody recognized you."

"They did?" I was surprised. We had talked with some cruisers our first afternoon in, but no one except Michael and Becca knew our names.

"One man remembered David," Polly said. "Called him 'the guy with the wild hair.' " We laughed together. "Another offered to drive us through the anchorage, looking."

"It really is a community," I said. "Cruisers."

We waited all afternoon to return to *Hei Tiki*. John, Walter, and Jeremy dinghied out to the boat around three, turned around, and came back. "Dave says the boat's not ready," Walter said, trying to sound cheerful. I was seething and embarrassed. How inhospitable. How hostile.

An hour later, I wasn't going to wait anymore. I rounded everyone up and said I would drive the dinghy. Polly, Alison, and Jeremy got in with me. I pulled the starter cord three, four times. The motor wouldn't go.

"Need some help?" somebody said. Turned out to be the guy who gave the Moores a lift out to our boat the night before. Greetings all around. John and Walter climbed into his inflatable and held on to our bow line. His motor started up right away, and we puttered past sailboats, toward *Hei Tiki*.

Dave was in the cockpit, drinking a beer, reading a book. He didn't say a word. His face didn't greet us. Mechanically, he helped us aboard.

"I couldn't get the motor started," I explained.

Still saying nothing, he climbed into the dinghy, now tied up behind us, and fiddled with the motor. It revved up in less than a minute.

"Flooded?" Walter asked.

"Yup," Dave grunted. That word eased the tension. At least he was talking.

Alison wanted to see her new books. David had rearranged all the Moores' possessions tightly into the port quarterberth. Polly started pulling out bags in search of the right backpack. Jeremy squeezed into the head and tried to lock the door behind him. He plunged the flush valve twice and came out. David shot an angry glance my way and followed after, plunging ten times with the valve open, then another ten with the valve shut. He passed me in the galley, still glaring. "You have to teach them," I whispered. "They don't know."

Polly offered to make dinner, but I had to shadow her, helping start up the stove. A little blue flame sputtered.

"Can I turn it on now?" she asked.

"No, wait another minute or two."

"Beer, Walter?"

"No, thanks, Dave."

"What's for dinner?" John squeezed between me and Polly.

"Do we have to move the boat tomorrow, Dad?" Alison pleaded.

"Can I turn it on yet?" Polly asked.

Too much was going on. I took over on the stove, turning the dial just so, giving a little puff. A circlet of blue arose.

"I'll never learn," Polly joked.

People crowded the cockpit bench. Cooking heated up the

cabin. Polly sat at the companionway, handing up full plates. We all loosened up over dinner.

"So where to tomorrow?" David asked jovially. It was a rhetorical question. He knew where we were heading and how far we might get. We were still sailing east, nose into the trades, and we had to outwit them. We would skip along the south coast of Puerto Rico, sailing the night breezes as they fell out of the mountains and waiting out the trades from midmorning on. Puerto Rico had plenty of southern harbors. On our first sail, we would round Cabo Rojo, the "red cape" on the island's southwest corner, and head toward Ponce, fifty miles east.

Michael scooted up in his dinghy as we were talking over plans. "Come aboard," David greeted him.

"There's no room," Michael chuckled, as if commiserating in code with David. We hadn't seen much of Michael and Becca since arriving at Boquerón. Polly and I had seen them on the sidewalk this morning. They just waved, as if we were fellow cruisers but not partners in sail anymore. I feared David was right: the Moores' visit marked the end of our sail with *Aerial.* "Becca and I want to head out as early as we can in the morning," said Michael. "We want to hit Ponce by noon."

"Or earlier," said David. "So what time are we out of here?"

"We think three," Michael said.

Jeremy gasped.

"Come on over and look at the charts with us," Michael said, pushing off.

David jumped at the chance. Without a word, he climbed into the dinghy and rowed away, his eyes on the sunset rather than on me.

Walter insisted on helping me wash dishes. We squatted together on the forward bow.

"So how has it been?" he asked me quietly.

"Oh, good and bad," I said. Then silence. Walter works as a counselor. He listens patiently.

"I love the life," I continued. "The water, the swimming, the beauty. I'm getting to love the sailing." I looked out at the sunset, too. It had dissolved from rose and purple to a dusky orange. "Being with the children has been better than I expected. It's great to see them learn, rather than going for weeks and then realizing they've jumped ahead without my noticing."

He nodded.

"David and I are a lot tighter than we used to be," I added. "We finally found something we can share, a long-term project. It feels good."

Walter bowed his head, still listening.

"I miss my friends." Warm tears clouded my eyesight. "We've met some people along the way. Michael and Becca. We've been sailing with them since the Bahamas. But there's nobody I can really talk to. I really miss my close woman friends." Tears were streaming.

"Hey, Mom, are you going to read to us tonight?" John's face popped through the forward hatch, right behind us.

Walter tossed the dirty dishwater into the drink.

I wiped my eyes with the heels of my hand. "Thanks," I said to him.

Three of us—David, Walter, and myself—woke at three and followed the green glow of *Aerial*'s wake out of Boquerón harbor. By daylight we were rounding the cape. Waves fisted up with a vengeance, four and five feet tall, coming close together, so that we had to sail, bang, bang, bang, bang, right into them. Jeremy moved nervously between cockpit and quarterberth, unable to get comfortable. Polly sat with her eyes closed, her face ashen. I stood at the helm, paying attention to nothing but driving the boat through the waves.

"What's that out in the water?" Walter asked, pointing behind us.

It was a buoy the size of a bowling ball, the color of dirty water.

"Fish pot!" John yelled. I scanned the horizon ahead. Four more. They looked like innocent, oversized fishing bobbers, but below them stretched cord that could wrap our propeller and make a mess.

"Somebody better spot from the bow," I said.

Walter jumped up eagerly. He hung from the forestay like a whaler, right hand shading his eyes. He gestured right. I turned the boat right. "No, no! Dead ahead!" he called back. I veered left. He pointed left. "Fish pot! Fish pot!" he yelled. Then he pointed right, yelling "fish pot" again. I glanced at David. Over these months, we had developed a system that was silent and subtle. The spotter points, the helmsman drives in that direction. Walter didn't understand. He was pointing at the fish pots.

"Just drive straight," David muttered.

I shouted into the wind, getting Walter's attention. "Point your hand in the direction the boat ought to go."

"Got it," he yelled. He really did want to help.

All I could do was keep on driving. The trades were picking up and the waves were taller and tougher than ever. David suggested we shorten our sail, turning in at Playa Santa rather than Ponce.

"Okay with you, Polly?" I asked. She nodded, not even opening her eyes, as if she were dreaming herself somewhere else and did not want to wake up. David radioed *Aerial*. They were heading in, too.

It was ten in the morning by the time we anchored—almost seven hours of a long, nerve-racking sail. We were going to do it again that night: anchor up at four, Ponce by nine. David and I were worn out. He popped a beer. I fell asleep.

I woke up at noon to the sound of jet skis. Guests at the beachside hotel were coming out to play. Walter, John, and Jeremy were snorkeling. Polly was helping Alison read. "She's doing great," she said. Polly taught elementary schoolchildren. She knew what first-graders could accomplish. It meant a lot to hear a professional's opinion of Alison's progress.

"You think so?" I said. "I can't get her to sound out words."

"She sounded out some words with me. John's reading really well, too," she said. "Look." She handed me his notebook.

First I read the cramped last entry he had written with me.

Abraham Lincoln (1809-1865)
He was assassinated 5 days after the
civil war ended.

Then, a new entry from this morning.

Andrew Johnson (1808-1875)
Andrew Johnson started out
his life as a tailor's
apprentice at the age of
13. Then he ran away to
Greenville, Tennesse. There
he Started a tailor job.
At the age of 27 he learned
how to read and write from
his wife. He was drunk during his
inaugration Speech. During his presid-
incy you wiere not allowed
to fire any government officials, but
Johnson did. He was impeeched by
Congress but still was the
President Because he won by one vote.

"How did you do it?" I asked.

"Do what?" Polly said.

"Get him to write this much. This is five times as much as he has written before," I said, flipping back through the pages.

"I didn't do anything," she laughed.

"Well, thank you," I said. She shrugged and smiled.

Walter splashed up alongside us, treading water. "You kids want a look at this?" he said. On his outstretched hand lay a sea cucumber. We saw them everywhere we snorkeled: eight, ten inches long, fleshy underwater blobs, like bloated garden grubs wallowing on the ocean floor. This one was putrid brown. John and Jeremy made faces.

"Walter," I said, "you're the only person I know who would pick up one of those things."

He grinned. "Want a look at a sea urchin?"

In Puerto Rico, the lights stay on. We sailed out of Playa Santa in the middle of the night, but even then, looking back at the island, we could see the roadways lit up along the coastline and into the mountains. It might not surprise many Americans, but it surprised me. We had been sailing for months through countries where electricity is expensive. At night the lights go out, revealing the darkness of nature. Then, the stars seemed a blessing, the moon a guide. Here, the lights of Ponce shone from twenty miles away.

To our visitors, the city of Ponce was a place to tour. For us, it was a place to restock. So the Moores took our children touring while David and I shopped. We were anchored within walking distance of big, modern, warehouse-sized stores. David bought a new marine battery. Next door, we spent $125 on food—cases of tomato sauce, beans, sardines, tuna, vegetables.

When the children returned, we were still packing down, stowing cans in the storage space under the galley settee. Polly heaved a shopping bag full of fresh fruits and vegetables aboard. It was a generous offer, but all I saw was more to store. John kept talking about eating lunch at the Ponce McDonald's.

"It's the city's three hundredth anniversary," Polly reported. "Carnival every night."

From the boat, we could just see the glint of amusement park rides not two blocks away. By late afternoon, the rides were cranking up and the smell of meat smoke was in the air. We all agreed on our evening's entertainment.

It felt like a county fair. Loudspeakers blaring conflicting music, rides grinding around to oompah sounds. Steamy windows stacked with hot fried dough. Teenaged couples clinging to each other, preteens squealing and traveling in packs. Skin colors from olive to ebony, hair from golden to pitch-black. Onstage, an announcer introduced a twelve-piece jazz band, dressed in matching blue sequins. Their music struggled against all the other noise.

"Choose one ride," I said into John's ear. Alison stayed tightly at my side. John and Jeremy boarded the Ferris wheel. "I'll go with you," I invited Alison. In a few minutes we were dangling at the top. It wasn't as tall as the ones I was used to in the States, but we still got a bird's-eye view of the color and chaos below.

Then the ride began to spin. We swooped down to the bottom and up again. Every time we crested the top of the wheel and skidded down, my stomach surged. With one hand I clutched the cab, with the other, Alison. The speed was picking up, faster than any Ferris wheel I had ever been on, and then even faster. I had to shriek—not a shriek of fun, but a shriek of release, as if my head would explode otherwise.

Alison was terrified, her face muscles clenched. I blurted out, "Screaming makes me feel better. Try it." Up around the top, and I screamed again. Alison was too scared to make a sound.

Finally the wheel began to slow down. It took forever to let us out. My legs felt shaky, my head light. I wanted to puke. With my arm around Alison, I stumbled down the ramp. Her face had lost all color. "How was that?" David greeted us, Mr. Joviality. I didn't say a word. All I wanted to do was stand in one place.

The noise of the festival carried late into the night, all the way to *Hei Tiki*. The volume seemed to grow as the night went on, and from the boat it was a cacophonous din, one melody line mingling with songs and bells and whistles. I put my head down and tried to fall asleep.

I sat bolt upright, grabbed my watch from the cubby. Three A.M. What had awakened me? I listened. Nothing. That was it. I had been awakened by the end of the noise. By instant, earsplitting silence. I fell back into the night.

It was a short predawn sail from Ponce to Salinas, the most picture-perfect harbor since Luperón. Past the narrow mangrove-lined entrance opened a lake of water, broad and flat, protected from waves and wind. Marinas scattered the water's edge and a postcard panorama painted the horizon to the north, with sandy foothills lifting up to blue-green peaks, clean white clouds silhouetted against a lapis lazuli sky. We spotted *Aerial*—they had left Ponce a day ahead of us—and anchored near them along the western shore.

We managed a trip to the inland town of Salinas, all seven of us climbing into a *publico*, a private van with a local circuit. We swerved five miles up and inland, from the cruising community into the heart of another country. People spoke Spanish. The aromas of fresh bread and fried plantain filled the air. Tinsel wrapped the street lamps, first reminder that Christmas was near. Here we were, sweating in shorts and sandals, going into the second week of December. At home all sights would be set on the holidays. Gift lists on the refrigerator, parties crowding the calendar, a tree erected in the living room, stockings and ornaments exhumed.

This year it was different. Presents were not even on my mind; making down-island progress was. We had places to go and people to meet. Soon after Christmas, David's sister Anne, with her husband and two teenaged children, would fly to St. Maarten. Then my father and stepmother, Janet, with hotel reservations in Antigua, planned a late-January rendezvous.

It had seemed such a good idea when we planned it. Now I was not so sure. It meant that all our efforts, once the Moores went home, had to focus on moving from Puerto Rico through the Virgin Islands, then across the Anegada Passage to St. Maarten. Somewhere in there we would celebrate Christmas, too. We had less than a month to progress two hundred miles. Members of David's and my family had arranged their winter vacations to see us. We couldn't let them down. I couldn't talk it over with David, though, afraid he would categorically refuse any more visitors.

He was acting so rudely. He didn't even talk to Polly or Jeremy. He shoved their belongings around whenever he found them out of place in the cabin, glaring at me as he did it. If

Jeremy or Walter left a shell or sea biscuit on deck, David would toss it overboard. He wanted the decks clear and the boat ship-shape, whether we were at anchor or under sail.

An hour into our visit in Salinas, he brusquely stated he was going back to the boat. He strode off toward a *publico*.

"David, wait," I called after him.

"We're running low on water," he said. "These people act like it comes out of the ground."

"Why are you being so mean?" I asked in an intense undertone.

"Somebody has to take care of things."

I frowned at him. We were on such different wavelengths. "Do you want help?" I asked.

"John can come with me. And Walter."

The two men and two boys hopped a *publico*. I felt a cer-tain relief. Alison, Polly, and I meandered back a few city blocks, discovering a bakery and a market, filling our go-bag with good things to eat. When we got back to Playa Salinas, nei-ther the dinghy nor *Hei Tiki* were where we had left them.

I walked up and down the dock, surveying the harbor. I suspected that David had up anchored and driven somewhere to tank up on water. We were hot and tired, overburdened with groceries. I befriended an older couple on a sailboat, tied up at the dock, and used their radio. No answer from *Hei Tiki*. I did raise Michael, who helped me spot David on the far side of the harbor.

"Let me give you a lift," said the man with the radio. "You've got quite a load there." The four of us, plus groceries, weighed his inflatable dinghy down. He kept the motor running low and puttered us across the harbor.

I sensed the tension even before we climbed on board. David was shouting to John about water tanks overflowing. Walter was nervously guiding the flow from the hose into the hole on the deck. John's face strained with panic, looking to me to save him.

"Where should we unload?" asked the man who had driven us over. I didn't even know his name. I called out to David, who clearly ignored me. We wrangled the groceries on board and I said thank you as our driver revved his dinghy motor.

Then David was on top of me. "Never, ever, beg a ride from anyone," he drilled.

I stuttered and tried to explain.

"Never again," he repeated, his eyes red with anger.

"I think we're full, Dave," Walter called from the foredeck. David moved forward, almost knocking into me.

I withered. I wanted to be somewhere else. I retreated into the galley and put food away.

Becca called on the radio. Cruisers' potluck at the marina. She and Michael were going. We couldn't, I told her. I didn't have to say why. She knew. Too many people. Too much trouble. "We'll just eat here," I said, turning to David.

"Didn't you say we had laundry?" he asked me. It seemed a non sequitur.

"It has been a week."

"Get it together and I'll do it."

I glanced at the clock. "Put it in the washers, then come have dinner."

"Right," he said. He dinghied off, beer in one hand, a small bag of laundry in the bow.

Polly took dinner over. She lit the stove without my help. Alison eagerly wrapped dinnerware in cloth napkins, as if we were having a party. John, Jeremy, and Walter paged through our biggest fish book, trying to find the scientific name for every creature they had seen. For once it felt like life as usual, even with three more people aboard.

The beans and rice were steamy, carrots tender, tomatoes sliced. I glanced toward the dock. All I could see was our dinghy, tied up, empty. It was 6:30. David had left half an hour ago. At 6:50 I proposed we eat.

"Great meal," said Walter. Seven-fifteen. We were politely ignoring David's absence. Walter rounded up the two boys to help him wash dishes. Seven-twenty-five. They brought the clean dishes back to the galley.

"Where's Dad?" John asked.

"He wanted to get away from you," I joked. John turned away.

"Maybe he needed a drink," Walter said quietly. David's absence spoke even more loudly.

I went up to stand alone on the bow. Night lights gleamed all along the harbor's edge.

"Do you want to talk?" Walter came up to join me.

I shrugged. I didn't.

"Well, I do," he said gently.

Silence.

"I think you've got a problem here," he continued quietly. My teeth clenched. "In my work I see a lot of things. Maybe I shouldn't speak up."

He was asking my permission. "Go ahead," I murmured.

"I'd be careful what I say to John," Walter told me. "David's pretty hard on him."

I nodded. My comment had felt wrong the moment I said it.

Walter drew in a breath. "David's got all the signs of an alcoholic," he said. I gulped. "It's all about control. You might want to look into some family counseling or maybe join Al-Anon when you get home. Learn to recognize the patterns, see what you can do to help."

I stared at Walter, mouth open. What was this all about? Control, maybe. Alcoholic, I didn't think so. David never drank under sail. It was his way of unwinding once we were at anchor, and with all this night sailing, sometimes he unwound and slept in the middle of the day. He wasn't perfect. Family dynamics could get rough. But alcoholic? I wouldn't accept this assessment.

"He has overreacted to your visit," I said. "He does feel out of control." I wanted Walter to see how circumstances drove David's behavior.

"Well, it has been really hard on all of us," said Walter. "Polly wanted to leave the second day we were here."

"She did?" I said. "She kept it to herself."

He nodded.

"I'm sorry," I said.

We heard the snare of a dinghy approaching. I recognized the motor as ours.

"I'm sorry," I repeated. *Three more days,* I thought to myself.

David climbed aboard, jovial and unsuspecting, handing up the bag of clean laundry. I spat out something about his being later than he promised. But I didn't say a word of what had just gone on.

The next day we pressed further east. I didn't know what Walter had told Polly, but they insisted on staying aboard with the children while Dave and I went ashore to the town of Patillas. We waited ten minutes for a *publico,* then agreed we wouldn't mind the walk. It turned out to be a good three miles. The road curved around, overhanging the ocean, then cut through pastures golden with ripening grain.

It felt good to have some time alone. A billboard about U.S. road improvements got David animated, arguing the issues of Puerto Rican statehood. I listened without much to say. My mind was swimming with family matters, still thrashing through the flood of Walter's analysis. I wasn't about to tell David all, but I needed to say something.

Finally I just bluntly changed the subject. "You're different when we have visitors, do you know that?" I asked.

"What I do know is that my back has started hurting again," he said.

"You clench up," I said. "As if you've got to have everything under control."

"Well, I do," he said. "I'm the skipper. Got to have control."

"Of everything?" I questioned. "You act as if there can't be one towel out of place, not one duffel bag poking a little too far out from the quarterberth. You're a lot less tolerant with them than with us."

"It's my responsibility to keep the boat safe and afloat. It all comes down to that," he said.

"Sometimes you're downright rude."

"Sometimes I am." It didn't bother him one bit.

"Are you going to act this way when your sister Anne comes?"

"She knows how to sail."

A flippant answer. "What about Chris and Kathy?" I pressed. Our best friends, godparents to our children. Kathy was collecting our rent, paying our bills. We were scheduled to rendezvous in February. Not only did we owe her a good visit, I didn't want to jeopardize our friendship.

"That's different. They know us," David said. "They're like family."

I didn't stop. "It really hurt and embarrassed me last night when you disappeared. It was dinnertime. Everybody noticed. John asked where you were. Why did you do that?"

He had nothing to say.

"I don't want the Moores to go home to Virginia wishing they had never come," I said. "If they left today, that's how they would feel."

"I hear you," said David, and I believed that he did.

The next day we sailed ten long hours across glossy waters, from four in the morning until two in the afternoon, from the southeast corner of mainland Puerto Rico to the islands scattered to the east, called by some the Spanish Virgin Islands. By the time we reached Culebra, twenty miles off the coast of P.R., we could see St. Thomas, first of the U.S. Virgin Islands, a solid hump on the eastern horizon.

In Culebra, the Moores made departure plans. A ferry took off at seven each morning. One more day with us, then they would be on their way. "We'll get going early tomorrow and find some good dives," said David.

In Culebra, we also caught up with *Aerial*, but not for long. They were headed for the Virgins in the morning, Becca told us. "We've got friends in St. John," she said, handing us a slip of paper. "Look us up. Maybe we'll still be there." *Just like that?* I thought, watching her dinghy away. I had imagined we would reconnect and travel down-island together. Christmas with Michael and Becca, we had hoped. Now it sounded like they had other plans.

Still, we had to approach our last day with the Moores positively. David especially seemed dedicated to making them happy, even though back pain was bending him over. We set out early for diving sites. When we had explored one, he drove us to another. By three in the afternoon, we had anchored four times, and David was still offering more.

"Jeremy, tie a line off the back and I'll drag you," he said. "Give me a yell when you see something, and we'll stop." Jeremy thought it was great sport. John jumped into the dinghy and rode behind, too. David stood crooked at the wheel and drove *Hei Tiki* at near-zero speed, chunking in and out of gear, even into reverse, to keep the ride comfortable. Jeremy's hand shot up out of the water. David held the boat in place. Walter jumped in, holding his mask against his face. The two of them disappeared below the water's surface, then Jeremy shot up. He grabbed the dinghy and scrambled into it. "A shark," he called out, ripping off his mask. "I saw a shark." His face beamed. For him, the trip was complete.

During those dives, I stayed aboard to finish my next magazine column. I was writing about coral reefs and the lesson Tina had taught me way back in George Town.

I had started a month before, writing arduously in long-hand. Now, thanks to my mother, I had a little typewriter, delivered by the Moores. I plunked away at the little portable, balanced on the galley table.

> "I don't see how you can see anything if you don't get your face right down there in the coral," Tina says as we snorkel together. She kicks under, hangs head down, pulls her face right up into the coral. She sees moray eels and lobsters where I just see shadows and light.
>
> I carry Tina's example now in these waters. My inclination is to linger on the edges, but I try to let these waters

engulf me. I dive deep into this vast other world. The closer
I pull myself into it, the more this world becomes mine.
Maybe by the end of this journey, I will see it in my dreams.

I finished the essay and folded it into an envelope for the
Moores to carry home.

The Moores had arrived with nine bags, and they said they
didn't mind carrying the same number back. I combed the boat
their last evening aboard, finding things we needed to send
home. Terry cloth towels so thick they never dried after saltwater soaking. Books we had read. Prize shells and bits of coral.
Polly and I stuffed travel bags full, then shoved and balanced
them back into the quarterberth. I set the alarm for four-thirty.
The ferry left at seven, but with this many bags, it would take
three dinghy trips.

The alarm rang. I snapped it off. Everyone else stayed
snoozing. I tiptoed around, pumping water into the kettle, lighting the burner. Soon I would have to rouse everyone, but I
wanted to wake up alone.

I was sitting on the lazarette, sipping hot coffee, when it
started to sprinkle. Dense darkness all around. A few lights
glimmered from the island. Three boats, far across the anchorage, had their mast lights on, but there were a dozen closer by.
Light rain pattered against the bimini. "Quarter of five," I whispered to David.

The raindrops were turning into a downpour. I scooted
forward through the cabin and pulled the front hatch shut.
Polly was up, coaxing Jeremy awake. Walter unzipped his bag,
looking for a rainjacket. David stood in the companionway, taking first sips of coffee.

Then I noticed. Right off our stern. Through sheets of rain,
I could see it. The shape of another boat. Last night, it was
thirty feet away. Now it was ten, and drawing closer. The dinghy
would be crushed in between.

"We're dragging!" I yelled.

Without another word, David and I surged into action.

He slid in at the helm, turned the key, cranked the engine. I ran up to the bow, planted my feet, and pulled up on the anchor line. No tension at all. I glanced back and tossed Dave a thumbs-up through curtains of rain. I could barely see him, stretching forward from the helm, straining to see me. He inched the boat forward. I swung my arm out. If he could see me, he would angle right. I hoisted in anchor line as fast as I could, then heaved the anchor itself aboard. Six feet of chain had tangled into the cleft of its hooks. I pulled and pushed, untangling, then shot a glance back at David, who was urgently motioning thumbs-down. I lowered the anchor, felt it hook, pulled back, felt it hold. I cleated it in one quick move.

As far as I could see through sheets of rain, we were in a safe position. I stood another moment on the bow just to feel sure. Hair plastered down. Rain and salt stinging my eyes, seeping into my lips. Clothing soaked through to the skin.

No matter. David and I had saved our boat together. No words, no planning, no discussion, no debate. We moved fast together, instinctively. We did what had to be done.

I felt proud. I felt vindicated. We were not a broken family. We were a team.

No matter how infuriating, even hurtful, David could be, he was my partner. What problems his character had, they were a part of the man I had chosen to marry. He would not be the same strong, interesting, complicated, demanding person without them. I did not want a simpler marriage. I wanted to strengthen the one I had.

That was why we had come sailing.

11

Holidays

Frst DAY BACK AS A FAMILY OF FOUR ON *HEI Tiki*. It felt like a gift.

Alison and I made Christmas cards in the morning: primitive construction paper collages combining palm trees and beaches with stars and wreaths. I took pleasure in boxing up a few small items for my mother and brother, too: Dominican coffee, a straw basket from George Town, a Taino wood figure from Luperón.

I wrote a long letter to Kathy. I needed to talk it all out with a friend. She knew us and the Moores well, so she could imagine the dynamics. I poured out the words, as if I was writing my own diary. I admitted our problems and that they were part of the maddening, rewarding feeling of being married to my husband.

The sun broke through by noon, and we spent the afternoon in the water. We dinghied to a reef a quarter mile offshore, where tumbled calcite columns strewed the ocean bottom. John pointed out the lidless eyes of a bloated porcupinefish, peering out from a crevice. Ten minutes later he pointed to two-foot antennae sticking out from a coral cave, signs of a spiny lobster. He shot his spear into the hole, but the creature pulled back out of sight. By then the falling sun shed slant rays, and what at one o'clock seemed crystal-clear water now appeared scattered with tiny white flecks. It was time for our family to go home.

At bedtime, David and I mingled feet in the forward berth, languishing in our privacy.

"I just hope they had a good visit," he said.

I laughed. "I can't believe you said that."

"Why?" he asked, oblivious. I gently stroked his body. Cheek, chin, shoulder, nipple, waist. His taut, thin body. I didn't want to think about the Moores anymore.

As we made love, his hands moved down between my legs. His mouth moved to my nipple. I breathed deeply. I felt the pleasure. I rose just to the verge of coming, then backed off again. And then again.

"It's taking me so long," I whispered.

"Never mind," he said. "Don't talk."

He stayed with me. My mind and body melted, relaxing in his patience. Slowly I surged, up and finally over in an explosion of delight. I reared up. I engulfed him. I pulled him into me and out of himself. We shuddered together and held tight.

"Thank you," I said to him. His body smiled.

Charlotte Amalie, capital of St. Thomas, teemed with Christmas shoppers, most unloaded from cruise ships. Pressed white clothing, lobster-red sunburn on backs and legs. We gawked, knowing how different we looked from them.

We didn't even shop in the same places. Habit herded them from one air-conditioned designer boutique to the next, with a break outside among T-shirt tables. We gravitated to the marine supply to buy a few Christmas presents. A cruising guide to the Virgins. A calendar for the coming year. New sponges to scrub the hull.

We found a bookstore, where I bought a few more gifts. For John, an ornate picture book by Graeme Base, *The Sign of the Seahorse,* a fantastical story about coral reef creatures. For Alison, a picture book from the island Saba, called *Old Grey Grizzly Grunt the Brave Iguana.* For David, a Marxist history of the Caribbean and a documentary album on the Rolling Stones.

For myself, I found Libby Purves' *One Summer's Grace*, the story of a family of four, with children even younger than ours, who sailed around the British Isles.

Even between islands in the American Virgins, you saw crowds. Distances were short: ten miles from St. Thomas to St. John. Winds were brisk, but the water stayed level. Good sport for anyone who wanted a quick sail and an easy anchorage. You could tell at a glance who were liveaboards and who were vacationers. It was the difference between our own house and a room at a hotel, between a boat that looked lived in—its deck cluttered with water jugs, fuel cans, spare parts, and laundry on the lifelines—and a boat with sparkling brightwork and a pristine deck.

Always we kept our eyes peeled for *Aerial*. We knew they were hurrying toward St. John, so we hoped if we hurried, too, we might catch up with them. We poked into Cruz Bay, St. John's major anchorage, but it was a tight hole with too many boats already. We skirted the south of the island and found our way into Reef Bay.

Three-quarters of the island of St. John is protected national parkland. The Rockefeller family acquired the property early in this century, then donated it to the U.S., contingent on its remaining wild. While houses pack neighboring St. Thomas, thick green thatch covers St. John. We snorkeled along rich, colorful coral edges, the prettiest we had seen since Turks and Caicos. A little beach invited us to land the dinghy and explore by foot. Signs pointed toward the ruins of a sugar factory. John and Alison scrambled up and down its weatherworn staircases, pretending to be slaves heaving loads of cane to the mills.

A gift awaited us on *Hei Tiki*: a rum bottle, lying in the cockpit. My first thought was that some rude sailor had tossed his trash aboard. "There's a note inside," said John. He pulled the cork excitedly and drew out a roll of paper.

Hei Tiki Tribe—
  Saw your boat as we sailed by. We'll be in Leinster Bay

overnight. Touring rest of BVIs this week. Baths on
Tuesday.
Christmas?
Hope we'll see you soon!!
Radio contact schedule channel 72 at 8:00 A.M. & 6:00 P.M.
We monitor 72 most of the time.

Luv,
The Aerials

We got out the cruising guide. Leinster Bay was north, on
the far side of the island. We couldn't make it before dark.

"What's today?" asked David.

"Saturday," Alison answered. She kept the days straight
better than the rest of us.

"I say we head for Jost Van Dyke tomorrow," said David.
"If we don't see *Aerial* there, we'll meet up at the Baths on
Tuesday."

"What's the Baths?" asked Alison.

"It's this neat place near here," John answered. He found
the new calendar to show her. Great round rocks, some a hundred feet high, clustered together on a beach of Virgin Gorda,
the easternmost of the British Virgin Islands. "That's where
Michael and Becca will be on Tuesday." And so, we agreed,
would we.

By traveling from St. John to Jost Van Dyke, we were leaving
the U.S. Virgins for the British. By sailing on to the Baths, we
were heading toward the eastern tip of Virgin Gorda, called the
Bitter End, where we would sit, watching weather, preparing for
our last long ocean sail, across the Anegada Passage to St.
Maarten. "From there, it's an island-hop down," David said,
and the chart bore out his promise. St. Maarten was the first of
the string-of-pearls archipelago that stretched along the eastern
edge of the Caribbean, all the way down to Grenada. When I
compared distances between Guadeloupe and Dominica, Martinique and St. Lucia, St. Vincent and Carriacou, they did look

like hops compared to the long, blue stretches we had already crossed. I was ready for some easy sailing, lots of islands in between.

Jost Van Dyke took my breath away. It was the perfect Caribbean island. The harbor water modulated from sapphire blue to aquamarine, up to a crescent sweep of white sand. A few thatch-roofed shanties, a few brilliantly whitewashed buildings, and a stand of graceful palms punctuated the line where sand met bush. Behind them, a perfectly conic, blue-green island arose, silhouetted against a pure blue sky.

We were one of twenty boats there. Some were as small and lived-in as *Hei Tiki*; others were long, lean, and sparkling clean. It was Sunday, and a few families had spread out for leisure on the beach. Alison soon was running and laughing with a wiry little straw-headed girl. I sat down beside the girl's father. "They made friends quickly," I said.

"It's like that when you're cruising, isn't it?" he said, holding out his hand. "Claw," he said. He had a friendly face, gnarly features, verging on handsome. I repeated his name. "Short for Clawson," he explained. He looked out across the water. "You make friends where you find 'em, then you leave friends behind," he spoke philosophically.

"Which is your boat?" I asked.

"Green one over there," he said, pointing. Glistening emerald hull, green sail boot to match. "Looks great right now. Just got new sail and cushion covers. Worked at a sail shop. Got paid in kind."

"What's your boat's name?" I asked.

"You're never going to remember."

"Try me."

"*Tir Na N'Og.*"

"Spell it."

He did. "It means 'Land of Eternal Youth' in Gaelic." I repeated the name, to remember. "Mary's Irish," he added.

"What did she do in St. Thomas?"

"Nursing. Worked at the hospital there. They wanted to give her another contract, but we were ready to split."

He talked freely, told me how they used to live in Hawaii, where they made a lot of money and saved up to buy this boat. Took off from Florida and made it to Charlotte Amalie in a straight two-week sail.

"It took us three months," I said, laughing.

"We had to. She had a job. Had to get there on time."

The girls ran over, giggling, and started burying Claw in sand. He stretched out, still talking.

"So where to now?" I asked.

"South as far as our money will take us," he answered. "I hear there's a guy in Grenada that rows around the anchorage every morning, selling spleef. Sounds good to me." He shoved his hat down his nose and fell back. "My old lady won't let me buy more than a couple of beers a night. Says we're broke."

"And with Christmas coming," I said.

"She didn't say that, but she probably thought it," he said. "Women are like that. They spend so much energy doing things for other people. My feeling is, what's Christmas? Just another day. Who needs presents when you're in a place like this?"

I leaned way back on my elbows, soaking in the setting sun.

"You ought to meet Mary," he said, standing up and shaking off the sand. "You'd like her."

It was a smooth anchorage, but the winds kept shifting. All afternoon, the boat had faced east on the anchor. In just twenty minutes, the winds switched and the boat turned, bow heading west. With the windshift came a thunderstorm, which drove us into the cabin. The sounds of a reggae band beat through the rain from a beachside bar. As the rain lifted, the music got louder. Monotonous drum, sloppy guitar, fuzzy amplified voice singing all the standards: "Red Red Wine," "Jammin'," "No Woman No Cry." Between songs, hoots and applause carried over the water. On a catamaran behind us, a vacation-load of twenty-year-olds were laughing too loudly.

The noise kept me awake. I read a little, wrote a little, looking up often. David read by flashlight. He could turn off any noise when he needed to. "They found jobs down here," I said, making conversation happen. "Claw worked in a sail shop and Mary worked in a hospital. They lived on their boat."

David closed his book.

"I could see doing something like that," I said.

David nodded. "I thought I would work along the way, but I've decided you've got to fit into the community. I can't just breeze in, fix engines, and breeze out again. No one would hire me."

"With my work, I don't have that problem. I could write anywhere." David agreed. "Of course, I do have to sell my work. Right now, all I'm doing is scribbling in a journal. There's a lot more to turning it into a book." Party noise became a featureless backdrop to our conversation. "I need more space, though, David. I wish I had my own little island. An island of my mind, where I could be all by myself. Everyone expects my help. I can't say no. I end up leading their lives, not mine."

"That's your fault," said David.

"You could help."

"How?"

"Help me have some time to myself. Make there be times when you have *both* children. Whether it's on the boat or off, let me be alone sometimes."

"I'll try," he replied. *I'll try, too,* I resolved within.

The next morning David told the children to play on the beach while he checked in with customs. That left me free. I took the circle walk, around the cluster of houses fronting the beach. Bright batik creations—coral, turquoise, fuchsia, yellow, and red—fluttered from one woman's laundry line. A half-grown goat, tied to a palmetto, gazed at me tentatively. A flash of fur dashed into the bush. The color of a groundhog, the shape of a ferret, it was the first mongoose I had ever seen.

I paused to breathe in a flowering shrub. Tall and full, it had delicate flowers, like miniature poinsettias in parchment white.

"You like the flowers?" rang a voice. I stepped back. A cocoa-skinned woman, about my age, round in face and body,

stood on her back stoop. She repeated her question with a smile.
I nodded.

"It's the Christmas bush. That's what we call her. Christmas bush." She repeated the name, as if she liked to say it. "Go ahead, break off a bunch. Help yourself."

I snapped off one branch, a modest nosegay.

"Take more than that," she urged. Her teeth were brown and broken. Her feet were bare. Her eyes sparkled with generosity. She reached in and broke off a larger bough.

"We live on a boat," I said. "We don't have much room for flowers."

"On a boat?" she asked.

"On a sailboat," I said. "My husband, myself, two children."

She smiled and shook her head. She broke off four more sprays and handed them to me. "You and your family, you have a happy holiday," she said. "God bless you."

I thanked her.

As I walked away, I understood. I was bringing home our Christmas tree.

We reached the Baths Tuesday morning before eight-thirty. Even so, we weren't the first ones there. T-shirt vendors were already clothespinning their wares up between palm trees.

"Here comes *Aerial!*" John cried. He pointed a good half mile out.

"*Hei Tiki, Aerial,*" came a familiar voice over the radio. I felt a chill of pleasure, hearing Michael on the radio again. I picked up the microphone.

"Hey, *Aerial. Tiki.* Good to see you guys."

Michael circled around our bow. He and Becca stood and waved. Willie the cat perched majestically in the cockpit with them. Alison and John ran up and down the length of our deck, hooting and cheering, as our friends climbed into their dinghy. What a grand reunion. Lots to catch up on.

"Hey, guys, how ya doin'?" Becca asked with a grin.

"We were afraid we might never see you again," I admitted.

Hugs all around. We talked and laughed over all that had happened since we had last sailed together. The Charlotte Amalie hustle. The cheap price of Virgin Islands rum. The Moores' departure. The stress of too many people on board.

"I know how you feel," said Michael. "This weekend we had—how many, Becca?—seven aboard. Came on with muddy feet. Kept flushing the head. The sail was smooth, but two of them still looked green."

I wanted to press the conversation on to Christmas. "So what are your plans from here?"

"Our friends in St. John invited us back there for the holidays," Becca answered.

"No way," Michael said.

"But Michael says no way," Becca echoed. We laughed. Clearly it was still a topic of discussion.

"What are you guys doing?" Michael asked.

"Looking for you!" I blurted out.

"We thought the Bitter End for Christmas," David said.

"Good plan," said Becca.

As David and Michael moved the conversation into the realm of engines, Becca pulled me aside. "Michael's birthday is on Christmas Day," she whispered. "He doesn't like anyone to know it."

I gave her a knowing look.

We made no final plans, but I sensed that we would sail with *Aerial* through the holidays.

For a short jaunt, the sail up Virgin Gorda was hard. Winds right on the nose through short, choppy waves. We ran it on engine alone. The motion nauseated Alison. She curled in and shut her eyes. John rode the seas more easily.

Out of nowhere came a question from him. "Why does Alison have more friends?"

I jumped to his defense. "She doesn't."

"She has made more friends on this trip."

I paused. He was right. Girl in Marsh Harbour, girl in

George Town, girl in Samaná, now another girl in Jost. I tried to boost his ego. "It's just coincidence, John. We've met more girls."

He scowled. I thought further. There were boys in George Town. He simply didn't attach himself the way Alison did.

"There's another thing," I said. "It might just have to do with your characters."

"What's wrong with my character?" he asked.

"Nothing's wrong. Alison makes friends differently."

He listened, still scowling.

"Maybe she finds it easier than you do to talk with people she doesn't know. Like the difference between me and Dad."

"Really?"

"You've seen how Dad can talk to anyone. For me, it takes more time. Maybe you're more like me. That's all right."

"But she gets all the kids to play with."

"You have other things."

He scowled, still not satisfied, and went back to studying his fish book.

The long, lumpy island of Virgin Gorda got its name, so they say, when Columbus and his voyagers envisioned a fat virgin reclining in these waters. Our all-day sail took us from toes, at the Baths, to topknot, at the Bitter End. We squeezed through the narrow passage at Anguilla Point, entering Gorda Sound. At the far eastern end, tidy bungalows lined the hillside. This was the Bitter End Yacht Club, a favorite charter destination. Sailboats crowded the docks. There had to be two hundred boats there. "I suggest we head over here," David said, pointing south, close to the yacht club but outside the crowd.

I read the depth indicated on the chart. "Fifty-six?" I couldn't believe it. We had been anchoring in twenty, fifteen, twelve feet of water.

"Sixty over near the dock," David said. "Only shallow water I see is over here"—he pointed north of the yacht club— "and that puts you wide open to the trades."

"Too bumpy," I agreed. We headed for the southern anchorage.

"Definitely a two-anchor situation," David said. We shifted positions: he took the helm, I handled the anchors. We had this routine down. I heaved the second, smaller anchor and its bucket of line up to the bow. "We'll put the smaller anchor down first," said David. "Then I'll back up slowly. Give me the sign when you feel it hook. Then we'll ride up and drop the big anchor."

I nodded. Set one anchor, hang back, reposition, drop the other. The ultimate goal was a symmetrical V spreading forward from the bow, each anchor line roughly the same length and tension as the other. We had done this before, many times, but it was always unnerving.

The sun was dropping. The water below was inky deep. I dropped the first anchor. I let the line go and go, feeling nothing. I was so used to an anchor hitting bottom twenty feet down. I told myself, *This is three times as deep.* I thought I felt it reach the bottom. I motioned to David to back up the boat. I thought I felt it hook. When I pulled on the line, it pulled back.

I gave David a thumbs-up and motioned for us now to go forward. The first anchor line fell slack. I had to worry about it at the same time I held the second ready. If we drove over the drooping first anchor line, it could wrap around the propeller, seize up, and make a mess. I shot a glance back at David. He was jerking his thumb down impatiently, trying to tell me to drop number two.

This anchor, twice as heavy, splashed into black water. Again I couldn't sense when it hit bottom. I pulled on the second anchor line. It felt as if it pulled back. I motioned to David to reverse. He did. But I wasn't sure. I let the line go further and pulled again. I felt my confidence wane. Was it just resistance through the water, or was the anchor really hooked fifty feet below? What about the first anchor? I reached to pull on it. My mind was racing. Then, like a snake in the forest, the very end of the first anchor line flashed by and into the deep.

I gasped.

David saw it. He threw the boat into neutral and charged forward. "Shit," he said, ripping off his shirt and diving in. He surfaced, gasping. "Mask and snorkel!" he yelled. John scrambled. David dove under.

"You won't be able to find it that way," I called out, knowing he wouldn't hear me. I noticed Michael in his cockpit, watching. I felt stupid.

David charged up out of the water and pulled himself aboard, dripping wet. My mind kept racing, trying to explain. "I can't believe it wasn't tied down at the end. It's so deep here. I couldn't feel it. How long is that line anyway? I've never seen so much anchor line go out. I was trying to work this line, and—"

"Just shut up and get out of the way."

It felt like a jab to the heart.

And yet it felt warranted. Should I stand on the bow? Take the helm? What could I do? I felt like a useless lump. David, all muscle, pulled up hard on our one anchor line, cleating it more tightly. He brushed past me.

"John," he commanded. "Grappling hook."

John's face pulled taut.

"In the anchor locker!" David shouted. He was climbing into the dinghy. John fumbled the grappling hook over to him.

"What are you going to do?" I asked.

He didn't answer.

The children and I watched wordlessly. David rowed across the water, raking the grappling hook along the bottom. The light was growing dim. On shore, hotel lights were beginning to outline the hillside. It seemed so futile, but David kept raking.

Then he rowed over to *Aerial*. He spoke a moment to Michael, then he tied up the dinghy and climbed aboard.

I felt shamed and abandoned. I felt furious, too. I needed comfort, not scorn. Presence, not absence. Together, not apart. That's not what I got.

"It's not going to be a very good Christmas," John muttered.

It was December 23.

The next morning we didn't speak much. Becca came over for half an hour—a welcome relief—and brought our repaired bimini curtains. She had sewn on plastic zippers, to replace the rusty snaps. We confirmed plans for Christmas dinner.

David didn't even say where he was going when he dinghied off in the middle of the day. When he came back two hours later, he was a bit more jocular.

"I found the guy who'll do it," he said.

"Do what?"

"Scrape the bottom for us. Dive master at the club here. He's got tanks. Can't do it without tanks."

"He'll do it today? Christmas Eve?"

"In half an hour. I want everyone off the boat."

"Why?" I dared to question.

"No distractions."

I didn't question further. The children and I went ashore. We walked through landscaped pathways, past boutiques and cabanas, out to a rocky point of land from which we could watch the rescue operation. Dave pointed the diver to an area thirty feet forward of the boat. The guy splashed in. Bubbles surfaced. In five minutes he was up, anchor in hand. Now we could get back to celebrating Christmas.

We went ashore to soak in the scene. We sat in the beachside bar and let the children wander. We ordered them Shirley Temples, a special treat. John came racing back, reporting that the peepers we heard were fake. No frogs anywhere, he said. He had found the speakers amplifying the noise. Conversation with David was a little halted. I was still feeling like a child who had done wrong. But when the pontoon passed through the anchorage, carrying a reggae band led by a limber, black-faced Santa, suited up in red, who sang "You better not cry, you better not pout" with a West Indian lilt, I glowed. David laughed. The children cheered and pointed. Christmas at the Bitter End.

John pulled up a chair right beside me. "Mom," he whispered in my ear. "Isn't it true that you and Dad buy the presents that Santa gives us?"

"No," I scoffed, but I looked into his eyes and he knew I meant something different. "Just don't tell your sister," I whispered back. "Let her have her fun." He smiled.

We tried to follow Christmas traditions, but things on the boat just had to be different from home. The Christmas bush bouquet sat in a plastic cup in the corner of the galley. For Christmas stockings, I pulled out a pair of gray anklets. "How will he know which is mine?" Alison asked. She remembered the beautiful stocking my mother had knitted for her, with her name emblazoned, red on green, across the top.

"He'll decide," I answered. "You'll find out in the morning."

"We have to leave something for the reindeers," she said, rummaging in the food drawer for some carrots.

"Where are they going to land?" John asked devilishly. "We can't fit twelve reindeer on the deck of this boat."

"You already saw what happens here. Santa drives around the anchorage in a pontoon," I said.

"That wasn't Santa," Alison insisted.

"No, you're right," I said, quickstepping out of that one. "But they leave that pontoon at the dock for Santa to use."

"We have to leave something for Santa, too," said John. "We always do." He didn't want to give up childish ways yet. He pulled out a cellophane-wrapped cupcake.

Alison wrote a note:

Dear Santa
Merry Christmas + the Carots are For the Reindeers + the Drink + Cakes are for you
Love John + Alison

John added a note along the margin:

Dear Santa,
Sorry about the cake but they are two week old. Merry Christmas
love John

I found *The Polar Express* in one of the book tubs. Tonight was the very reason we had brought it. The children snuggled up on either side of me in the forward berth, and I read aloud. "The first gift of Christmas!" I tried to make my voice ring.

When I sensed heavy breathing, I slipped out. David was snoring. "Wake up," I shook him. "We've got to play Santa." He dragged up obligatorily and nursed a muddy cup of instant coffee while I bustled through the boat, pulling presents out from hideaway corners, hanging paper rings on the Christmas bush, stacking goodies on the galley table. Besides the ones we had bought in Charlotte Amalie, my mother had sent gifts along with the Moores. They piled the table high. Thank goodness the anchorage wasn't rocky.

I may have fallen asleep before one o'clock. The children may have awakened by four. I heard them pattering, giggling, whispering. "You only open your stockings before the big people get up," I grunted, and fell back into fitful sleep.

At seven, I figured I should greet the morning. I pushed on David, too, and offered to make us both some coffee. We sat in the cockpit, doing our best to prolong the waking hour, knowing that when we gave the signal, wrapping and ribbon would fly.

The pinks of dawn were fading. The sky was a velvet blue. Even tucked behind land, shielded, we could feel the trade winds pumping from the east. I stepped up on deck to stretch. Out in the air, it was just another morning.

Close to us stretched a glossy yacht, hull and sail boot a matching midnight blue. Sheets and halyards, so white they looked unused, coiled perfectly on the deck. Two people could be seen. A woman with long fingers and bright red nails sat sipping coffee, staring out at the sky. Near her stood a man, tanned and handsome, wearing a polo shirt, midnight blue. Probably had the boat's name embroidered on his breast pocket. He was crew. He looked in another direction entirely, polishing brasswork, scrubbing away.

It was seven-thirty on Christmas morning. I was glad to have my life to live.

By half past eight, David and I conceded. We were both still bleary-eyed, but we let the children start opening packages. They were gleeful. John loved his fishing lure best, iridescent streamers coming off a big-eyed, silver body. Alison played with her sticker book immediately, pressing colorful animals into a jungle background. I held up the red cotton pants my mother had sent me. They were enormous, size eighteen, but they may well have fit me last time she saw me. Not any more. This sailing life was turning me lean and muscular.

I saved my secret envelope for David until the children were sated and happily playing. I sat beside him and handed it to him. "I didn't buy much for you, but here," I said. On the outside of the envelope, I had written a doggerel rhyme:

> *Sometimes the feelings well up*
> *Without any words to say*
> *Next time that happens, reach inside*
> *Any time, any night, any noon, any day.*

Love from Susan

Inside were twenty little snips of paper, each with a different proposition, like:

Hey, baby—your place or mine? V-berth or cockpit?

and

Time for a little lovin'.

and

Voulez-vous coucher avec moi ce soir?

and

Do I have to spell it out for you? H-O-R-N-Y.

and

Let's rock the boat.

David pulled a few out and read them, smiling. He got the point. He slipped the envelope into his pocket.

"I guess you could call it an early New Year's resolution," I said. "Let's keep in touch." I gave him a juicy kiss.

We whiled away the day, then had Christmas dinner aboard *Aerial*. Michael almost blushed when we sang him "Happy Birthday." Becca presented us with a flag, a bright red heart on a blue field.

"You made this?" asked John. He was impressed.

"Who needs courtesy flags? We sail in the nation of love," I drawled.

We hoisted that flag up the starboard rigging, and it flew there for the rest of our trip.

Christmas over, we were ready to move on. Crowds of boats kept milling around, anchoring too close on either side and threatening to slice our anchor line by driving too close in front of us. Food was way too expensive, even at the grocery. Nine-fifty for a snack-pack of American cereals. Three dollars for an ice cream bar.

But the trade winds kept thrashing. Becca and I walked the hillside one day to look east, toward the Anegada Passage. The wind whipped our faces. The ocean churned, capped with white as far as we could see.

"The oh-my-God-a passage," I said, remembering Pat in George Town, more than two months back.

"Are we ever going to get out of here?" Becca said, and the wind gusted in answer.

One day, as the children and I were beach-lounging among hotel guests, we spied *Tir Na N'Og*'s distinctive green on the other side of the crowd. Back aboard, we radioed. Good to hear

Claw's voice. He suggested we get together at Pirate's Roost for a beer.

It was the first time I had met Mary, his wife. She was wiry and intense, with fine Irish features, blue-green eyes, and dark wavy hair. We talked together as easily as Claw and I had, and soon she was telling me their sailing plans.

"We'd love to live aboard among these islands, but there's the money we have to worry about," she said. "We haven't got six hundred dollars aboard right now."

We had ten times that much, and it felt risky.

"So we've got a friend who will meet us in Grenada. He might lend us some money. Then we head for the Panama Canal. We hear you can pick up paying boarders going through. From there, Hawaii."

"You'll sail to Hawaii?" I asked.

"Got to. This boat's all the home we have. If I can just keep Claw from drinking away those six hundred, we'll make it." She shot a glance over at our two husbands, joshing each other over beers. She smiled and shook her head. This was a lifelong game for her. He drinks, and she scolds. It didn't seem to worry her deeply.

"Did you hear me on the radio this morning?" she asked, turning the conversation.

I hadn't. Hadn't known to listen.

"We keep our radio on channel sixteen a good bit of the time. Eavesdropping, you know. Great sport. This morning these two idiots get on the tube—on sixteen, no less—and one says to the other, 'Swedish boat coming by. Check out the boobs. Big boobs.' "

I smiled. I had seen the very boat. Beautiful blond women, carefree and topless.

"So I get on the horn," said Mary, devilish look in her eyes, "and with my best Swedish accent I say, 'You filthy male chauvinist pigs.' Shut them right up."

We convulsed in laughter together. I liked this woman.

———

So then there were three boats waiting together for weather: *Tir Na N'Og* was going east, too. But even a short conversation between David, Michael, and Claw showed that this threesome might not be as balanced as our partnership with *Aerial* had been.

"I'll sail in thirty knots, no problem," Claw said.

"On the nose?" asked Michael skeptically. I could tell from his demeanor he did not trust our new friend.

"Just tack. That's how we got here," Claw said.

"You've still got to choose your weather to tack," said David.

"Hell, I've flown through a hurricane," Claw said over David. We had learned in days past that not only was Claw a pilot, he and Mary skydived and motorcycled together. These people took risks for fun—in the air, on land, and on the water.

Michael shook his head. "No more than twenty for us. Seventeen's what I'm looking for."

"I don't think we're going to get seventeen," David said. "Hasn't gone below twenty all week."

"No big deal," Claw rumbled. "Check you later." He struggled with his dinghy motor for a minute, then sped away.

Michael watched him go. "I don't know about that guy, Dave."

"He's a wild man," David agreed.

If anything, the crowd of boats grew bigger between Christmas and New Year's. We found ourselves pinned in by bigger, fancier boats. David and I decided one evening to move *Hei Tiki* to the far side of the pack.

"Let's try a different anchor maneuver," he suggested. "I'll work the bow. You drive. We drop one, then instead of hanging back on it, we drive straight across and drop the other one, then pull back simultaneously on both." He looked at me. "Got it?" he asked.

"I guess so." I understood the principle, but I wasn't sure I could pull it off. It was hard for me to triangulate from an anchor that had disappeared fifty feet under water.

"Just watch me," he said.

We pulled up both anchors without a hitch. I was driving against the wind, and I had to give it more gas than I wanted. David's gestures became more urgent. The boat surged forward. He shot a panicked hand back. I thrust it into reverse. I didn't have good enough control. I felt the motor stumble. I heard it hesitate. Flipped it into neutral.

"What's the matter?" David called from the bow.

"I don't know," I called back. I shifted the engine into forward, gingerly gave it some gas. It was straining, going nowhere.

"Out of gear," David yelled, running back to the cockpit. "You've wrapped it."

"We've what?"

"Wrapped the line." He was already in the water, clothes and all. Then I saw it, rising up white alongside us: an anchor line swooped from the bow back to the propeller. It had wrapped around the turning shaft and jammed it.

David dove down under. It was twilight, barely enough light to see what he was doing. "Michael and Becca have a waterproof searchlight," I said.

"No," he demanded. He never wanted to ask for help, not even from friends.

I was about to argue the point when I saw Michael climb into his dinghy, three boats away.

David's teeth chattered. "T-too cold," he said. By the time Michael reached us, I had on my mask. I had more body fat than David.

Michael and I jumped in together. I held my breath, held the flashlight, and surveyed the damage. "You turn the prop," Michael said. Our bodies almost intertwined as we struggled together. A jellyfish raked my shoulder, but I didn't care. I grabbed another breath of air and shoved again on the prop. One turn free. Michael pulled on the line. Another turn, and then the line burst loose. It floated into the underwater gloom, back between bow and anchor.

Michael and I hung, panting, off the sides of the dinghy. David sat there, shivering. "Thanks, man," he said.

"Good job," I gasped.

Michael gulped and smiled. "You guys do have your share of anchoring episodes, don't you?"

I nodded, thinking, *I may have played a role in creating this problem, but I also jumped in and worked us out.* I felt cold and stung, exhausted and strong.

We kept waiting. Sailors warned of these Christmas winds, and now I knew why. One night, Michael told us, his wind gauge clocked fifty miles per hour. Michael kept radioing in to Herb every evening. It seemed we would never leave the Bitter End.

The crowd of boats shifted, but hardly diminished, until the very afternoon of New Year's Eve. Sleek hundred-foot yachts with smoked-glass windows fired up their engines and glided away. Word around the anchorage was that the hot place for New Year's Eve was back at Jost Van Dyke. We stayed put.

"Might as well make the most of it," Michael said that afternoon.

"Yeah, let's party," I agreed.

Miraculously, like a gift to the adults, the children fell asleep by eight. "Do you think we can leave them?" I asked out loud.

"We'll check back on them," said David.

I yanked on the anchor lines to see that they were holding, and David whispered a prayer in each child's ear:

Angels guard you through the night
And keep you safe till morning light.

The four of us party-hopped through the Bitter End. Watched a steel-drum band set up. Stole desserts from a hotel buffet. Eavesdropped on a rock band, but the lead guitar kept sliding out of the tune and the drummer was sloppy. Dinghied around to Biras Creek, peering in on the children on the way, and laughed our way past the sign requiring gentlemen to wear ties. We were all in shorts and sandals, and we didn't care. The four of us danced together to a grinding "Louie, Louie." Checked again on the children—still asleep—and back to the steel-drum band. Now they were hot, transitioning from "Brazil" to wild, pumping improvisations. The musicians, nine of them, nodded, pranced, danced at their drums. A burst of fireworks lit up the anchorage.

Boats shot off Roman candles against a background of honking airhorns. The drumming mounted. Throbbing bodies, throbbing rhythms. A dozen flares shot up from boats out on the water. Their bright red trajectories flashed, peaked, and tumbled down.

I looked around for David. He was standing next to Michael and Becca. I went over and grabbed him. He put his beer bottle down. We hugged and circled around.

Happy New Year.

12

Rough Passage

THE WIND KEPT PUMPING FROM THE EAST, blowing rain clouds through the Bitter End anchorage. It had become a familiar cycle: strong gusts, thick cloud cover, downpour, rain growing lighter, clouds lifting, and, finally, an evanescent rainbow. We saw two or three rainbows daily, but even they were starting to lose their magic. We needed to move on.

"When are Don and Anne coming?" asked David.

"The seventh," I answered, raising my voice a little, wanting to sear the answer into his brain. I must have told him that ten times in the past week. David's sister Anne, her husband Don, and their two teenaged children, were flying to meet us in St. Maarten. They had round-trip tickets. Plus they had chartered a boat. They would sail along with us to Antigua. There were definite dates to meet: pick up the boat in St. Maarten on one day, deliver the boat to Antigua a week later. We had a deadline, and then we had a sailing plan, and all those dates were pressing in upon us.

But St. Maarten was a long sail away. Between Virgin Gorda and St. Maarten stretched eighty miles of the worst ocean yet, the Anegada Passage. Like a massive ocean inlet on the northeast corner of the Caribbean, here the vast arc of the Greater and Lesser Antilles opens up like a barrel uncorked, except that the forces stream inward, from the east. It's far enough south to feel the full brunt of steady trade winds and far enough east that nothing slows down the waves and weather building up all the way from Africa.

We wanted to leave. We had sat through forty-knot winds over the holidays. We were looking for a nice easy fifteen to eighteen. Even twenty would do.

Just before eight, a harmonica warbled on the VHF radio.

David picked up the microphone. "You there, Claw?"

The harmonica warbled again as if to answer.

A familiar voice chimed in. *"Hei Tiki, Aerial."*

"We're all three on," said Dave. Without even saying it, we knew we would sail this passage with *Aerial.* Now there seemed some loose assumption that *Tir Na N'Og* would sail to St. Maarten with us, too.

"November Mike says no significant features," said Dave. "Seas four to eight feet, winds fifteen to twenty-five knots."

"Herb says to sit still," said Michael. "I did get a radio call from that guy who left here last night," Michael continued. "Bill on *Runninfree.* He made it to St. Maarten early this morning. Said it wasn't bad at all. Four-foot waves at the most."

"I don't know," said David. He scratched his head and looked out. We couldn't see the waves or feel the wind, anchored in the lee of the island, but it was still blowing plenty hard.

"What time you thinking of leaving?" Claw asked.

"Four o'clock," said David. "Put us there midday tomorrow."

"I was thinking more like noon," said Claw.

"If we have a good run, leaving at noon would get us there in the middle of the night," said Michael.

Claw was silent. David said nothing either, but I knew he agreed with Michael.

They left the point unresolved. "Becca's going to the market," Michael said. "Need anything?" David looked at me.

"Ask her to get us a few potatoes," I said.

He signed off, as if shopping had been the main subject of the conversation.

"Well?" I asked. I would never leave a decision like that hanging.

"We'll see," said David.

So there we were, still waiting.

It was hard to settle into a morning routine, not knowing where we would be that afternoon—stuck here longer or out there sailing. On the bet that we would sail, I became cabin-compulsive, stashing away anything loose. I tried to read with Alison, but we were both restless. The children built Lego armies in the forward cabin and battled out their tensions. David read Winston Churchill.

By eleven, a rainstorm had swept across, leaving a glorious rainbow behind. The wind kept pumping, but the skies to the east looked blue. Another radio conference.

"Not much different," David said. "Blowing pretty hard. Right on the nose."

"My wind gauge calls it a steady twenty-four," said Michael. "You know I never go out in anything over eighteen." I could just imagine his half-joking smile.

"I can't afford to sit here any longer," said Claw. "I've got to get somewhere that beer costs less than two-fifty a bottle."

David stood silent for a full minute, calculating. Finally, he just said, "No go."

We heard Michael sigh into the microphone. Then he echoed, "No go."

Claw was silent. Then he said, "We're out of here."

Dave and I looked at each other. Claw and Mary may be funny and friendly, but their style of sailing was not ours. They took risks. Made us look conservative.

Half an hour later, John spotted them through the tangled crowd of boats. *Tir Na N'Og*, that bright green ketch, moved into open waters.

Three in the afternoon. Skies still clear, wind still throbbing. Michael's voice came over the radio. "Becca and I want to go out and just see what it's like. This wind is going to kick up even taller waves for tomorrow."

David and I agreed. Nothing lost, out and back. It gave us something to do. And everything gained if we did keep on going. David spread charts on the galley table.

Alison curled up in the corner of the cockpit, sulking. "I don't want to move," she said.

I sat down and tried to cradle her. She knew it would be a long, hard passage. She knew she would get seasick again. She was scared.

"We'll be okay. And if we're not, we'll come back," I said.

I dressed for the worst, for rain and cold and a long night of it. If we kept on sailing—boat pounding through steep waves, heeling at a raucous angle—I knew how hard it would be just to change clothes. Four shirt layers, rain jacket easy to grab. Even a pair of socks zipped into my jacket pocket. I could count on one hand the times I had worn socks in the last four months, but tonight I might need them to keep my feet warm. I pulled on the pants my mother had sent for Christmas. They looked baggy, but who cared? They were one more layer, and somehow it felt as if their red color would keep me warm.

At four in the afternoon, our two boats stoked out of the Bitter End anchorage. Becca moved up and down their deck, already wearing her yellow slicker, readying the sails. She motioned to me, then strung a plastic bag off the end of a twelve-foot boat hook. David steered us in closer. I plucked the bag off the hook. Four potatoes. Our passage dinner. I put them on to boil, thinking, *Cook them now, fix dinner later.*

In half an hour, Virgin Gorda lay behind us. We tried to radio *Tir Na N'Og*. No answer. "His radio was konking out," David said. "He couldn't talk with anyone more than half a mile away." Claw, Mary, and their daughter, Crystal, were out there alone somewhere. I was glad we were sailing this with friends.

By five we could look back west to see the sun near the

horizon, tinting that whole half a sky with eerie stripes of purple and orange. Michael radioed, saying it was time to decide. Last chance to return by light into Gorda Sound.

I looked east, projecting my thoughts through the long, dark hours ahead, coming to grips with the prospect of sailing like this for another eighteen hours. The wind was blowing as fiercely as we had expected. The waves stood steadily six feet tall, sharp on top and close together. If we were to sail straight for St. Maarten, we would plough right into them perpendicularly. But instead, slicing through for the best speed we could manage, we angled just off the perpendicular. Boat met wave, again and again, no two meetings quite the same. Sometimes we surged through the middle, sometimes we arced over the top, and sometimes we smashed flat-face into one. You could feel the bow smack up against the wave, and you ducked, knowing that in a split second this one would shatter cold salt water across the bow and over all of us. The whole boat would shudder. The brass bell, attached to the cabin bulkhead, would clang helplessly.

David slid in beside me to read the tachometer: 2600 rpm. He pushed it up to 2900. We had hauled in the mainsail as tightly as we could, but still got pushed south of our track. The wind wouldn't give. It pressed down upon us; the boat heeled over thirty degrees. Sitting at the helm, I had to brace my body, right foot up against solid fiberglass. I rode the helm like a cowboy on a bucking Brahman. The boat plunged through the waves. All I could do was to concentrate on moving through this chaos.

My vote came through intuition, based on these sensations. It was rough, but we could make it. David decided rationally. He braced himself in the cabin. He poked at the buttons on the GPS, read out position and speed, measured distance. He calculated.

"We're only making four knots," he said, angling up the companionway steps. "At the best."

"Four knots, eighty miles. Get there at noon." He was six feet away, but I had to yell.

"Two or three." Worst scenario.

"I say it's no fun, but it's not going to get any better in the next few days. I vote go."

He stared at the turmoil all around us. In the dwindling light, one's sense of distance imploded. It was difficult to distinguish sea from sky. David competed with the wind for a last puff on his cigarette, then flicked it overboard. "No go," he said.

I was amazed. He was the one who had sailed through nor'easters. He was the one always urging us on to harder challenges. He was the veteran sailor. And he was the one voting no.

We radioed *Aerial*. Three votes to go, one vote—David's vote—no.

The ayes had it.

He signed off and looked out ahead. As if in comment, a wave cracked over the forward deck. We ducked. The hull shook. The bell clanged. Salt water slapped our faces. "You feel okay about this?" I asked. Now I wasn't so sure.

"We'll be fine," he said. Stoic control had taken over.

"We could radio back," I said. "I guess I was thinking—"

"We took a vote," he said. "We keep on sailing." He wrestled open the companionway for another engine check.

I still felt confident, but something made me uneasy. The most experienced among us had voted to turn back.

By six at night we were plunging through darkness. Our red and green running lights barely penetrated the gloom. The waxing moon, three days short of full, shone straight ahead, an amber glow through streaks of black cloud. *If the clouds don't pile up,* I remember thinking, *we'll have moonlight on the water to guide us.* Cold white moonlight makes the whitecaps shine.

Wave upon wave, we kept beating into them. Wave upon wave, we shattered those whitecaps into foam. All I was sure of were the waves. No rhythm, no letup, just hours of wave upon wave. Clouds clotted the sky. My senses drew in, so that all I could see for sure were the waves so close by that they reflected our humble little running lights. Now and then, a wave would take us by surprise, jerking the boat sidelong, flinging the bell into a futile alarm.

Alison lay curled up, introverted, sleeping through it. John was still wide awake, nonplussed, reporting hunger. "Help yourself," I said to him. He stumbled down into the galley, holding on to keep from being thrown around. He jerked open a drawer and grabbed a handful of cookies. He held them up and looked out at me with questioning eyes. I glanced down and nodded. "If you can stomach them," I said into the wind.

An eight-foot wave exploded down the length of the boat, drenching us with cold salt water. John shrieked. David shivered. Alison curled up more tightly. My rational mind fought off the vision of a torrent, surging into the cockpit and carrying my fifty-pound daughter away. Water swirled down the drain between my feet. I licked my lips, blinked the sting out of my eyes, and kept on driving.

"You doing all right?" David spoke out over the din. He had just checked the engine again. He was doing it every half hour. I nodded. The clock in the cabin said just after eight. "I'm going to lie down."

"Put Alison inside the cabin," I yelled. Bracing his body, he lifted our daughter, a tight little ball of life, and wedged her into the port quarterberth, up against laundry baskets filled with sheets and towels. She had no room to stretch, but it didn't matter. It was dry and protected. She stayed a fetal huddle, drawn in and shut down. John lay down in the starboard quarterberth, wrapped mummylike in a sheet.

Even while he rested, David checked the engine. Every half hour he stood up, knees stiff-locked, and pivoted open the heavy companionway panel. A churning roar and the stench of diesel fumes would escape. The beam of his flashlight would dart back and forth at the machinery, eyeing belts and pulleys and inky-black bilgewater sloshing in the trough beneath the engine.

At his nine-thirty engine check, something had gone wrong. He plunged his arm deep in at the engine. "We've got a problem," he yelled up to me. "Bilge pump." He dove back down into the engine.

The bilge pump should switch on when the boat takes on too much water, spewing excess out. If it doesn't, water fills the hull. That could sink the boat.

My mind tensed in apprehension; my body couldn't tense any more. David re-emerged, his arm black with grease, his face clenched with worry. "I can't turn it on manually," he yelled. "Got to go at it from the back side."

David slid past John and jerked open the sliding door that led back behind the engine. He angled his body in behind the grinding monster, the 350-pound motor he and his father had installed a year ago.

There was nothing I could do but drive.

And believe.

I applauded and pitied David. If I had to do what he was doing, I would be sick for the rest of the passage. All I could see were his feet, flapping with the effort of his upper body. He fumbled in the dark, he groped in the murky bilgewater. His nostrils filled with noxious fumes. His feet disappeared as he dove deeper. I wanted to be by his side, but all I could do was drive through the relentless waves.

His feet reappeared. Then his body. His hands and face were smudged with black. He panted as if he had been running. "Get it going?" I yelled.

He nodded.

He smoked a cigarette, then finally he talked. "Piece of trash lodged in the switch. I jerked it loose and the pump started right up. Have to keep an eye on it. I'm lying down."

He wrapped a sheet around himself and lay down on his side in the cabin. With every jolt from a wave, his body bounced. He squeezed his face shut and seemed to shiver.

Clouds had condensed, masking the moon. The sky above was thick and gray. The sea below was deep and gray. It was only ten o'clock. The whole night lay ahead of us.

Ten-forty. David jerked up and looked around as if he didn't know where he was. We had agreed on trading watches, but during these past three hours he had raised up seven times to check the bilge. Once he had had to fish trash out from the bilge pump again.

"Course?" he yelled.

I glanced down at the compass. "One-oh-nine," I yelled back.

He held tight within the bucking cabin, read the GPS, scrawled those numbers into the logbook, then drew a faint pencil line on the chart.

"Bring it up a little if you can," he said. But when I verged more eastward, I could hear the sail flap. I strained to look up at the white sail above me, dimly lit by the running lights, and pushed the wheel back until the leech edge pulled tight as wind filled the sail again. Ninety-five on the compass. I tried to keep the boat there. The closer we sailed to ninety, I thought, the shorter this misery would be.

David wedged his body in beside me. "Want a break?" he asked.

"I'm fine."

"You need to rest," he insisted.

The truth was, I felt so uncomfortable I didn't want to move at all. I didn't want to change positions for fear the next one would be even more miserable. I sat gripping the wheel, bracing my body by jamming my right leg out against the downwind side. My butt bones hurt from bouncing up and down on fiberglass. My neck and shoulders were tensed up like a fist ready to punch. Cold salt water soaked through all five layers of clothing. My hands were stiff. My fingers were pruny. My mouth tasted sour and salty. The insides of my lips were chapped from grimacing.

I did need a break. I inched around the cockpit bench sideways. I huddled, paralyzed, gathering the strength to move down into the cabin.

When I finally lay down, water puddled under me on the vinyl settee cover. My mind darted—dry clothing in my cubby— but no way could I keep my balance and change my clothes. Anyway, what was the use? They would be dripping wet as soon as I went back out into the cockpit again.

I lay there as the heeling boat banged into the waves. Amidst the roar of wind, waves, and churning engine, I could hear cans of food, stored in the cupboard right behind me, jerking and rolling around. My mind wandered off into those images that precede sleep.

A blast, a jolt, a shudder, a clang of the bell. I sat straight up. "Everything all right?" I yelled at David. I could see him at the helm, squinting into the elements. He nodded. I lay back down.

More wandering images. Another jolt. Eyes wide open. A double jolt.

Twelve more hours of this. We had only been sailing seven.

I must have slept some, because the clock read eleven-fifty. My mouth felt dry and fuzzy. I pumped myself a cup of water at the galley sink. It tasted warm and dirty—warm because the pipes ran right past the engine; dirty from sludge stirred up in the tank.

David radioed *Aerial*. We hadn't spoken for hours.

"Aerial, Hei Tiki."

No response.

"What does that mean?" I asked.

"It means they're more than ten miles away."

We were on our own. Nothing we could do but keep on sailing.

He checked the GPS coordinates, scrawled another line on the chart. Flashlight into the engine compartment, in, around, down at the bilge. Then he lay down. He fell asleep quickly, flat on his back, mouth wide open. He slept for more than two hours, then jerked upright, as if he had just remembered something important. He groped for a mug, spooned in instant coffee, and pumped in that warm, dirty water. He downed it.

"I really have to pee," I said. No way I was going overboard, and I couldn't stomach the head.

"Just pee on the floor," David said.

He took the helm. I struggled into the center of the cockpit. I held both sides of the bench and squatted, sopping pants pulled down around my ankles. In the midst of so much discomfort, emptying my bladder gave me great pleasure. So much water kept sloshing across the cockpit floor, I didn't catch a whiff of ammonia. Then a wave blasted down on us, and the pee washed away.

This time when I lay down, all I could think of was the horrid taste in my mouth. A cottony, sour taste of salt and fear. I thought about the little bag of strawberry candies that we had bought in Ponce. I knew exactly where it was: on top of the cans of tomato sauce and pinto beans in the galley cupboard.

I lay there, braced against the violence of the boat as it pitched and plummeted, plotting how to get some candy into my mouth. The way I was lying, it would be possible to scootch my body down the settee, slide open the cupboard door without even rising, reach in, and get a handful of strawberry.

I lay there thinking. It seemed a tremendous challenge. The boat kept heaving and jerking. I moved my body into position and thought some more. I was ready. I knew I could do it.

I slid the cupboard door halfway open. Cans tumbled everywhere. I shoved my hand in among them and grabbed a handful of candy. I shoved cans back and jerked the door closed.

I froglegged my body back up the length of the cushion and stretched out flat again. I unwrapped one of the candies. It melted into my mouth.

First strawberry sweetness, then sleep engulfed me.

The clock said eight minutes before four. I awoke from a long, black, dreamless sleep. I lay there stiffly, listening. Waves crashing, wind blasting, engine droning, sailboat heaving. Occasionally the boat would slam into a wave and shudder. The bell would ding a futile ding. I knew I had to drag myself up and take over the helm again.

"Drove through rain. Big hard drops. No lightning," said David.

"Shows how soundly I was sleeping," I said.

"I've been holding it at a hundred." He climbed down and plotted our position on the chart again.

He looked up at me and yelled a word. I read his lips through the din. "Course?" he had asked. I pushed the boat down into the wind a little more. Ninety-eight, ninety-six, ninety-five. The closer we kept to ninety, the straighter our track to St. Maarten. David had been saying that I was becoming a better helmsman than he was, and here was proof of it. I could slice in closer to the wind.

"Ninety-five," I yelled down. He gave me a thumbs-up, then lay down.

There was no moon now. The clouds were parting to show a sweep of stars toward the east. I selected a bright pair and steered by them, keeping the mast right between them. We were still bucking wind and waves, but now I felt used to it.

Then I heard a noise. A flapping. Something loose on high. I shot a look up the sail. There seemed to be some flutter along the leech: a sign I was pushing it too hard to windward. I eased up on the wheel, falling off. The noise continued. I could see the flutter still. I pulled back more. Now 100°, now 105°. The flutter kept growing.

Then I heard a massive ripping noise, and I looked up to the see the mainsail tear in two.

"David!" I cried. He flung himself awake. I pointed. Halfway up the sail, a great horizontal rip stretched from the leech inward. The two halves flogged wildly, held together only by the line sewn into the leech of the sail.

"Point up!" he cried, already loosing the mainsheet and handing it to me. "We've got to get it down." He climbed spiderlike up onto the middeck, letting loose the mainsail halyard and yanking down armfuls of sail, draping his body across the swaying boom, the most stable thing in the midst of this chaos. I held the wheel with my left hand, the sheet with my right, and drove us as straight as I could into the wind, straight on at the waves, knowing that only my accuracy kept the wind from swinging the boom and flinging my husband into the indifferent sea.

Sail doused and tied down, David collapsed in the cockpit, lit a cigarette, didn't say a word.

I kept on driving. Now, without it, I could feel how the sail had steadied the ride. We were more than ever at the mercy of the waves. Thrusting forward then thrown back, pushed over, thrown around. The engine strained on.

David read numbers off the GPS. "Three-one. Two-eight. Two-seven. Three-three." Three knots. Half our usual speed. That put us into St. Maarten at two or three, not noon. Ten more hours.

"How did it happen?" David finally asked.

"I must have been letting the sail luff too much. I thought you said a little luff was all right."

"Not in this kind of wind."

That's all: no blame, no guilt, no anger. We were working too hard.

After six in the morning, the whole sky lightened to a steely gray, then dawn stretched pink across the eastern horizon. It felt like a promise: the beginning of the day when this passage would end. But it also felt like torment. Sometimes we dipped so low into the trough between waves that the gray-green swill surrounded us. Sometimes we lifted to the crest of a wave, so we could see far on every side, and still all that showed was water, white ridges and unctuous surface, far out to the horizon. No islands in sight.

The passage was feeling endless.

By ten in the morning the sun was blasting heat on us. I had stripped off outer layers. My shirt was stiff with salt. A pair of brown boobies appeared, those hefty waterbirds, swooping into the tops of the waves. They seemed harbingers of progress. Maybe land was out there somewhere.

John and Alison now sat side by side in the cockpit. John had his arm around his sister, trying to cheer her out of her mal-de-mer. "Close your eyes and open the book," he said. They were playing a game they had invented, using Graeme Base's alphabet book, *Animalia*. Alison opened to the letter *M*. Beady-eyed mice stared at monitors, wearing monocles with microphones nearby.

"This is my page," she said. "Read it to me, Johnny."

"Meticulous Mice Monitoring Mysterious Mathematical Messages," he read.

She pointed out objects she could recognize. "I get mice. I get a map. I get a moose. I get a monster. I get—what's this thing called, Johnny?"

"A microscope."

"I get a microscope. I get Monopoly. I get a monkey. Look, Johnny, there's the boy." On every page, Baese had hidden a little boy in a striped shirt. "Your turn, Johnny."

The waves were beginning to flatten out—four to six feet instead of six to eight. We surged through them, only occasionally blasted. The children leaned with the movement. John opened the book to the letter *H*.

Just after one-thirty, David leaned over and quietly said to me, "Do you see it?"

"See what?"

"Land."

I stood up at the helm and sighted beyond the immediate. Far out ahead, a faintly darker line floated on the horizon. It had no bulk, no features, just a definiteness about it.

"I'm not going to tell the children yet," David whispered. "Let them notice for themselves."

"Hei Tiki, Hei Tiki. Aerial," came a voice over the VHF. We cheered to hear it.

"Where you been, buddy?" David answered.

"We tacked through the night, way south of course. I see something now, and I think it must be Saba." Saba is a tiny Dutch possession, twenty-five miles south of St. Maarten. "We've turned on the engine, just to get into Philipsburg before dark. You?"

"We're out here somewhere," answered Dave. "Mainsail ripped in the night. We're on engine alone. Quite a ride."

"Something to write home about," said Michael. He and

David recited longitude and latitude. They were south, but just as far from St. Maarten as we were.

"Keep in touch, man," said David. "We didn't like it when we couldn't hear you."

"We're heading in the same direction now," Michael said, and signed off.

Sitting between the two children in the cockpit, I leaned back and let my face drink in the sunshine. The waves had calmed—or was I just getting used to them? My hair clung in stiff curls to my scalp. My face felt grainy and salt-caked. I could pull pinches of sea salt off my ear lobes.

Then John saw land. He pointed it out to Alison, and they bounced up and down on their butts, clapping.

"Tell me a story, Mommy," Alison asked.

"Not another animal story," I said. I only had so many, and I told them over and over.

"Tell me a story about when Johnny was a baby," she said. John beamed.

I thought about it for a minute. "I remember the day when John turned eighteen months old," I said. "Dad was working on the part of the house that's now his office. You can look right out the kitchen window and see that roof, right?"

Both children nodded.

"Dad had climbed up there and was hammering away. I was standing in the kitchen, and I looked out the window, and there was baby John at the top of the ladder, just as happy as he could be."

The children giggled.

"I was terrified," I said. "And you know what Dad did?"

"What?" asked John.

"He invited you up onto the roof. He thought it was great that you had climbed the ladder." We laughed. "You stayed up there, watching him work on the roof." It had been one of those moments, I thought to myself, when I had learned to trust my husband.

"Tell me a story about *me* now," said Alison.

"All right," I said. I wasn't sure if I could put this memory into words.

"When you were only a week old, Alison, I remember a special afternoon. We had a brown velvet sofa then, and I was tired all the time." Alison listened with wide eyes. "I lay down on that sofa with you right beside me, face to face, so we were breathing the same air. I must have been dreaming, or maybe I was just falling asleep, but I had the most wonderful feeling, like I was floating in heaven or surrounded by magic." I faded off.

"And then what?" Alison asked.

"And then somebody drove up the driveway and woke me up, and that was the end of it. But I've never forgotten it."

"Tell us another, Mom," said John.

"That's all for now," I said. "I'm exhausted."

The engine droned on. By four in the afternoon we could distinguish orange roofs on the hillside. I could begin to see the coastline's ins and outs.

We were all sitting in the cockpit, hopes set on land. The engine whirred at a high pitch for a split second, then dropped back down to a drone. David looked at me. He jumped down into the cabin, pulled open the engine compartment. I smelled the familiar gust of diesel, I heard that unmuffled roar. David reached in and jiggled on the fuel pump, shrugged his shoulders, and shut the door.

Five minutes later the motor spun out again, then sputtered and died. The children and I looked at David, slack jawed. He dove into the engine compartment. He rattled parts. He sucked on lines.

"Crank it," he yelled up at me.

The engine started slowly, revved up fast, sputtered, and died.

"Again," David yelled. He grabbed a wrench and a screwdriver as if they were weapons. He sucked and spewed something on the cabin floor. By now his forearms and face were smudged with grease and exhaust. "Again," he gasped.

Nothing.

I could feel David's intensity as he tried tactic after tactic. I tried to steer the boat forward, but with neither sail nor motor, we were losing momentum, and the waves were gaining the upper hand. I could see palm trees and pink houses on St. Maarten. We were that close, but we had no power. The sun was only a hand's width from the horizon.

"*Aerial, Hei Tiki,*" David breathed into the microphone. "Michael, we're in trouble. Engine died. I think it's air in the gas lines. We're dead in the water."

Michael asked our position. "We're just south of you," he said.

"There they are!" John pointed.

"Keep at it, Dave," said Michael. "I'm getting out the tow rope."

I sat there, futilely steering. I tried to imagine the scene: *Aerial* sails up alongside, we hitch their line to our bow, they rev their engine, and we become the coal car pulled by the locomotive. Into a crowded harbor? How do we anchor? Then how do we repair the engine? The solutions eluded me. I sat and steered, getting nowhere.

Not David. He had stuck his head back into the bowels of the boat, sucking again on the fuel line. "Crank!" his voice cried out from the depths. The motor ground slowly, two, three, four times.

"Again!" David commanded. Motor did the same thing. David's body jerked; he grappled with engine parts. "Again!" Such persistence.

The motor ground two, three times. It began to pick up. It cycled faster, kept on going. David leapt into the cockpit, pushed me over, and thrust the throttle forward. The motor roared with power. "Twenty-eight hundred!" David yelled in triumph. I slipped back behind the wheel. David reached for the radio. "*Aerial, Hei Tiki.* We've got power. See you at anchor."

We rounded St. Maarten's southwest corner and headed for Philipsburg harbor, neck and neck with *Aerial*.

"I thought we would never get here," I said.

"We're not there yet," said David.

"Not till the anchor's down," Alison recited.

Two monster cruise liners hogged the space at the mouth of the harbor. Past them were crowds of sailboats, their masts like so many compass needles, all floating toward north. *Aerial* passed between us and one of the cruise liners, her silhouette dwarfed against the massive black hull. Looking toward shore, I saw lights, hundreds of lights. Anchor lights atop masts, swaying back and forth with the harbor ripples. Marina lights, restaurant lights, hotel lights, even auto lights that crept up the hills. No sleepy tropical island here. St. Maarten was turned on.

Alison was wired, too. After sleeping a good two-thirds of the twenty-six hours we had just been sailing, she was ready to party. She coiled every one of the sail lines up pretty, then she clamored, "Let's go to town!" She sashayed up and down the deck.

"Tomorrow," said David.

Too weary to say anything, I let my silence speak.

I ran a little tap water in the galley sink and splashed my face. I brushed my teeth. I peeled off my clothing, stiff with sun-dried salt. I stepped naked into the shower stall. I didn't feel guilty about using fresh water. We had just filled up at Virgin Gorda, and we could fill up again here.

"Mom's taking a shower!" Alison reported, policing me.

"She deserves one," David said. "She did a great job driving."

Half a minute later I stepped out, dripping wet, grinning beatifically. I luxuriated in the feeling of clean, dry clothes.

A little pot still sat on the galley stove. After a rum and lime and a half hour of doing nothing, I was ready to exert one final effort. Four boiled potatoes, one small can of mixed vegetables, toss them in a vinaigrette dressing: there's dinner.

Best potato salad I've ever had.

13

Family Vacations

A CRUISING FAMILY IS NOT ON VACATION. THE boat is home, and on it we try to live a normal, everyday life. When visitors join us, though, they are on vacation, which ups the pace and dictates the pathway.

We made it to St. Maarten three days before our first set of family visitors. David's sister, her husband, and two teenagers were to charter a sailboat, boarding it in St. Maarten and sailing in tandem with us, delivering it a week later to Antigua, 120 miles south and east.

A few days after they were to fly home, my father and stepmother would arrive in Antigua for a week. We would share a few days, then leave them to their vacation while we resumed our cruising agenda.

Just a stroll through Philipsburg, the capital of Dutch St. Maarten, showed how different we were from the mass of holiday tourists. Giant cruise liners dumped crowds into the town square, plump white people with bathing suit silhouettes on their shoulders in painful red.

We stood back and watched them. By this point, four months into our life aboard, we were all deep brown. Tanless squint wrinkles feathered my eyes. Both children had gone white-blond. David's graying hair had turned a shock of white. Even my salt-

and-pepper hair was taking on a golden sheen. Our wardrobes were plainly functional, in colors faded from the sun. Our shoes were caked with salt. We looked different from tourists, and I could tell by the way the merchants of fruit and T-shirts treated us that they knew we were different, too.

With visitors coming to see us, our partnership with *Aerial* loosened again. They had their own calendar: Becca's mother had a ticket to Grenada in a month. Here we were in St. Maarten, at the north end of the Lesser Antilles. Grenada was at the south end, almost five hundred miles away. While we visited with family, they would soon move on to theirs.

We met up again with Claw, Mary, and Crystal. *Tir Na N'Og* had been beat up by the Anegada crossing just as roughly as *Hei Tiki*. David helped Claw weld his rigging. Claw set up his sewing machine on the dock and helped Dave mend our mainsail.

Those winds that beat us up on the passage kept blowing, blowing from the east, so that even after Anne, Don, Skip, and Rhea arrived, even after they were scheduled to take possession of the shiny forty-two footer they were chartering, they stayed put. David used the layover time to install a new bilge pump and replace the frayed forestay that we had discovered months before. We were all eager to sail, but the easterlies kept pumping. Still, we got together daily, tooling around St. Maarten in the car Don had rented, gathering together for dinner every night.

Finally we couldn't wait any longer. We were 120 miles from Antigua, and we had to get there. Charter return date, air tickets out and in—it all forced us further east. Against our better judgment, we let the appointment book rule again.

First stop, St. Barts. We tucked into an idyllic west-coast beach, Anse de Colombier, wild Caribbean nature at its best. Jewel-like turquoise waters lapped a white sand beach. Intricate coral reef grew just a swim away. Rocky crags reached up, supporting a few tough plant survivors. Paths led up to the ridge, from which one could look back to St. Maarten and out to the Atlantic, which splashed in foamy waves against an inhospitable shore. No other sign of habitation, save a farm shed up one slope and the gables of a house hidden high up on the hill.

John and I snorkeled over shapes and colors, toward a cluster of rocks he had spotted. "Mom! Look!" We surfaced, and he pointed back underwater. "A flying gurnard."

He pointed out a warty brown fish, motionlessly blending into the white sand bottom, ten feet below.

"That's a toadfish, John," I scoffed.

"No, really," he said. "Watch." He dove down and prodded the fish, which spread peacock-blue fins and seemed to fly five feet forward along the sand. John shot me an underwater grin. All those hours spent during passages, soaking in information from marine life books. All those hours spent snorkeling, gazing, hunting. He was becoming the family expert.

From Barts, we intended to sail to St. Kitts, or even Nevis. These were not easy waters. The waves reached eight to twelve feet high, but we were moving more south than east, cutting across them rather than sailing into them. I stood at the wheel, surging on, riding the waves. A fishy smell swept through the cockpit. Two dozen flying fish grazed the wave just ahead of our bow. I cast a glance behind to see Anne, standing at the wheel of her sailboat, smiling and waving. It felt good to be driving these waves with her.

But the sail was too hard to make Kitts or Nevis. We detoured to St. Eustatius, a Dutch island with a history. Statia, as it is known, was a mercantile outpost in the heyday of Caribbean colonialism, busier in the eighteenth century than it ever gets today. We walked up the Old Slave Road, worn cobblestones climbing to the old town center, only half-alive, the ruins of eighteenth-century buildings better tended than the few modern wooden shanties nearby.

We followed sidewalks up even further, past a cemetery with graves bearing dates from the early 1800s and Hebrew inscriptions carved in stone. Up beyond the perimeter of what must have been town two hundred years ago, a new neighborhood began. Brick ranchers, blossoming gardens, cars and driveways, laundry on the line. This was where the people lived.

We all liked Statia, but we had to keep moving on. We pulled up anchor in the early morning, and there was *Tir Na N'Og*, just arriving. We circled around, close enough to yell hello.

"Where next?" Mary shouted.

"Nevis. You?" I cried.

"Montserrat. Hope we see you."

We waved frantically. We had had some fun together. You could never tell in this cruising life. We might see each other again.

Time pressed us on. Don and Anne had to return their boat in Antigua, fifty miles further, excruciatingly eastward. The Christmas trades were letting up only a little. We were just going to have to sail into them.

We set out around the north coast of Nevis. Once outside the island's shadow, we were driving straight into stiff waves. Then Anne radioed to say she had driven over a fish pot. Something had wrapped the prop, and their boat was straining. We had to turn around and try it the next day.

Back at anchor well before noon, Don wasn't one to waste a half-day of touring. For the first time in five months, I found myself behind the wheel of an automobile, driving a rental Jeep almost ten times as fast as our sailboat could ever go. We zipped across to the ocean side of the island and lunched at a sugar-mill-turned-restaurant. We stopped at gift shops and art galleries. By the time we returned our cars, my head was throbbing with an anxiety I hadn't felt for months. Same feeling I used to have after a long day at work.

The next morning, we left at five. We sailed around the south coast. It wasn't any easier, but somehow we were all more prepared—teeth clenched, inner clocks set, ready for an all-day battle. By midafternoon, Antigua rose before us, but those strong easterly winds kept blowing. We zigzagged on long, broad tacks. We penetrated sheets of rain, so dense it all looked gray. I sat at the helm, my shoulders hunched in discomfort. I wrapped a blanket around my legs. My teeth chattered. My mind roamed into the realm of blame.

If it weren't for these visitors, we would skip Antigua. Don and Anne should have just chartered in St. Maarten. If Dad and Janet had only chosen some other holiday island, we wouldn't have to do this sail. We let other people, who have no concept of sailing, make our decisions.

Useless lines of thought.

We made Five Island Harbour in Antigua just at dark. All that misery faded behind us. We ate the last of the thick beef fillets that Don and Anne had brought from home. Dave and I raised a glass to each other. "Furthest east I'm ever sailing," I toasted.

But I was wrong. The next morning, we coasted around the island, further east to its southern shore, into English Harbour. Here, Don and Anne were to return their boat; here, in a few days, Jan and Dad had reservations at the Inn.

English Harbour is the British West Indies' museum on the water, the headquarters for Britain's navy during the peak of her colonial island hold. The map shows why: water winds through a series of rocky openings, each offering protection from wind and waves, then opens inland into two broad fingers, flat water with plenty of shoreline.

It was a lively sailing destination. Boats everywhere: lined up at the dock, anchored out. Rigging clanged, pennants flew, dinghies buzzed back and forth. Three boats away, a fifty-foot-long steel boat looked well lived-in: cluttered deck, laundry flying from every horizontal line.

"Kid boat!" John cried, pointing to it. Kid boat indeed. Two boys with bleached, cropped hair, not much older than John himself, climbed from the steel boat into a little skiff. By the end of the afternoon, John was learning to play cricket with them on the lawn of Nelson's Dockyard. We had made it east to Antigua, and for the time being, it was home.

"You think Don and Anne are doing okay?" David asked me the evening after they had taken off for home.

"Seemed fine to me," I answered. I had always admired their energy and enterprise. They traveled to the beach and to

Florida. They went overseas, all four of them. They had taken
two trips to New Zealand, to see the country and visit relatives.
These ten days with them had been exhausting, but it had been
fun to travel in their style.

David sat and looked over the water. He had other things
on his mind. "More sex," he said.

Did he mean us or them? I waited for him to say more.
When he didn't, I asked, "How can you possibly know that?"

Finally he spoke in a philosophical tone. "Sometimes I think
women just don't know the power they have over their men."

I was lost. I waited for more.

"When you're a teenager—no, all the way into your
twenties—you follow after your dick. That's all you care about.
That's every decision you make," he said.

"What?" I asked.

"Your dick," he said emphatically, looking straight at me.

"I heard that," I said. "*Your* dick."

"Whatever."

"Go on."

"If you're getting some, you feel good about life. You feel
good about yourself. You feel good about your woman. You
want her. You don't want to lose her. She's the one that makes
you feel that good." He looked out over the water. "Women
don't seem to understand what power they have."

I was beginning to understand.

When we made love that night, I watched David's face as
he thrust into me, as he felt it coming, as he came. His eyes
closed, as if he was tasting the most delicate sensations. His face
held the moment, as if he was diving through the air, and then
he let go and relaxed on top of me. And then he smiled.

It was easy to enjoy English Harbour. All within a short dinghy
ride, you had eighteenth-century forts and boatyards, bakeries
and groceries, an open-air market, and the post office. This was
a cruising community, comparable only to a few we had visited
so far—George Town in the Bahamas, Boquerón in Puerto Rico,
Philipsburg in St. Maarten. You could tell, just by looking, that

most of these boats were lived in. There was a chandlery and a sail shop, with all the tools and equipment one could ever need to outfit, repair, or improve a sailboat. Each day started out with a weather report on channel 68, spoken with a British clip and dry humor. And with all this came the feeling of a village, with faces that quickly became familiar and a sense that it was safe for the children to take off and play on their own.

"Mom, you've got to come up this hill with us this afternoon," Alison said. "It's really neat."

Plaintive little goat kids bleated from the hillside, echoing the invitation. We tied the dinghy up at a tumbledown dock and climbed the crumbling rock stairway to the fort.

She was right—it was spectacular up there. To the northwest, a view into English Harbour, looking down on scores of boats; to the southeast, a view out toward Guadeloupe and the Atlantic. The wind blew nonstop, roaring into my ears and whipping my short hair back. Whitecaps ridged the water east as far as I could see. Straight below, big waves shattered up against a rocky wall, blue-white foam spilling over red and ochre crags.

The children were already hoofing it up the hillside, up beyond the colonial crenellations. Thorny little bushes and bulbous cacti, bristly and green, were somehow succeeding in that dry, rocky, wind-blasted soil. Fat-leaved aloe plants were preparing to bloom. I broke off a leaf tip, and it oozed golden-brown sap. Against the backdrop of ocean roar, I heard a high-pitched hum as an iridescent gray-green hummingbird poked its curved beak into the rosy cactus bloom.

"Did you like that walk?" I asked Alison that afternoon. She nodded enthusiastically, wondering what came next. "Why don't you write about what you saw?"

I went to a Fort in English Harbour.
I Found a Nest.
We think its a Hummingbird's Nest.
it is Made out of Sticks, Grass,

And Fuzz. And I
Saw Some Cactuses

"Want to draw a picture of the nest?" I asked.
She shook her head. "I need to write more," she said.

Wiley and Janet, my father and stepmother, flew into Antigua later that week. The children and I had already scoped out their harborside hotel and left a little hello note for their arrival. In the early evening, we heard the radio hail.

"Hey, *Hei Tiki*! Greetings! We're here."

I jumped to answer. "Hi. Switch to channel eighteen." Might have sounded officious, but in a crowded anchorage, radio protocol prevailed.

"I've never spoken on a VHF radio before," my father said. His voice seemed to glow with childish excitement.

"We can see your hotel from where we are," I said, poking my head up out of the cabin. "Look for the boat with a bright blue deck."

"We've already spotted you," he said. "We had a nice chat with David's sister, and she told us where to look. Shall we meet on the beach after breakfast tomorrow?"

"We'll get some early school in before that," I agreed.

This reunion had been in the works for months. Dad and Janet always plan far ahead. They are prodigious academics, Wiley a musicologist, Janet an art historian. With no children of their own, they live an urbane life—Park Avenue condo, intense cultural calendar. They write books, conduct classes, attend concerts and openings all year round. They allow themselves a Caribbean beach week every winter. This year, instead of Jamaica, they came to Antigua, to meet up with us. They would have the privacy of their hotel, but we would share a taste of the cruising life with them.

It wasn't even nine-thirty. I recognized my father's stocky silhouette at the water's edge, stretching and gazing toward us. I walked up to the bow and waved. He waved back. My heart sang. I rounded up everyone and we dinghied over

"You look so brown," he said, giving me a hug.

"You look so white," I answered.

We spent all morning talking, stretched out on hotel beach chairs. So many stories, polished with retelling. Running aground in Green Turtle Cay. Meeting Michael and Becca in West Plana. Laundry in Luperón. Boat boys in Samaná. Christmas at the Bitter End. The Anegada Passage.

Janet joined us, looking statuesque in her two-piece. She and I talked some more as Dad played with John and Alison, swimming out to the float, diving off, swimming around. David bowed out politely, proffering boat chores as his reason. Then the rest of us sipped iced drinks under the beach bar's thatched roof—a vacationer's luxury.

"So tell me, what has been the best and the worst of the trip so far?" asked Dad, looking around the table.

John assumed his deep, grown-up voice.

"I would say worst was the Anegada Passage." He glanced at me, then his eyes lit up. "And best is catching big fish." Nods and smiles all around.

I spoke next. "The worst times have been when David has gotten hurt," I said. "I have two best: the city of Samaná, and snorkeling in the Bahamas."

Alison's turn. She screwed her face up, thinking. "Well, I would say—mmm—best was George Town."

"In the Bahamas, where we made a lot of friends," I expanded.

"And worst—mmm—worst is moving."

"*Moving?*" Dad echoed. We all laughed. "You mean when the boat is moving?"

John and I smiled. What an honest answer.

We all approached this rendezvous with the same sense of timing: we would overlap three or four days, then we aboard *Hei Tiki* would bid farewell and sail on, leaving Dad and Jan to vacation by themselves. The first night, we restauranted together.

Big mistake. While they eat fashionably late, we were used to dinner before dark. We compromised and ate at seven-thirty, but still the entrées did not arrive until after eight. Both children, sated by bread and butter, rested their heads on the table and fell asleep. The next night, we invited Dad and Jan aboard for drinks before dinner instead.

The third day, we planned a short sail together, even though the wind was still pumping up fiercely outside. We poked out of English Harbour. Three-foot waves from the east. We skirted the island westward and anchored near a crescent of rock and sand.

We reeled in a little tuna. Enough for a nibble, but not a meal, so I served typical fare: rice, canned chicken, vegetables, and fresh limeade. Neither Janet nor Dad felt like leaving *Hei Tiki*, but the children and I went exploring. Alison roamed the rocky beach. John and I snorkeled. The children dinghied around while I swam back. Time alone felt good. I pulled myself up onto the stern and toweled off. "Good swim?" asked my father. "You're braver than I am."

It was a hard sail back, pounding into waves and wind on the nose. I stood at the wheel and drove with my muscles.

"I'm not sure when we'll get out of here," I said once we were at anchor. "We have to sail fifty miles in this very direction."

"I see what you mean," said Janet. She understood then, when, despite all plans, we sat at anchor all that week. The winds just wouldn't die down or switch around, and finally—with nobody on the calendar—we could wait for the quiet sail we wanted. As the days went on, we gave each other space. We had things to attend to, and Janet and Dad wanted the isolation of a beach vacation.

In those days of waiting for weather, I finished the next essay to send home. I set myself to the task of describing our Anegada Passage. Looking back, it represented the toughest sail we had had, the kind of hardship many uninitiated might think we faced daily. It was a lot to get into eight hundred words. I typed a draft, counted words, cut, and typed again. I found a fax machine at the sail shop, and sent another essay off to Virginia.

———

Among the gifts from Janet and Dad were two books of mythology for the children. Alison gravitated toward Marcia Williams' *Greek Myths for Children*; its colorful illustrations turned the great myths into comics. At first I turned my nose up, then I began to see a plan.

Each of twelve myths was told on three different levels. There were the childish illustrations, which told a lot of the story right there. There was a narrative, and there were also dialogue bubbles, written in simple words. We could look at the pictures together, I could read the narrative, and Alison could read the bubbles. She quickly chose her favorite: the myth of Hercules.

"Heracles was a tough little baby," I began. "As he grew up, Heracles became stronger and stronger and stronger. He married and had many children."

"Let me read that part, Mommy," she said, and read, "How many at the last count, dear?" Her eyes feasted on the detail with which Hercules' twelve tasks were pictured. The more often we read the story, the more fluently she could read the dialogue that went along.

"You like that story, don't you?" I asked as we finished.

Her answer? "Let's read about Medusa."

Dreams about teaching kept troubling me. I would be late to class. I would arrive half-dressed. I would stand in front of the class and forget what I was talking about. I would have to take an exam, and I would not know any of the answers.

"I'm considering calling home to say I don't want to teach next year," I finally told David. It was the month when next year's fall appointments were made. If I had been there, I would be sitting in the department chair's office, talking schedule. If I wanted to teach, I should tell her. If I didn't, I should tell her, too.

"You sure?" said David. "It's a lot of money." For the past ten years, even a part-time teaching position had meant a regular paycheck, nine months out of the year.

"I'm never going to be a writer if I try to be a teacher, too,"

I said. "It stretches me too thin. I spend all my energy reading texts and grading papers."

"You should do what you want," he said. In this domain, we had always been good partners. Each of us respected the other's drive to shape work that suited us rather than to find a job. We forged a path of give-and-take, balancing incomes and recognizing needs.

"Do you think we can afford it?" I ventured.

"We'll make it," he said.

I made the call. When I hung up, it felt momentous. I had taken the plunge and declared myself a full-time writer.

We tanked up with fresh water. We stocked up on goods— English biscuits, a bag of limes, jam and butter. I discovered, in our calm pocket of English Harbour, that *Hei Tiki* was growing green fuzz. Over the next three days I scrubbed the whole hull. I wore mask and fins and carried a scrub brush, and with each gulp of air I could clear a square foot of fiberglass.

Each day we organized some little encounter, until the morning Dad and Jan were to leave. There, on the beach, that familiar silhouette waved goodbye. I stood alone on the bow and waved back. Home he would go, and on we would sail. I noticed an ancient sadness: leaving my father. Yet this time, there was a new sense of exhilaration. This life feels good. Dad noticed it; he admired it. Those little looks, those little comments. He saw how firmly I could hold the helm, he mentioned how well David and I anchored together. I had something new and strong, something all my own.

Tears warmed my eyes. Then I noticed that the winds were slackening.

Sunday night, the winds started shifting around. Tuesday, just after midnight, we crept out of English Harbour.

14

Laundry on River Rocks

WE PROBABLY WOULD HAVE ENJOYED GUADE-
loupe, but we had sat too long in Antigua. So we skated down
that next island's coastline all day long and anchored overnight
on its southwest corner. We kept sailing on the next day,
through choppy open waters, past the Iles des Saintes, and on to
Dominica. It was bright midafternoon as we approached that
tall, conic island.

We glided into an idyllic landscape. The harbor opened
its protective arms wide, five miles from one fingertip to the
other. Seaside shanties lined the beach to the left of us, palms
arced over the beach to the right. Between the two beaches a
steel-girdered dock stretched out into the harbor, built high for
workboats. The rusty rigging of a half-sunk tanker jutted up out
of the water. Beyond this scene of industry, the dense, green
steeps of Dominica rose into peaks lost in fog.

"I see a green boat over there," David whispered as we
scoped out Prince Rupert Bay. I looked where he nodded and
saw a familiar ketch: *Tir Na N'Og.*

We slid behind their stern and gave a yell. Claw climbed out
of the cabin, waving. As we anchored nearby, a native yola—a
long, low, wooden boat—approached *Tir Na N'Og* from the bow.
It worried me. Two men balanced in the yola, grabbing hold and

inching themselves down the length of the sailboat. Claw was aft, watching us. Mary and Crystal were nowhere to be seen. I yelled and pointed. Claw didn't notice. The yola edged closer.

Then Claw leaned down toward it, smiling and speaking. He knew these guys.

"Yeah, that's Randolph," Claw said minutes later, over for a visit. "He'll come around here soon enough, and then you won't be able to get rid of him."

It was good to see Claw again. His inflatable dinghy looked patched and sorry, like a day-old balloon, but his spirits were high. "Randolph's a wild man," he continued, climbing aboard. "He'll do anything for money. Eddie's a Carib Indian. He comes from the reserve on the other side of the island. They're cool. So where you guys been?"

We recounted our adventures, and he told theirs. They had gone to Saba and Montserrat, two islands we had missed on the path we had chosen.

"So you kids want to go to the movies?" Claw asked.

"Yeah, sure," John said sarcastically. I thought Claw was joking, too.

"No, seriously. *Home Alone Two* is playing in town."

John and Alison cheered. First movie in months.

That left David and me alone. We looked at each other and dove for the V-berth.

With daylight and plenty of time to spare, we dawdled in pleasure. We could be as deliberate and as noisy as we wanted, with only the buzz of an occasional fly to interrupt us. David twiddled with my breast, then his tongue teased my nipple. I stroked the inside of his legs, just short of my goal. I hovered over him, humping with my hips and letting my breasts just graze his lips. We rolled over and back again. He watched my face as I came, as I arced rhythmically like a dolphin, breaking the water again and again. Then I grabbed him and pulled him inside me, which made me blossom more, and he shot up into me, calling out in pleasure then wrapping around me in fatigue.

We lay there, dozing off together, melting into the sky-blue day outside. David jerked to. "We're adrift," he said, and shot up the hatch. I lay there, doubting. How could he tell from in-side the cabin? I heard the anchor line rub through the chock. I stuck my head up to see.

"You were right?" I asked, not yet believing.

"Wasn't even hooked," he said. "We must have moved twenty feet. Good thing it's not crowded."

I pulled on clothing, hoisted myself up through the hatch, and took over on the anchor. "I can't believe you knew that," I said.

"Something didn't feel right," he said. "Something about the way the boat was moving. I could tell." He was always at the ready, always tuned in, deeply intuitive about this boat of ours. Moments like this reminded me that I was still learning, but David had sailing in his bones.

The next morning, all four of us went ashore. We had to check in with customs. We dinghied around a bulky old workboat and eyed the dock, at least six feet above us. No ladder in sight, just old tractor tires nailed to the pylons. David and John climbed nimbly up them, then David hoisted Alison by the wrists. I groped for a good handhold, riding the slop as the dinghy bobbed up and down.

"Come on, Mom!" John yelled. Dave and Alison were no-where to be seen. *I can do it,* I told myself. I hooked my foot into the first tire, shoulder height, then I swung upward, trying not to notice how the rotting rubber flexed. Two more steps, and I was on solid wood.

We walked past piles of bananas. Massive banana stalks, six or eight feet tall, lay on the dock. Each stalk held dozens of green fruit, interlaced with crisp brown leaves. Men and women chattered to each other as they worked, using sharp kitchen knives or machetes to cut off small bunches. They piled them into bushel boxes, some marked "Bananas from the Windward Is-lands" and others pirated, labeled lettuce or motor oil. A young man heaved each full carton onto the workboat, which listed under the weight of bananas.

While John and David checked in with customs, I wanted to

explore. I took Alison by the hand. "Let's walk up this way," I suggested, leading her up a dusty road. I wanted to taste this island.

"I don't want to walk," she complained.

"Let's look at the flowers."

"I'm tired."

"It's only ten o'clock."

"I'm thirsty and hungry."

"There is no food and drink here. Come on."

She huffed, folded her arms, and stood still.

I could be just as ornery. I kept on walking. What little twinge of conscience I felt about my decision told me that the place was safe. I would stay within her sight, but I wasn't about to give in to her grumpiness.

I searched the roadside scrub for plants. So many island plants looked familiar, but I could name so few. At home I carried an index of plant names in my head, so a walk through the forest always called up words. But in the tropics, I walked through unnamed green.

I came to a fork in the road. I could turn left and walk deeper inland, maybe find a neighborhood, or I could turn right, through palms and mangroves, and head toward the beach.

I sensed Alison approaching, dragging her toes in the sand. I imagined her head hung down, moping. *What is her problem?* I asked myself. I just wished she would let me go free. I wanted to roam. There was something wild and wonderful and friendly about Dominica that drew me in to its greenery and its life, and I wanted to follow.

Then a voice inside answered. *She wants my attention. She wants my hand. She wants to know she isn't alone in this new and different world.*

The adventurer battled with the mother inside me. The mother won. I turned around. "Come on, Alison. Cheer up. Look, here's a path to the beach." I forced her hand into mine and led her through a mangrove thicket toward the water. We found a beach strewn with the rubbish of culture—faded beer cans, a rum bottle, a single sandal, a plastic motor oil jug. The waves lapped up at our toes as we squatted and looked out past

Hei Tiki and *Tir Na N'Og*, out to Guadeloupe in the hazy distance, out to the Caribbean Sea.

Same sort of thing happened in the town of Portsmouth. We walked ten blocks, from the edge to the center of town, to find immigration. Checking in here was a two-step affair.

We passed by flimsy shanties, cobbled together with found lumber and sheet metal, dingy curtains flapping in the tropic breeze. No matter how dreary the house, though, every one seemed adorned with flowers. Deep rose hibiscus drooped from bushes eight feet tall. Mottled red-and-green croton decorated many a front yard. Dense poinsettia hedges glowed true red up against unpainted wooden houses. Grapefruit branches bowed heavy with fruit. Grapefruit lay on the ground, on the street, ungathered. Such riches amid such poverty.

Unbuilt lots were strewn with trash. The remains of old stone houses crumbled in on themselves, and at the heart of them, bananas, aloes, palm trees grew in what were once living rooms and kitchens. Water trickled through the streetside gutters. Beyond the town, fields lifted up into dark green mountains, so that natural beauty refreshed every intersection.

We passed a front porch with an old woman sitting, crocheting, watching the world go by. Her hair was growing thin, her cinnamon skin old and weathered, but kindness lit up her eyes. I smiled at her. She grinned and waved like a child. It felt like a blessing.

I mused about why I liked this island so. Such an intersection of poverty and beauty. But how much more deeply I could look into these people's eyes than into the eyes of the people in St. Thomas or Antigua, where they saw me as just another rich American. I wanted to soak in this culture, and I found it so intriguing that a poorer country would seem to have so much more heart.

Then I heard a familiar cry. "Mommy. Wait up."

Alison ran up to me, grabbed my hand, and squeezed hard. "Pretty flowers, pretty smiles," I said. "I like this place, don't you?"

She just clung more tightly. At the moment, all she cared about was me.

"It must be some sort of phase," I said later, once both children had fallen asleep. "A response to being in so many different places."

"I don't remember this fear of new places earlier in the trip," said David.

"We have been in much more foreign places than this— Luperón, Samaná," I agreed. "They didn't even speak our language."

"Maybe it's just new culture overload."

"I hope it doesn't last long. It wears me out." I wanted to add, *And you keep leaving her with me,* but the mother inside kept me quiet. "I already like this island. People look you in the eye. Lots of fruits and flowers. Those steep, green mountains." I looked out over the water, to the mist-covered island heights. "You know, Dave, sometimes it feels as if all we see is the edge of every island we come to. We park the boat and walk ashore, but we never get much deeper."

"If we were going to rent a car and see an island from the inside, this would be the one," David said. "Fifty miles from one end to the other. We could drive it in a day, no problem."

"I like that idea. It shouldn't cost too much."

"Less than a hundred."

"Let's do it tomorrow."

"Good school today, Alison," I cheered her on the next morning. We were playing our version of bingo designed to help her read more words. Meanwhile, the tone felt different in the cockpit. David was showing John simple algebra, and it was hard for him. One moment John was hooting and giggling, then the next he was stabbing the paper with his pencil, yelling "I can't!"

I poked my head out and reminded John that he hadn't eaten any breakfast. David glared.

"Well, he hasn't had anything all morning," I continued. "It's after ten."

"Don't interrupt our lesson," David shot back.

"Just trying to make it easier for both of you," I said, and I stalked back to the galley.

Later that morning the children, in a burst of independence, said they wanted to go to the beach by themselves. David and I returned to the conversation. "You're so hard on him sometimes, I feel as if I ought to save him," I said.

"I wasn't being hard on him."

"I see this look in his eyes," I said.

"He plays up to you."

"But he was hungry. I could tell."

"He wasn't going to starve." David wouldn't give an inch. "He wasn't paying attention. He wasn't doing his best. He needs to shape up and concentrate."

Then it hit me. I saw why it was so hard for me to let go. I had my own reasons for interfering with David's parenting. My voice got small. "Somehow I'm saving myself when I do it. I'm trying to save the sad little put-upon child that I was, and that I fear he is becoming."

David refused to lick my wounds. He kept to the subject and said intensely, "I'm not going to hurt him."

A noisy outboard motor interrupted us. Claw had been right. Now that they knew us, we couldn't get rid of them. Randolph and Eddie clunked up against our bow.

Randolph was a fast-talking salesman, with raisin-dark skin and bloodshot eyes that darted away as he talked. Eddie stayed quiet, in Randolph's shadow. He had nutmeg skin, angular features, and a transcendent innocence. When he spoke, he struggled. The only language he knew well was the Dominican patois.

After five minutes of obsequiousness, Randolph got to the point. "We have a big job this morning, to clean the bottom of that yacht over there, you seen it?"

"Yes?" So what did he want, congratulations?

"We have no masks," Randolph said. "We could do it without masks, but it's a lot easier . . ."

"I guess you could borrow ours." David had gone back to reading, tuning Randolph out.

I opened up the lazarette and pulled out two masks.

Randolph edged the yola down and peered into the lazarette. "I notice you have a brush. Could we borrow a brush, too?"

I pulled one out.

"Do you possibly have two?"

Deep breath. "I think so." I climbed down into the cabin and rummaged through the galley cupboard.

I handed over two masks and two scrub brushes—the very tools they needed for the job they had already agreed to do. "Anything else?" I asked. The sarcasm flew by them.

"We will bring them back this evening," Randolph said. He leaned up, trying to catch David's eye. "Bye, Captain. See you later."

We had said yes to the children's beach outing to reward their sense of independence. We had said yes, they could take the dinghy. But an hour and a half later, I started getting antsy. I couldn't see them anywhere.

"I'm going to swim over and find them," I said.

"They're fine," said Dave.

"I'd like the swim."

I rode a wave in and scrambled up the sand. John and Alison were right there, scouring the beach for fallen coconuts. "Do we have to go?" they pleaded.

"Where's the dinghy?" I asked. John pointed to the hotel dock stretching thirty feet out into the water. I saw the familiar shape of our dinghy, but something looked wrong. Three other dinghies, tied to the other side of the dock, were riding well, pulled back taut on their lines by the current. The children had tied ours so that the line wrapped under the dock and now, with the rising tide, the dinghy was trapped. It bumped up under the dock with each wave that lapped in.

"Oh, no," John moaned. He started ranting at himself hysterically. "How could I do this? It's all my fault."

Alison just stared.

"We have to get it out from under," I cried. "You pull on the bow line."

John was caving in, but I ignored it. I lowered my body and gingerly put my foot on the bow of the dinghy, inching it forward against the current. I shoved a little harder and forced the outboard motor out from under the dock joists.

"Get in, get in!" I yelled, holding the boat against the current. "Forget the coconuts."

Then I noticed. The gearshift lever was gone. I could start the motor, but I couldn't shift into forward. There, on the aft seat of the dinghy, lay the little gray piece of metal, ripped right off. "We'll have to row," I said.

"Oh, no. I'm in big trouble now," said John.

"Probably so," I told him, unsure whether to play disciplining parent or sympathizing pal.

"We'll to have to turn around. Abort the trip. No way we can continue."

David held the broken lever in his hand, just staring at it. He didn't express anger at anyone. He blanked out into despair.

"Abort?" I repeated, finding both the word and the concept ridiculous. It wasn't as if we could will ourselves home. We had a long way to sail in either direction.

"We have no dinghy," he said.

"We have a dinghy. We have no gear shift lever," I corrected.

"That amounts to no dinghy."

"There's no way to fix it? Glue it? Solder it?" I asked.

"Look at it." He held the piece out to me. "You can't glue that material."

"Couldn't we get a replacement part? Maybe there's a Yamaha dealer here in Dominica, or Martinique, or Bequia."

"You have to take the whole engine apart to replace it. I can't possibly do that."

We sat in glum silence.

After smoking two cigarettes, David gathered up a handful of tools. "John, pull up the dinghy," he said, and he climbed in. The little boat pulled back and rode on its bow line, carrying David ten feet off our stern.

A pall of uncertainty fell over *Hei Tiki*. I found it hard to do anything. Then I heard the blurt of the Yamaha motor. David was starting it up. It caught, kept running, moved forward on the bow line. David throttled it down and drove up alongside *Hei Tiki.*

"Untie me!" he yelled.

"Everything okay?" I asked, but he drove off without answering.

I watched him circle around, stop at *Tir Na N'Og* to talk with Claw, circle around slowly again. He glided in toward us, reaching up to tie the dinghy line to a cleat.

"Everything okay?" I repeated.

"No problem," he said. As if nothing had happened.

"What did you do?"

"Just leave it in forward. You can't shift into neutral, can't shift into reverse. Leave it in forward, throttle up, throttle down." His voice lilted with that tone of technogossip he adopted when he and his father shoptalked together. "Works fine," he said. "Never liked that reverse anyway."

What happened to "Abort!"?

In an instant, I saw my husband more clearly than ever. When things go wrong, he takes a plunge. He speaks in absolutes, in words of doom. But then he stands up, gets to work, and figures out how to fix things. And when he fixes things, he soars.

I saw him more clearly, and with that realization came a lesson in how to be his wife. Instead of plunging with him, I should keep on the level. I should banish the voice of the child inside who fears it's all her fault. I should ignore the voice only slightly older who feels it's her responsibility to fix everything up. Glide on through. It would be easier on both of us.

We all agreed: the children were not allowed to take the dinghy alone anymore. But I could. I dinghied across the bay to town, to spend a little time by myself in this place that so intrigued me. I found a souvenir shop, run by an oatmeal-skinned man with an educated way of speaking who ranted about drug addicts ruining Dominica. I peeked into a music shop, clerked by a

wild-eyed Rastafarian. CDs cost over forty U.S. dollars. I found
a corner bakery, back behind the main street, and bought four
little bread twists and four eggs. The middle-aged woman at the
counter never cracked a smile. I noticed a stack of journal
books, black with red bindings.

"How much are these?" I asked.

"Two dollars." In Eastern Caribbean currency, that's less
than our dollar.

"Good price," I said and smiled, trying to warm her up.

"You want to buy one?" she asked, key in hand to unlock
the case.

"I'll buy two. My daughter would like one, too."

"Your daughter writes? How old is she?"

"Almost seven."

"Very smart."

I handed her some money.

"You want to contribute to our education drive?" she asked,
lifting a pint jar with a handwritten label.

"Sure," I said, dropping an E.C. dollar coin into the jar.

She never cracked a smile, but we connected.

A car rental sign hung over the door of an appliance store.
I looked inside. Washers, dryers, televisions. Watches and calcu-
lators in the display case. "Yes, we rent cars," the young woman
said. It took forty-five minutes of looking up prices, dialing in
credit card numbers, and waiting for signatures, but I finally re-
served a Jeep for the next day.

"Got a car," I said, back at *Hei Tiki*. "Eight-thirty tomorrow."

"I spent the whole afternoon fixing Randolph's goddamn
motor," said David.

"You what?"

"He came by, brought back the masks and brushes, and
started asking questions about how to clean the carburetor. Before I knew it, I was sitting in his yola with that cheap-shit engine all in pieces."

"Did you fix it?"

"Can't be fixed. Doesn't drive any better after I worked on
it for three hours."

"Dave, you're something." I shook my head. He may have a gruff exterior, but he gives and gives.

The sun glinted through the mist on the hilltops as we picked up our little red Jeep. We were all so used to my taking the helm, Dave and I hardly discussed it. I jerked the car into forward, bungled over pockmarked pavement, and we were off. We headed down the western coastline toward Roseau, the capital. David and I had three dollars E.C., a U.S. fifty-dollar bill, and a fifty-dollar traveler's check between us. We needed to find a bank.

The road twisted and turned. We passed men and women working with machetes cutting down the roadside scrub, women carrying baskets on their heads, women carrying children on their hips, men sitting in twos and threes, playing dominoes.

Dipping inland, down into a valley and across a bridge, we passed a long, low warehouse. There, on top of the building, a man stood barefoot, raking some large brown balls. We rounded the bend and I saw a hillside orchard. Cocoa trees. The man on the rooftop must have been turning cocoa pods, spread on the roof to dry.

We entered Roseau from on high. A tiny airplane droned in toward the airport north of town. A cruise liner, small compared to those we sailed past in St. Maarten, lay at dock. Beyond it, the city was congested, street upon street of buildings, huddled together. Roseau is no metropolis—no building sits over two stories high, and from these heights, we could see the city's far edge—but it still felt daunting, a confused heap of life that we had to maneuver by motor. David rifled through guidebooks for a city map.

I just kept driving. Cars zipped past. I could feel the annoyance of drivers behind me who knew where they were going. We turned and turned again, and found ourselves heading east out of town, past a sign saying TRAFALGAR FALLS, 5 MILES. It was one of the sites we wanted to visit.

"But we have no cash," I said.

David shrugged. "We'll get by."

We plunged into jungle shadows as we climbed the road. We entered the mist. Slopes rose at fifty-degree angles. Banana

plants shot out of the hillside, banana fingerlings pointing upward, waxy blood-purple flowers at the tip of each bunch. I saw
the long, thin sheaths of dasheen, key ingredient of Caribbean
callaloo stew, unrolling into graceful arrowhead leaves.

At one turn we stopped to gawk. Thick white clouds drifted
past us, beneath us, now and then parting to reveal how steep
the slope dropped down. Down there, down in the valley below
us, sat a village of tiny patchwork shanties, clustering together
against the ferocious landscape. I couldn't look for long. It felt
as if I might fall downhill, it was so steep.

We began to hear the pounding of water. We passed a cluster of utilitarian buildings. Huge sluice pipes funneled down
into a generating center from which high-tension wires shot down
the ravine. Concrete pavement defined a public space. Men clustered as I parked the car. They hovered around David, each one
offering to be our guide. Dave reached into his pocket, bringing
out three E.C. dollar coins. "It's all I have," he said. All but one
guy disappeared.

"We don't have much money," I explained, shrugging my
shoulders. He shrugged back and smiled mildly, then gestured
for us to follow. I asked his name. Ervin. Three inches taller
than David, he probably weighed half again as much, all muscle.
His skin shone the color of darkest chocolate. He wore a torn
khaki work shirt, dingy brown pants cut at the knees. He walked
barefoot, so fast we all ran to keep up with him.

We climbed a well-worn pathway. The air throbbed with
falling water. There was moistness everywhere—plants glistening, vines dripping, boulders slick and slippery. The smell of
clean water filled the air. Ervin led us down to a pebbly stream-
bed. We stood barefoot in icy water and, from there, got our
first glimpse of the falls as they plunged through the greenery.

"Come this way," said Ervin, inviting us to step from one
slick boulder onto the next. He gave me, then John, a hand, then
lifted Alison by the armpits. We passed by the spicy white blooms
of ginger, basking in this hothouse world. We ducked under
the umbrella of great ancient tree ferns, plants that belong in
dinosaur dioramas. And always the wetness, and always the noise.

As we drew closer to the thunder, great rocks lay strewn like fallen ruins. This was not one waterfall, but many, joining and dividing, pooling up and shooting down. I stripped down to my bathing suit and waded in. I heard the laughter of my children through the water's crash. They had followed Ervin to a pool, perhaps twelve feet in diameter, fed by two flows of water.

I eased my body under. Cold, clean, fresh water, ever replenished. What a luxury to those of us who had been surrounded by salt water for months. I sank into momentary oblivion.

"Mom! You gotta try this!" said John, and he dog-paddled from one side of the pool to the other.

I followed him, swimming from icy cold on one edge of the pool to bathtub hot on the other. Two falls, one hot, one cold, coalesced in one pool. I hooted for joy.

Ervin sat on a stone slab above us, smiling at our play. John found a slippery rock to slide down. He scrambled up, slid down again, squealing every time. Alison was more cautious. She found a hot tub just her size, and she sat, dangling her head back like a glamorous lady taking a bath. David found a cranny where the cold water fell straight down on him. I swam back and forth, enjoying the little body shock every time.

A new fleet of tourists broke the magic. I wanted the place all to ourselves. We pulled our shorts on over our wet bathing suits and started the trek back down the mountain, down to concrete, power lines, the city, and the traffic, away from the force of these falls.

We didn't say much—it's hard to talk, even shout, with that din all around—and yet some powerful feeling of togetherness formed between the five of us. We four, delighted by this tropical wonderland, and Ervin, equally delighted, even though he must have known it all his life. He loved this place so much, he wanted to share it, no matter how little we could pay. We gave him two oranges and a ride to his village, trying to find some way to thank him more.

The next day was market day in Portsmouth. "Get there early, just at sunrise," we had heard, so the alarm rang at five-fifteen.

By six, we all were climbing into the dinghy, empty go-bag in hand.

Portsmouth has no market building. "Just down there, on the corner," as a shopkeeper had told me, a handful of people sat on folding stools and overturned buckets, tending produce spread out on the sidewalk. Little piles of tomatoes, potatoes, eggplants, and peppers. Larger piles, even feed bags, full of grapefruit. Bunches of plantains, bunches of bananas. From one woman, I bought a sprig of thyme, a dozen little purple onions, and the ripest tomatoes she had. Then I asked her about those deep-red seedpods.

"That's sorrel," she answered.

I picked one up. A hollow, waxy lantern, the shape of a pepper but the size of a walnut.

"For sorrel tea, you know?" she said. I had seen sorrel tea in the restaurants, served cold, a brilliant ruby-red.

"I'll buy some if you tell me how to make it," I said.

"How you make sorrel tea?" she echoed. She looked over at two women selling vegetables alongside her. *Get a load of the stranger,* her eyes seemed to say. *Doesn't know how to make sorrel tea.*

"First you tear de sorrel from de stalk like dis," she said, pinching the flower. Red juice oozed onto her thick black fingers. "T'row away de stalks. Then you put your sorrel into a pot of boiling water, along wit' a little cinnamon bark and cloves. Let it simmer twenty, t'irty minutes. Strain out de sorrel. Add sugar, and let it sit and cool down. Dat's all, dat's it, to make sorrel tea. How much you want?"

She picked up all her sorrel.

"That looks like a lot. How much?"

"Two dollar."

"Give me half." A single E.C. coin for a handful of red flowers. I laid the sorrel on top of the grapefruit plumping up our go-bag. "I'll think of you as I make sorrel tea," I said.

And I did. My own fingers turned spicy red, and in the heat of the afternoon we enjoyed glasses of sorrel tea, tangy and refreshing, even without ice.

During the few days we anchored at Portsmouth, Randolph and Eddie came around at least once a day. They wanted to give us a tour up the Peaceful River. After Trafalgar Falls, it seemed anticlimactic.

"But it's different, very different," Randolph insisted. "I can show you many birds. Do it for the children." What a salesman.

I gave in. "Four o'clock?"

"Four," Randolph agreed. He fiddled with the fuel valve and started up his outboard with a high-pitched snare, then a stutter. "Goodbye, Captain," called out Randolph. He noticed David lighting up, and gestured. He took two Camels, shoving one behind his ear.

"He ought to take us for free," I grumbled after them. "You worked on his motor. They borrowed that equipment."

"Oh, I'll pay him. That's the way he makes a living," said David. "I just wish he wouldn't smoke up all my cigarettes."

The ride up the Peaceful River did turn out to be a trip worth taking. We ducked under a city bridge, past rusting barges that brought bananas out to the bay. We passed vast mangrove thickets, glided under palm archways. The water was so still, it reflected every tree. A steel-blue heron stepped gingerly along the riverbank. We rounded the bend and the water beneath us was filled with mullet, schooling by.

Randolph slowed the motor as we slid through a curtain of hanging vines. He grabbed one and hoisted himself twelve feet up, while the yola kept on going without him. "I want to try!" John cried. Eddie circled the yola around. Randolph dropped back in and gave John a boost. His feet dangled nervously, six feet above the water.

"We'll pick you up on the way back," Randolph yelled. We all laughed, and Eddie brought the yola back around.

Randolph promised more birds, and headed us into marsh grass. We ran aground. Eddie and I used paddles to push sideways. Pried loose, we ran aground again. Randolph jumped into the knee-deep water and pushed the yola around.

"So what do I owe you?" David asked when we returned to *Hei Tiki*.

"Forty E.C.," said Randolph, eyes darting. Eddie looked on inscrutably.

David paid him the forty.

"It's the way he makes his living," David repeated as we watched them go. The outboard clattered into the distance, then died again. We watched the yola drift across the bay, Randolph fiddling with the motor, Eddie watching silently.

Super Bowl Sunday might have gone unnoticed, but we had Claw to remind us. "It's a celebration of everything that's American, man," he said.

"Everything that's male and American," Mary spat out in her Irish way. She and I laughed.

"I just watch it for the ads anyway," I said.

"Claw uses it as an excuse to get roaring drunk once a year," she said. I had come to expect Mary's gripes. Mary dished it out, Claw shrugged it off. It seemed the constant patter of their life.

We rendezvoused with Mary, Claw, and Crystal at the open-air bar of the Coconut Beach Hotel. The place was packed. All white faces, except for the bartenders and waitresses, who snaked through the crowd with trays held high. Portsmouth is home for a catch-up medical school for Americans, and the entire student body must have come to watch the game.

I sipped on a beer and watched football. I didn't care about the game, but it made me think of home. I found a pay phone and called Chris and Kathy, soon flying down for a visit aboard.

Chris answered. "It wouldn't be the Stupid Bowl without you," I joked. We had shared many a "Stupid Bowl," as Kathy and I liked to call it. There was the year we shoveled through foot-deep snow to drive from our house to theirs, then, after the game was over, found ourselves snowed in two feet deeper and stayed all night. Chris asked a few questions, but I could tell he wanted to get back to the game. He gave the phone to Kathy.

"Hi, Suze." Great to hear her. "Bequia on Dave's birthday. February eleventh, right?"

"That soon?" I said.

"You sure you want us to come?" she asked. "Last chance to say no."

"Yes," I said urgently. "We're counting on it."

"We check into the Hotel Frangipani on the eleventh. See you for dinner." It felt so odd, making a date three weeks and 175 miles away.

I got back to the television for Michael Jackson's halftime. There he was, glitter and moonwalk, surrounded by hundreds of children, all singing about making the world a better place. It was so corny, and so American, it brought tears to my eyes. The best and the worst of my United States, right there in halftime. Emotions of longing and belonging cascaded through me.

That night, we bid our friends on *Tir Na N'Og* a sad good-bye. They were sailing straight on to Grenada, then west through the Panama Canal, then across the Pacific to Hawaii and home. Out of money, no more island hopping for them.

"They live closer to the edge than I could," I said to David. "Mary told me in the Virgins they had six hundred dollars."

He just shook his head. People back home thought we were taking a risk, leaving house, work, and paychecks behind. But we still had more than five thousand dollars, and by the calendar's reckoning, we had reached the halfway mark. It was costing us less to sail the Caribbean than it cost to live our everyday life in Virginia. We were living frugally, but neither of us would ever let us get down to our last few hundred.

"Hey, what do you expect?" he said, looking out at *Tir Na N'Og* in the moonlight. "They're skydivers. Motorcyclists. They approach life that way."

To meet Chris and Kathy for David's birthday, we had a long way to go. From Dominica, we had to pass by Martinique, St. Lucia, and St. Vincent, before Bequia, largest of the St. Vincent Grenadines. Beyond Bequia, I wanted to get to Carriacou, the island north of Grenada, where Michael and Becca had headed. They had decided to settle there, and I wanted to see their island.

We left Dominica in the deep of the night, destination St.-Pierre, Martinique. I swatted the alarm clock when it rang at two-thirty. I pulled on my favorite passage clothes—a worn white T-shirt with tails knotted at my midriff and cotton knit shorts, bleached to oblivion. I stood on the deck and felt as if I were the only one awake in the world. The dinghy rocked a little, slapping the water. The night was very dark, no moon at all. An immense sky arched overhead, splattered with more stars than I ever see back home, even in the Virginia countryside. A shooting star streaked across the sky. I stood, opened my arms, and stared. I wanted to memorize this vision for all time.

But we had to get sailing. "David, quarter of three," I whispered. We sat together, sipping Dominican coffee. "I like this place," I said. "It's the first place that has made me have fantasies about living here."

"I've had fantasies like that all the way along," he said. "Bahamas, Dominican Republic, Puerto Rico."

"I know you have. Not me. But this place is different. I like the people. I like it that they grow so much here. Portsmouth and Roseau are both so poor, but these places have spirit."

By three-fifteen, David had turned on the GPS, checked our waypoints, opened the logbook, and written a heading for yet another sail. He sat at the helm, I stood at the bow in the light of the running lights. I could only dimly see the anchor line as I pulled, using my muscle to bring *Hei Tiki* up over the anchor, then giving that last great tug and unhooking the anchor from the floor of the bay. David revved the engine. We moved, unnoticed, out of Prince Rupert Bay.

It was a long sail, but not a hard one. Well past daylight, we sailed past Roseau, which from the water looked as if some giant had tossed a sackful of buildings down the mountain slope. They lay scattered, piling up as they reached water's edge, a confusion of the Caribbean colors: turquoise, yellow, pink, coral, sea-foam green. Martinique loomed beyond, a firm blue ridge on the shimmering horizon.

Alison woke well after sunrise, wrapped herself in a blanket and started to whine. "I need candy."

"We had breakfast an hour ago, and you wouldn't eat," David said. "No candy."

Her face contorted. "My stomach hurts," she said. I sat at the helm and let David handle it. "I'm thirsty," she groaned, trying a new tack.

"I'll get you a glass of water," David said.

"I don't like water."

"Water or nothing."

She said nothing, but looked me in the eye then abruptly sat up, gagged, and dry-retched over the back of the cockpit bench. She looked at me again, hugged the blanket, and shivered. David brought a cup. "Drink some water," he commanded. She sipped, then fell back weakly. A moment later, she dry-retched again. David was at the galley table, checking the chart. "Alison, would Gatorade taste better than water?" I asked.

She sat up straighter. "I want some *candy*," she said.

We're playing a little game here, I thought.

"It's obvious what has happened," David said that afternoon. We had reached the wind shadow of Martinique. John was in the forward cabin, building with Legos. Alison was fast asleep, head draped back, mouth wide open. "She has been getting positive reinforcement for acting seasick."

"This was not a rough ride," I said, agreeing. It looked more like an act than a reality today. Sometimes tough parenting was right.

Approaching St.-Pierre, we saw the sign of French culture. Red tile roofs atop sturdy houses and, above them all, a steeple pointing toward a Catholic God. Overtowering all stood Mount Pelée, its peak lost in clouds.

More than any other in the Caribbean, this volcano has made history. St.-Pierre was Martinique's elegant capital, the Paris of the Antilles. In 1902, Pelée burst forth, killing thirty thousand and turning the city into rubble in one day. One man survived, a criminal imprisoned underground. The French government set him free, and he joined the Barnum & Bailey sideshow.

Fort-de-France, further south, became Martinique's capital while St.-Pierre rebuilt upon its ruins. It still has the feel of a European city—narrow, cobbled streets, wrought-iron balconies hung with pots full of begonias and fuchsias. Blackboards on the sidewalks beckon into cafés with dark coffee, rich pastries, crusty bread, and smelly cheese.

We looked for the sign DOUANES and found the office open. A man in uniform with almond skin and a Clark Gable mustache greeted us. Slowly my French came back to me, and I played interpreter for David. We interacted officially, then something caught the official's fancy. *"Vous habitez la Virginie?"* he asked. I nodded politely.

He grinned and started chattering away, telling me—as far as I could tell—that he raised fighting cocks, that he bought them from many different locations, including the United States. He showed us a loading slip listing three roosters from Alabama.

"What's he saying?" David asked.

"He's into fighting cocks. He bought some from Alabama."

David smiled and nodded, and the customs official smiled back, talking all the while about fighting cocks as he rubber-stamped our paperwork without even reading it, shook David's hand, and bowed to me.

"Easiest check-in of the whole trip," David said once we were out of the office.

We stayed in St.-Pierre for Saturday market. Twenty, thirty women, each with her own still-life arrangement. Whenever eyes engaged, I nodded. Sometimes someone would chatter at me in fast French, showing me handfuls of string beans or okra or skinny eggplants.

Closer by the beach stood the fishmongers, including one tough-faced woman who wielded a machete, sharpened so often that the blade curved in. She was shouting and pointing, arguing some sort of deal, then slicing up the silky red meat of a massive half a tuna on the cutting block. Its midriff measured bigger around than hers.

David and I gravitated toward the *boucherie*—our chances for red meat came so infrequently. Two men, one black and one white, bantered with customers before us. I knew none of the words for cuts of meat. David just pointed at pork chops and gestured "four."

Magical aromas drew me on. One woman offered whole cloves, whole allspice, whole nutmeg, boughs of dried bay leaves, boughs of dried sage. She had bouquets of fresh thyme, sage, oregano. She had black peppercorns and cracked black pepper. Rolls of cinnamon bark and black vanilla beans. She had little bottles with tinctures of who-knows-what, with handwritten labels and corks poked tight. I stuck my nose down into a bright orange spice mix.

"*Qu'est-ce que c'est?*" I asked.

"*Le masala,*" she answered. "*Pour le viande, le poisson, le pot-au-feu.*" Caribbean curry paste. I bought some, along with a cluster of fresh thyme leaves. Drawing herbs under my nose brought back memories of my own garden, so far away, so long ago.

Add to our market purchases half-a-dozen bottles of wine, and we had an unwieldy load. The children battled over who should carry which packages. Alison ran ahead, carrying nothing, and John dropped the canvas bag with the wine bottles in it. We argued our way back to the boat and on through dinner. Pork chops mollified the children. Later, David and I polished off a bottle of wine.

"What's gotten into him?" David asked.

"What?" I asked. His question came out of the blue.

"John. He's useless."

"That's extreme, Dave. Come on."

"What do you mean, extreme? I can't get any work out of him."

"I still worry about how you and John interact," I said.

"What does that have to do with it?"

"All he hears from you is negatives. How he's too slow doing this and he's not doing that right."

"He puts on an act for you, you know."

"What?"

"He's much more miserable when you're around than when he's alone with me." Sometimes I did feel drawn into a triangle.

I returned to my original tack. "I'm not convinced that criticism is the best way to teach our children. The more John hears, 'You're not doing right,' the more he thinks he *can't* do right."

David uttered some skeptical remark.

"You love him. You say you don't want to hurt him," I said. "He needs to know that. He needs to feel that."

David flicked his cigarette butt into the water. "Okay," he said. "I'll try it your way. We'll have a no-negativity campaign."

David did set to trying. The next morning, when John worked himself up into a snit over math, David used humor to cajole him. He tickled him, put his arm around his shoulder, and said, "Come on, man. You can get this. Try again."

Meanwhile, Alison was playing helpless on me. We were working through a book about baby chicks. She had heard it many times, but she still stumbled over words.

"Come on, Alison. What do the letters sound like?"

"I don't know."

"Well, at least try. *H* sounds like—"

She made the sound of *W*.

"Alison. *H* is for *horse*, and *house*, and *Hitchcock*, and *ha-ha-ha*. So what does *H* sound like?" I repeated *horse*, pausing on its opening consonant sound. She echoed the sound.

"Okay. Next letters, *A* and *R*. What do they sound like together? *Ahh-rr*."

She formed her mouth uncomfortably and said something resembling *ar*.

"Good," I said. "Now put the *H* in front of the *ar*."

"I can't." She didn't even try.

"Well, if you can't, then I can't either." I lost my cool. I slapped the book shut and squeezed my way out from behind the galley table.

"Mom," she moaned. "Don't leave me." She started to cry.

No-negativity campaign, I reminded myself.

I sat back down and tried to show her how to sound out *harvest.*

It felt as if we were hurrying. From St.-Pierre, we anchored overnight at a southern beach in Martinique, but we didn't go ashore. We spent another night at Rodney Bay, on the northwest corner of St. Lucia, then sailed the afternoon down the island's west coast. Ever since I had seen their silhouettes in Caribbean travel guides, I had dreamed of anchoring at the foot of the Pitons.

"Throw me your line!" yelled one boy from a yola. "Give me your line!" another yelled. We had furled the mainsail; I had throttled way down. David stood forward, spotting. John was rummaging for a line in the lazarette. "Just ignore them," I said.

Abruptly, David gestured to turn around. The yolas peeled off as we headed outward.

"What were they yelling at us for?" I asked Dave.

"I'm not sure. We don't have to give them anything," he said.

The sun had already slipped below the horizon. The western view was brilliant gold. To the east, we were skirting dark, unknown territory. Deep waters, steep beaches, dense greenery to the waterline. "This water is so deep, we couldn't possibly anchor," I realized. "That's why they kept yelling 'Give me your line.' " What I was beginning to understand was that the ocean floor dropped as sharply as the slopes of these volcanic islands. An anchor could only hold if we were to hook bow out and tie a line from stern to shore.

We sailed further up the coastline to a little strip of sand. There was no sign of life except a shanty among the palm trees. Even close to shore, the water was so deep and the light so faint, I could not see a sandy bottom. I dropped the anchor and felt it plummet. The boat seemed to circle aimlessly on the anchor line.

All four of us fell to work, determined to anchor before dark. Alison stood on the bow and manned the anchor line, pulling up tight and checking the cleat wrap. John found a line in the lazarette. He held one end and handed the other to David, who rowed to shore and disappeared into shadows. We felt a tug on line. John and I pulled back and the boat kept revolving, stern pointing toward the palms. "Anchor holding?" I called to Alison. She yanked and nodded. I gave our line one more pull, then a quick cleat knot. Success. We had anchored ourselves, Windward Island style.

A wisp of cooking smoke arose from the shanty. I gave up my dream of anchoring at the foot of the Pitons, satisfied instead with this secret tropic spot. The sunset faded into pink, purple, and green, then a universe of stars dusted the pitch-black sky. We ate and read and fell asleep early.

We woke in the middle of the night, prepared for another long sail. A deep calm surrounded us. Languid waves lapped the hull. A steady breeze whistled through the halyards. We moved without speaking, above deck, below. David checked the rigging. I reached up above the heads of the children, fast asleep in the V-berth, and shut the forward hatch. David unfolded the chart and reached for a pencil. "How far today?" I whispered.

He read numbers off the GPS. "Forty-three miles."

More than eight hours. Another long sail. It was the ninth of February. Chris and Kathy expected us in Bequia the day after tomorrow.

Once we passed out of St. Lucia's wind shadow, the seas kicked up. There was a strong northeasterly, and waves pounded us sidelong, a rolling corduroy that threw us side to side without any rhythm. Occasionally the boat shuddered. Blast of salt water in the face. It wasn't fun. It wasn't easy. I was tired of long, hard sails.

By seven-thirty Alison had climbed into the cockpit, huddled, ashen, wrapped in a sheet. Occasionally she peered out miserably at the sea. She stretched her neck and dry-puked into the gutter, then retreated into herself again. "Wouldn't you feel better if you went back and lay down?" I asked. She shook her head listlessly.

An hour later, she opened her eyes. "Look, Mom," she

said, emerging. Behind my right shoulder was the most spectacular rainbow I have ever seen. A full bow, horizon to horizon, growing brighter as we watched.

"It's a double!" John said, and I began to see, tucked into the arch, a second sequence of colors, a pale reflection of the first.

As we skirted the St. Vincent coastline, a yola drew closer. I watched the steadily pumping muscles of its rower. His oars were nothing but straight-hewn saplings. He was a young man, under twenty, with cappuccino skin and a haircut trimmed close around the ears, tall and curly on top. His boat, bright yellow with red trim, was named *Sunset*, handpainted on its hull. He matched our speed and overtook us, never missing a beat as he rowed and spoke.

"You visiting St. Vincent?" He spoke with the lilt of the West Indies, the pout of French, as if English were not his native language. "Where are you heading?"

"Kingstown," I called, naming the capital, still far south. Far enough that he won't offer to show us the way, I figured.

"Big city," he called back, still rowing vigorously. "You ought to visit Wallilabu Bay. Beautiful anchorage." He looked at David. "*Capitain,* come to Wallilabu. When you come, ask for me, Kali. Kali is your man."

He slacked off rowing and waved as we left him behind.

"That kid must have rowed out a mile and a half," David muttered as we watched his yola head back toward land.

The landscape of St. Vincent changed as we moved south, from steep untouched green to gentler hillsides shaped into terraces, with rows of fruit trees. I joyed in the symmetry, the control of nature, the productivity.

But the island seemed to go on forever. We could not see the southern end. We had been sailing eight hours, and it looked as if we might not make it to Kingstown by dark. "Let's go back to Wallilabu Bay," I said. "Kali seemed to know what he was talking about."

David nodded.

"Coming about," I said, and as John worked the mainsheet, I turned the boat in closer toward land. We approached one little bay with a cluster of shanties, dingy yolas, and worn-out fishing skiffs. From the beach, someone waved his arms above his head.

"It's Kali!" both children cried, as if finding a long-lost friend. He rowed toward us energetically, another young man now in the bow of his yola with him.

"You convinced us," I called to him. "Where's Wallilabu Bay?"

"Kali is your man," he smiled. "Do you have a line? You could tie a line behind and pull me." We wrapped a line around a stern cleat and threw him the end, following his directions to Wallilabu Bay.

Great rocks lifted up tall and jagged, as if standing guard for this little nest of water. The harbor was clear and clean, yet the ocean floor dropped so steeply that the water changed from turquoise to slate ten feet from shore. A beach curved gently, strewn with soft brown rock. Five buildings skirted the waterfront: three little weatherworn houses, a whitewashed restaurant, and a row of tiny offices, so new they were vacant. A few coconut palms rattled in the wind. A rainbow shimmered in the air, arcing down over the mountain river.

Along the river just beyond the buildings, a dusty Jeep putted out. A man drove a donkey. Two women walked behind him, one with a basket perched on her head. A jungle yodel reverberated in the air. For a moment I was in Africa.

By entering the bay with our man Kali tied on behind, we repelled other boat boys. At least half a dozen noted our arrival, though, and as soon as Kali left us, carrying our line to shore, the swarm descended.

"Capitain! Capitain!" a voice cried from one side.

"Missus! Missus! Lady! We bring you bread, fruits, water!" came another.

"You got business for me?"

"Want to buy shells?"

No one has told them that it takes concentration to anchor.

"Tomatoes? Mangoes? Breadfruit?"

We've been sailing since four in the morning, and we just want to anchor and go to sleep.

"Lady! We have grapefruit. Want some fruit?"

That does it. "Nothing!" I yelled out. "I want nothing! Leave us alone."

One yola retreated, but the guy in the dinghy came closer, grabbing the side of our boat. "Lady!" he said again.

"No!" I looked right at him and finally swatted him away.

"How much do I owe you?" David asked Kali once we were tied, anchored, and secure.

Kali shrugged. "Three dollar U.S." David gave him five. "You need anything else?" he asked. "Bread? They make it in my village. Very good." I gave him two more U.S. dollars to bring us bread in the morning. "I go home now, to Barouallie, where you saw me waving. But just remember, Kali is your man." He smiled sweetly and rowed away. John and Alison stood on the bow and waved.

David took the children ashore, having learned that in one of the vacant-looking offices was the customs official. This was yet another country, and we had to check in. I went down into the galley, feeling thirsty. The air below was hot and still. Dozens of flies had found their way in. They buzzed and circled. I searched for the swatter.

Then I heard a voice: "My sister she want to do your laundry."

A small hand gripped the side of our boat. A young man and a girl, kneeling in front of him, balanced on a beat-up surfboard. She looked up and smiled as if she didn't know my language. Her skin was a deeper brown than her round brown eyes. He repeated, "My sister will do your laundry." She smiled more broadly.

I really didn't need laundry done. I had become quite self-sufficient, ever since paying thirty-five dollars a load in Antigua. I did a few pieces at a time by hand, planning around sailing and weather, so I could pin wet clothing onto the lifelines and get it dry by late afternoon.

But I liked these two, coming alongside on their humble surfboard. "How much?" I asked.

"Depend on how much laundry."

I gathered up a few pieces, mostly T-shirts, a couple of kitchen towels. "Five dollar E.C.," he said. I handed it over.

"I need soap. You have soap?" said the girl, now coming alive. She grabbed hold of the boat and craned her neck to look inside.

I scrambled to the galley, sensing that if I didn't act fast enough, she would come in and look for soap herself. Detergent and cleanser tumbled out on the floor.

"I need bleach. And a brush. You have a brush?"

I was handing things over when David and the children returned. The laundry girl spied Alison, but her brother paddled her away, taking our laundry, detergent, bleach, and scrub brush. We watched the girl carry our laundry over to the broad, flat rocks where the mountain river flowed into the sea. Two other women stood ankle-deep in the river, bending down and scrubbing against the stones. Three other girls, closer to Alison's age, joined the girl doing our laundry.

"I want to go," Alison said.

"Then go," I urged.

"Can I take the dinghy?"

"Just swim. It's only thirty feet away."

She jumped right into the water, swimming with the straight-armed freestyle that was becoming so second nature to her. She climbed, dripping, up out of the water and coyly approached the laundry scene.

In five minutes she was the queen of the river rocks. Five or six girls gathered around her, laughing and splashing and running up and down the beach. It was a little girls' party on the occasion of doing laundry. Shrieks of glee traveled out to *Hei Tiki* on the wind. I looked out to see a gaggle of girls, Alison golden among them.

An hour later, my laundry was delivered. The young man paddled up, carrying Alison, her friend, and our laundry on his surfboard. He handed up our clothing, dripping wet.

"Can Dyan see the boat? She wants to see the boat," Alison said. Before I could say no, both girls were aboard, also dripping wet. Dyan shot straight into the cabin, eyes gorging on everything. She gravitated toward the V-berth and the shelves with toys. She grabbed Alison's doll and hugged her to her chest.

I felt invaded. "You two are sopping wet," I said, herding them back into the cockpit.

Dyan told me she was twelve. Taller than I, with sinewy limbs and breasts just budding, she could barely sit still. She kept peering below, hungry to see and touch more.

"Can Alison play some more?" she asked with the same desperate yearning.

Dyan's brother paddled them back to shore. I wrung river water out of our laundry and pinned it up on the lifelines. Bleach spots speckled my red T-shirt. I wondered what other damage had been done. From the beach I heard the squeal of girls. There was Dyan, running on spidery legs, tallest among the girls who surrounded Alison. She was still a child. She might not even know what bleach does. I liked her enough that I couldn't get mad.

"She's really nice, and she's got these sisters, or cousins, or something, and I like them all except one," Alison said at dinner. "I told that one a secret, and I even *told* her it was a secret, but she went and told everyone else. So I don't like her."

Girl games happen in every culture.

"I wonder if we have any books we could give them," I mused. We found a few we could do without: a book about horses, a book about pirate treasure, two easy readers, a couple of picture books. "We'll give them to the girls tomorrow," I said.

I hadn't even had my morning coffee when Kali rowed up the next day. "Fresh bread," he said. "Baked this morning." He handed us five golden dough twists, wrapped in brown paper. "Something special for you," he said to John. He held out a treasure, ivory an inch long.

"It's a whale's tooth," said Kali. He smiled at John. Suspicion glimmered momentarily in my mind, but I could see it in his eyes: Kali wasn't asking for anything in return. He brought this gift in genuine friendship. John was delighted.

In the afternoon, Alison and I walked up the mountain road and down again, studying banana plants and cocoa trees close up. We met Dyan on the beach. "We would like to give you some books," I said. "Do you read books?"

"Oh yes," she said, although I wasn't convinced. "You bring candy, too?" she said eagerly. "Alison says you have candy."

"Yes, we have candy," I said quietly. That wasn't my idea of a cultural exchange.

Leaving Alison on the beach to play, I went back to *Hei Tiki* and gathered up the books in a paper bag. I added a copy of *Vogue* left behind by Janet and a handful of butterscotch candies, especially for Dyan.

As I approached the dinghy dock, more people came to greet me. One, a woman with close-cropped hair, I took to be Dyan's mother, coming to say thank you. Why else would she be moving in on me?

I had not even tied up the dinghy securely when I felt hands reaching, pushing, grabbing from me. A press of people moved in. Not all children, not all girls. Alison got buffeted in the middle, her face in tears. She reached out for me, helpless. Pieces of candy, spilling out of the bag, got swooped up. Hands grabbed the books. A young man ran down the beach, tossing a candy wrapper behind him. The shorthaired woman ran down the beach, too, coveting the book on pirate treasure. I watched and wondered if she could even read. There I stood, empty-handed. Alison wrapped herself around me, dissolving in fear and disappointment.

"I didn't get to give out anything," she cried.

"Neither did I," I said, slack jawed. I asked Dyan if she had gotten anything. She opened her hand. Two pieces of candy. I yelled down the beach at a man twice her age, "That's what they mean, taking candy from babies." A futile gesture.

Alison was still sobbing. I knelt down and held her in my

arms. "They just took things from us," she spouted, unbeliev-
ing. Dyan and three other girls clustered around, pawing Alison
to try and make her feel better.

It was hard to explain the scene to a six-year-old. I wasn't
sure I understood it myself. In a land of little, our naive gifts
brought out greed. Better, perhaps, not to try to give at all.

On David's birthday, the eleventh of February, I awoke to an
alarm clock well before dawn. I quietly prepared myself: comfortable clothing, contact lenses in. Water boiling. Three cups of
coffee.

"Dave," I whispered. I shook his shoulder. "Five o'clock.
Happy birthday."

We came awake quietly in the dark cool of Wallilabu Bay.
Nothing else seemed moving. No other cruisers were awake. No
boat boys around us. No flies in the galley. Even the water
around us seemed asleep.

We worked silently together. I stood at the stern, hands on
the line, while David rowed to shore and untied the other end
from the tree where two days ago Kali had tied it. As I pulled
him in, hand over hand, the boat began to drift around on the
anchor. David turned the key. I heard the familiar muffled roar
of our engine. I leaned over, put my whole back into it, and
pulled up the anchor. David steered the boat out between rocks
into the Caribbean Sea.

We motored a good mile out before turning to coast the island. By then, the sun's first rays were glinting above the slopes
of St. Vincent. I looked back to Wallilabu Bay. There, silhouetted against the rocks, glided a single figure, rowing a yola,
silently, patiently, through the dawn.

15

Turning Toward Home

CERTAIN THINGS ABOUT PORT ELIZABETH, Bequia, tell you it's a boating town. Fancy dinghy docks, shops and cafés lined up to face the water, and in front of them a footpath along the water's edge. It was also a tourist town: plenty of bright white shorts and gold jewelry. In the town center, streets were built for autos, hawkers sold shells and shark's teeth, and the garbage dumpsters were always overflowing.

It was here, on David's forty-ninth birthday, that we were to meet our visitors: Chris and Kathy, friends, neighbors, godparents to our children. I had known them for twenty years.

By choice, Kathy has no children, and yet she nurtures from the heart. When John was delivered last-minute by cesarean, Kathy understood my needs—not only because she is a nurse practitioner, but because she instinctively cares for people. That first week of my motherhood, she visited daily, bearing casseroles, lanolin, alcohol wipes, and wine. Now she was counting on us for a winter vacation, especially since her octogenarian father had moved in, making home life just as demanding as work. Kathy's plan was to sail with us for a month.

Chris would stay for a week, then fly home to prune his vineyards and care for his father-in-law. As much as Kathy, he gives from the heart. Tall and sweet, he speaks with a Southern stutter. He's so unassuming, some who meet him may take him for a bumpkin, but he's smart, quick, literate, and loving. With a master's degree in horticulture, he still calls himself a farmer. He charms everyone he meets, and he sometimes wears himself out with friendliness. But we know each other well enough that Chris can usually say no to us when he needs to.

David and I had suffered through many wins and losses with these neighbors and friends. Some nights, when our marriage had reached the depths, I would pass out on their sofa, too full of wine and food. Other nights, it was David who fell out so soundly that I would drive home alone, two toddlers in tow.

As our marriage regained its balance, Chris and Kathy traveled through hard times themselves. First her mother died, then her father slid mentally, requiring full-time attention. Chris and Kathy brought him into their home. They hired caregivers in the day, but through the night, they kept the vigil, always on the alert for this eighty-four-year-old, who was liable to rewire a lamp or light a fire or roam about in the middle of the night.

We had shared highs, we had shared lows, and Chris and Kathy still loved us. A visit with them was like a visit with family. We would have the room.

First I spotted Chris. His six-foot-four body and sandy gray head of hair stood above the crowd.

"Chris Hill!" I called out loud. Then, beside him, I saw Kathy, her angular face glowing.

"Suze!" Kathy cried. Hugs all around. We bantered through comments on how tall the children had grown, how white David's hair looked, how tan we all were. They proposed two more nights in their Bequia hotel, then all six on *Hei Tiki* heading south for Carriacou.

"I want to be sure you feel c-c-comfortable with this plan," Chris said, looking straight at me. Chris knew what a trial that week with the Moores had been. He was giving us one last out.

"No way," I said. "We've been looking forward to this day."

To celebrate our reunion, and David's birthday, too, Chris and Kathy treated us to an all-you-can-eat hotel buffet dinner.

Cocktails all around, live music, barbecue, and island salads. John wolfed down four T-bone steaks.

The next night, we started to face the reality of all six aboard for dinner. I thought about buying something fancy, but I figured Chris and Kathy would rather taste our ordinary cuisine. I minced garlic, onions, and hot little peppers, let them sizzle in olive oil, then added tomatoes, two cans of beans, and a generous pinch of Martinique masala. I chopped cabbage, carrots, and onions together. I heaped beans, rice, and salad on each plate and handed dinner up the companionway. We squeezed into the cockpit and balanced plates on our knees. Chris led us in a blessing about food, friends, and safe travel. We talked late into the night.

I woke up feeling gray and fuzzy. I had drunk more in the last two nights than I had for months. David was moving slowly, too, still drinking coffee at a quarter to eight.

I dressed to go meet Chris and Kathy, to help them bring bags aboard. I fumbled with my contacts and finally got them in. The right one felt a little scratchy. The left one started to sting. The right one felt worse. My lenses were burning excruciatingly.

Then I remembered the pepper I minced last night. One little lantern-shaped pepper, bought green in Martinique and ripened to red. I had minced that pepper into tiny pieces. Then I had removed my contact lenses.

The sting had struck both eyes. I was afraid to take out my contacts, for fear I would hurt my eyes more. I stomped, I yelled. I had to let out the pain.

"Are you okay?" asked Alison.

"My eyes," I said, almost incoherent. I felt overwhelmed by pain and fear. Then I heard the voice of other feelings, mingling with the pain in my eyes. *I am so scared that something will go wrong during this visit. I'm nervous about sharing my private life, afraid of being seen. I don't want to alienate these dear friends.* I listened, then I surfaced and steeled myself. Having faced all those thoughts, I felt more in control. I made myself remove one, then the other contact. It hurt, but then my eyes relaxed. I wore my glasses ashore, hoping that red eyes wouldn't give away my premonitions.

For our first night out, we just sailed around the corner to Petit Nevis, uninhabited but famous as a whalers' outpost. We anchored on the lee side. Some of us dinghied, some swam ashore. We roamed the hillside, sharing it with no one but a pair of skittish goats. The beach facing the ocean looked like an ancient burial ground, strewn with bleached white bones.

"They're whale bones," said Kathy. "I'm sure of it. That's a scapula. That's a vertebra."

"Coral," David contended. I wanted to believe Kathy, but I suspected Dave was right.

We ate, we drank, we communed like a family.

"So where to tomorrow?" I mused out loud.

"What are our choices?" asked Kathy.

David unfolded the chart. "Canouan, Mayreau, Mustique, the Tobago Cays."

"Mustique!" John cried. "We can visit Mick Jagger."

We agreed to skirt by Canouan and go on to the Tobago Cays. There we settled for two nights, despite the crowds. It was a pleasure to be back in water warm and shallow enough for snorkeling.

John and I swam hand-in-hand against the current. He showed me the surgeonfish. With their pursed lips and wide-open eyes, they look as if they take themselves so seriously, each one protecting its own little coral nook. Move in on a surgeonfish, poke at it with your finger, and it darts back in tiny attack.

"Great snorkeling," Kathy said. "I could have stayed till dark."

"Too shallow," I said. "The current kept bumping me up against the coral."

"Not as much color as the Bahamas," David said.

"You guys," said Kathy. "Picky, picky, picky."

"Darn right they're picky," said Chris. "They've got the whole Caribbean to choose from."

———

"We're twenty-five miles from Carriacou. Let's see what we can get," said David. *"Aerial, Aerial. Hei Tiki,"* he spoke into the microphone.

"Hei Tiki, Aerial," answered a familiar voice.

"Becca!" we cried.

"Hey, guys," she said. "Where the hell are you?"

"Tobago Cays. Coming your way. Where are you?"

"Tyrrel Bay. Tyrrel Bay." Becca still had that radio manner, repeating phrases to be sure she was heard. "Southwest corner of Carriacou."

I took the microphone. "Hey, Becca, we're coming your way."

"We'll keep an eye out for you." We chitchatted some more, then signed off. I turned to Kathy. "You're really going to like them."

We sailed without engine to Carriacou. John did nav. Chris took the helm. We put up the jib. The winds were brisk, the waters gentle. Clear, keen sailing.

Hillsborough, Carriacou's main town, lay on the way to Tyrrel Bay. While the men checked in with customs, the women got to know the town. Soca beats blared from radios through open windows. Men sat on a concrete stoop, arguing politics, waving their hands. A pickup truck rumbled by, kicking up street dust. The municipal trash can was overflowing, and a mangey brown mutt sniffed at the pile. So this was Carriacou, Michael and Becca's dream island.

My heart pounded faster as we rounded the island, into sight of Tyrrel Bay. We scanned the masts, a good two dozen.

"There's *Aerial!*" Alison cried. She and John ran forward, yelling and waving.

And then I saw her: that golden brown mainmast, the white radar globe, the brown sail boots. I thought I saw Michael, glasses on, reading. He went down into the cabin, unawares. The kids yelled louder. Then two people climbed up out of the cabin.

This time they saw us. They waved and yelled, too. Soon that familiar red rubber dinghy eased up to *Hei Tiki* and they climbed aboard.

"We had our bets you wouldn't make it down this far," Michael said, giving David a warm man-hug.

"If it wasn't for you, we'd be heading north," David said, broad smile.

"Yeah, hey, you're making us late," I added. "We'll have to sail straight from Martinique home."

"How are you guys?" Becca asked, drawing John and Alison to her. "So, Juan, speared many fish since we saw you last?"

"Not since Puerto Rico," John said seriously.

"Becca, we got to do laundry on the rocks in Wallilabu Bay," Alison said excitedly. "And this girl poured bleach all over Mommy's shirt, and we were going to give her books and candy, but a bunch of adults came and grabbed them."

"Quite a story," said Becca, tousling Alison's hair.

"We stopped at Palm Island," Michael told us. "There might be some possibility of selling a wind-solar system to the hotel there. Long shot, though. And we met a guy who runs a boat charter business. He lined up someone for us to take out next week already."

"Day sail?"

"Out and back. Feed them native fruits and rum punch, show them how to snorkel, green flash at sunset, the whole scene. I don't know how we'll like it, but it's money."

Then Alison cornered Becca with her journal. She read every page and discussed every drawing. It was good for my soul, and even better for Alison's.

"Last night for just the four of us for a while," I said to David. Kathy and Chris had checked into a hotel for their last night together.

"How long is Kathy staying?" David said.

"Almost a month," I reminded him.

"Great." And he meant it.

"Hope it's great." I was worried.

"Great to see Michael and Becca again."

"And in Carriacou," I said. "I don't know if this would be the island I'd choose, though."

We looked up at the stars together.

"They ought to keep cruising," David said.

"They want a home."

"*Aerial*'s their home."

"I don't know, Dave. A moving boat just isn't the same as a house, with a yard and garden and people living next door." *We're really talking about us here,* I thought. "And a community," I added. "Being with Chris and Kathy again makes me long for a community. You just don't get that sailing around on a boat."

"Your community is the community of cruisers," said David. "I share more with the sailors we have met than I do with most people at home."

"I get scared when we have this conversation," I answered. "We are different this way. I haven't made that many friends." Tears warmed my eyelids.

"The plan ought to be both," said David. "Summer garden, winter sail."

"What a dream."

"Some people do it. Look at Ed and Marge on *Windsong*."

I was skeptical. "Things worked out for us because we live in a university town, so we could rent out our house for the academic year. But that's more than half."

"So nine and three, or eight and four."

"I don't know, Dave," I sighed. I had come to love this life on the water, but I felt so aware of what I was missing. And what I missed seemed not to matter so much to my husband. We were unearthing differences between us, yet I felt us moving closer, too. I edged my body over onto his along the narrow cockpit bench, humping through clothing and blankets, inviting a response. Slowly we found a way for skin to meet skin, then I slipped under him and we made love slowly, sweetly, until he came and we separated. I crawled into the forward bunk with Alison. David, as usual, slept out alone.

So as not to dwell upon missing Chris, who flew home the next morning, Kathy proposed a girls' trip to town.

To me, Hillsborough looked like so many other island towns. Its store fronts needed paint, too many buildings were abandoned, and trash overflowed onto the street. But Kathy came with unjaded eyes. She led us energetically through the museum—dimly lit handwritten displays celebrating the Indians, then the slaves, populating this island.

She led us on to the market. It looked dreary to me. An insistent Rastafarian hawked beads and leather at the doorway. Beyond him, we entered a dark space. The vegetables looked tired, and so did the people selling them. But Kathy's enthusiasm engaged one elderly man, who began to show us oranges, grapefruit, peppers, tomatoes.

"What's this?" Kathy pointed to chestnut-brown confections.

"Tamarind," the woman said. "Tamarind balls. Take some for de children." She reached with bamboo tongs and dropped five sugary balls into a waxed-paper bag.

"Bay?" Kathy asked, walking to the next table and fingering gray-green leaves.

"Sweet bay," said the woman, elderly and diminutive. Kathy pinched and lifted her fingers to her nose, then mine. Musky cinnamon. She bought a bouquet.

We caught a bus back to Tyrrel Bay. Bass speakers throbbed from behind the back seat, and the woman sitting next to me danced along, her eyes shut to the outside world, her wiry arms gyrating.

"Boom boom shorts, boom boom shorts," Alison, Kathy, and I sang as the van bounced away. We cracked up. It was the closest we could come to the lyrics that had been throbbing us along.

Meanwhile, John and David had been on an adventure. Returning to *Hei Tiki* at sunset, John held up their prey. "Look what we caught," he said, pulling a long, pink body out of a plastic bag. They had been iguana hunting, and they had brought back dinner.

It had all started the day before, when Alison came running down the road in Tyrrel Bay. "Mom! You gotta see this," she said. We followed her to a rusty pickup, where two young guys dangled scaly treasures by the neck: three-foot iguanas, limp and gutted, their scaly skin still beige, black, and green, with a smattering of scarlet around the head.

"You want to buy one?" one guy asked.

"Why would we?" Kathy and I answered.

"To eat. Very good white meat."

Come to find out that evening, John and David had met up with the same two men.

"So I said to this guy, Trevor, 'No, man, I don't want a dead iguana,'" David recounted. " 'But we'll go hunting with you.' "

"Trevor gave us a taste of iguana he had cooked," said John. "It was good, wasn't it, Dad? Cooked in barbecue sauce. Tasted like chicken."

So I had said I would cook iguana if John sacked it. And the very next night, he brought home the iguana.

"The mighty hunter," I said to him.

"Let me see, let me see," said Alison.

"We just brought home one of them," John said seriously. "We got nine. Trevor is keeping the smallest as a pet for his daughter."

"How did you catch them?" I asked.

David described the scene. The iguanas live high on cliffs above the ocean, and they climb the tamarind trees, grazing for leaves. Trevor would climb a tree and reach out along the branches, using a noose on a pole to snag an iguana by the neck. Those he missed jumped down into the sea and swam away.

"Look at this thing," Kathy said, holding up the lizard by the tip of the tail. It was headless, but otherwise intact, two feet long, stubby little legs hanging limp off the sides.

"Eeugh," Alison said. She held her nose.

"It doesn't stink," I said. "It's a good fresh meat. So how are we doing to cook it?"

"Get out *The Joy of Cooking*," said Kathy.

"Look in the index under *I* for iguana. Right."

"You're the one who said you'd cook it if John killed it," she said. "It's all yours."

I began by cutting it into pieces: front legs, back legs, right and left rib cage, then five chunks of tail, which looked the most promising meat. I cooked it the way I had been cooking our occasional chicken: roll the meat in seasoned flour, brown it in the pan, put in cooked onions, add some bouillon, let it simmer away.

Maybe it didn't simmer long enough.

"A little tough," David said.

"It is cooked, isn't it?" I asked. Strings of meat slid between my teeth. It was hard to bite them off the bone.

"Interesting," Kathy said.

"Good seasoning," David said.

"Like it, John?" I asked.

"Trevor cooked it better," he mumbled.

"I need more practice," I said. We gnawed on bones a little while longer, our fingers dripping.

"Got any crackers?" John said. It wasn't much of a meal.

"Weather's right. Time to get moving."

David was standing at the stern, looking out at the nighttime ocean. John had fallen asleep in the cockpit, Alison had trundled into the quarterberth. Even Kathy had bedded down early. I was writing in my journal by flashlight. David seemed to be talking to himself.

I answered anyway. "Moving?" I questioned. "Carnival's only two days away."

"Weather's right," he said, still talking as if nobody were listening. "Got to get the boat home." He walked up toward the bow and busied himself, checking the rigging, checking the anchor line.

I followed. "David? I thought we were staying here a few more days."

He lit up a cigarette and looked toward shore, past *Aerial.*

"David?" I repeated.

"A lot of things are being decided without ever consulting me," he growled.

"What—" I fumbled.

"I have no say in the matter," he snarled.

I got my grounding. He was accusing, and I wasn't going to take it. "You mean you don't *say* anything."

"What's the use? You guys will just do what you want anyway."

"You guys? Who is you guys?" My voice was rising, and I worried that the sound would travel and Kathy might hear.

David's voice dropped. "It's the middle of February. We have to have the boat back by June. We have eighteen hundred miles to sail. No one else seems to remember that."

"You won't let us forget it!" I shot back. Then I composed myself. "We're here in Carriacou, our last few days with Michael and Becca. Carnival starts two days from now and runs through Tuesday. It won't put us that much later."

"Do what you want. Let me know when you're ready to leave." It felt like a slap in the face.

"Don't pull that one on me," I retorted. "Say what you mean." I was almost yelling.

"No one listens," he almost yelled back.

"I'm listening!" I yelled.

And when I yelled, he retreated. He had done it for years. At home, at a point in conversation like this one, he would take a long walk outside. There on the boat, he couldn't go away.

"I think the same thing is happening now as happened when the Moores were with us," I said. "You don't speak up. You don't let us know what you want, or what you think we should do. You want to play the gracious host, but you also want to be skipper."

I stopped talking. I let the silence be, leaving room for David. But he just sat, looking out.

"You talk as if you think we're ganging up on you," I said.

Further silence.

Finally he spoke. "You guys do have a way of making decisions without any regard for me."

"Us guys being me and Kathy?"

He looked at me.

"I hear what you're saying," I said, looking back over the last few days. Kathy and I had taken off on our own, shopping, exploring, telling him where we were going rather than consulting with him. So what? He was used to being in charge, and all of a sudden he wasn't.

I had one more thing to say.

"As far as leaving Carriacou, I am going to insist that we stay to get a taste of carnival. Three or four more days."

He didn't answer. I had the last word. It made me uncomfortable, but I was going to get my way.

On the day before carnival, we day-sailed south of Carriacou. Great snorkeling, Michael and Becca reported. When we came upon light-green waters, David spotted from the bow. We motored straight for a picture-perfect island, white sand beaches and two graceful palms. I throttled way down. David pointed right. I felt a deep thump.

"John! Crank up the centerboard!" David cried.

John jerked on the crank at the front of the binnacle. The crank coiled a wire that drew the centerboard into the boat's keel, changing our draft from six to three and a half feet. But the whole mechanism was corroded and cantankerous. The boat wobbled, as if it was toe-dancing on the centerboard, then eased back, once again afloat.

When David checked the engine, his face went blank with shock. "We've got a big problem here," he called up at us. "We're filling up with water." I was sure he was overreacting until I saw bilge water backing up as high as the bottom edge of the engine, six inches above normal and rising still.

The kids could sense the panic. Alison huddled in the corner of the cockpit, gripping herself as if she was shivering. John was holding his head, staring into the cabin, muttering "I'm sorry" over and over again.

Kathy kept her cool. "What can I do?"

"Stay at the helm," David said to me. He found the hand

pump. "Lazarette. Bucket," he said, already pumping into the dish tub. Kathy took over on the pump while Dave wrestled with fittings under the floor.

"What's going to happen?" John asked in an undertone.

"Everything will be fine," I said, putting aside my own visions of *Hei Tiki* filling up with water and sinking right then and there.

David backed away from the fittings as if that battle had been won. I asked what had happened. He didn't answer. The engine still roared in low-pitched idle. Kathy pumped some more, and David checked the fittings, then stood at the galley sink and soaped his hands. "I think we'd better move back out a little and anchor somewhere else, don't you?" he said, his voice assuming an ironic calm. He climbed to the bow and pointed to starboard.

"Coming about," I said, even though we flew no sail.

Once we had reanchored, David finally talked.

"We backed up on the centerboard is what happened. The fitting jerked off." I asked what fitting. He explained, "Everything that goes from inside to outside the boat, like the cable to the centerboard, runs through a watertight seal. A fitting popped off, and that let water pour in. I knew what it was the minute it happened."

"Is it fixed?" I asked.

"It's a weak spot. Has been ever since we built the boat. Just have to keep an eye on it."

We sat in silence, letting our heartbeats return to normal.

We returned to the promise of a lobster dinner that evening. The day before, up to our boat had puttered a ragged old dinghy. *Not another boat boy,* I thought.

"You interested in fruit, vegetables, fish?" he asked. He handed us a business card. John Grimes. Native produce and seafood. "Lobster? Very good lobster."

Kathy's eyes lit up.

"How much?" I asked.

"Just six dollar a pound."

"Too much."

"Six is too much? If you buy a big lobster, the price goes down."

"Like to what?" I asked.

He looked out to sea for a moment, calculating. "You buy a lobster over eight pound, and I sell it to you for four-fifty a pound."

"Tomorrow," I had told him.

So now it was five-thirty, and I was wondering if lobster was really coming, or if we were going to have beans and rice again. It seemed hard to believe that he could simply go off with an order one day and bring back an eight-pound lobster the next. How many eight-pound lobsters are out there to be caught?

But here came John Grimes at a quarter to six. He reached down into the hold of his skiff and came up with two hands around the biggest lobster I had ever seen. When the body uncurled, it stretched eighteen inches, beady eyes to tail flippers. Its swimmerets thrashed and clicked helplessly. I took it, wrapping my fingers around the carapace. I dropped it into the cockpit. It struggled against the fiberglass.

"Eight and a half pounds," said Grimes. He smiled proudly. "I give it to you for the price of eight."

"Amazing," Kathy said.

"Where do you get a lobster like this?" I asked.

"Fishermen get them off reefs out there," he said, gesturing vaguely out to open water.

"Do they spear them?" I asked.

"No, nets. They drag nets."

"Amazing," Kathy said again.

"How are we ever going to cook it?" I asked Kathy. A four-quart saucepan was the biggest pot we had. "I guess we cut it into pieces."

"Cook it all in one piece. Much better," Grimes said, "I'll bring a pot." He motored over to his boat and came back with a stew pot. Even so, the animal didn't fit. We got water boiling, then dunked the lobster in head first. The tail draped out the

other side. After five minutes' boiling, I wrestled the front end
out and dunked the tail. By now the lobster was turning sunset
orange and a sweet shellfish smell was steaming up the cabin.

"How long do you cook an eight-and-a-half-pound lobster?" I asked Kathy. She just laughed.

Finally we declared it done and served it, stretched across
two dinner plates. Even the feathery swimmerets had a string of
succulent meat. All the lobster you can eat: one feeds five, and
then some.

Everybody was talking carnival. "Each neighborhood choose a
t'eme, you see," one woman told us. "Our t'eme Adam and Eve."
She showed us the papier maché costumes, leaves of green, red
apples dangling on a chicken wire frame, a black serpent writhing
around an archway.

Posters all over the island announced the Kiddie Carnival
on Friday afternoon. We entered a small arena where spectators
and officials were milling. Music pumped through huge loudspeakers, pounding drums, blaring horns. At twenty after four
the taped music ended abruptly. Someone blew into a microphone and announced that the parade would soon begin. Parents preened, children lined up, the taped music started all over.

Bands of dancing children paraded around. One group
commemorated "The World of Our Music," each age dressed as
an instrument—drums, bass viols, saxophones, guitars. Another
celebrated Columbus' five hundredth. A ten-year-old beauty, lips
bright red, darkened lashes fluttering, vamped around the ring,
dressed as Queen Isabella. The music throbbed. Its bass line vi-
brated through our bodies. Every one, old and young, danced to
the opening of carnival.

Saturday night, the streets still pounded with music. Every
restaurant, every hole in the wall, had dragged six- and eight-
foot speakers out onto the sidewalk, blasting out carnival rhythms
at earsplitting decibels. Single men swigged Carib beers together,
occasionally raising their bottles and swinging their hips with
abandon. Each new set of speakers, a block or two from the one

before, played a different carnival song, so we walked from one sphere of rhythm into another. Michael, walking ahead of me, strutted to the music.

Sweet, greasy smells led us around the corner where, in a cloud of smoke and sizzle, women poked at barbecue fires, turning dozens of leg quarters over and over. We ordered chicken all around.

As the night stretched on, the music seemed to pound more deeply. People began to link eyes, not just mill around. Wordlessly, physically, they moved toward some great shared climax. Men outnumbered women five or six to one.

"Tonight's Dirty Mas," an American yelled in my ear. He and his boyfriend, he told me, come for carnival in Carriacou every year. "Stick around until four in the morning. People dancing all together, smearing themselves and each other with mud and oil. It's very sensual. It's a religious ritual."

It was just after one. Maybe it was beginning already. Just the three of us were left in town—David, Kathy, and me. The children had stayed with a Tyrrell Bay family and Michael and Becca had headed home early. David danced along down the street, glad-handing many a Carriacou native. Kathy and I agreed: we felt threatened. We snaked our way through forty or fifty people, sweating bodies, hands high in the air. Chests and pelvises rubbed up against mine, hands caressed my waist. I pulled in. I was not ready for this.

I was too much an outsider, too much a Puritan at that, to descend into the chaos of Carriacou's Dirty Mas. On the other side of the crowd, we walked empty streets, saying nothing, the din of carnival behind us.

There was more. The next morning—Mardi Gras, Fat Tuesday—there was the match of the Pierrots. That was something I didn't want to miss.

I had agreed with David that we would stay through Tuesday morning, to see the Pierrots, then bid farewell to Carriacou at noon. It felt right: we would ride the wave of excitement out of Hillsborough. We would say goodbye to Michael and Becca and turn north toward home. No one said so, but everyone felt the weight of the coming moment.

Our search for the Pierrots took us to the outskirts of Hillsborough, where we found five men dressed in motley, walking down dusty roads. These players wore dresses of patchwork, mirrors, and bells. Lacy slips showed down under, tickling the top of their leather workboots. Most wore turbans, wrapped with straw and gauze. Some hid their faces behind fencing masks, which had been whitewashed and painted with red lips and black lashes. Each man wore a cap, lined with stiff brown paper, and each man carried a rubber switch.

They marched toward Hillsborough, attracting followers as if they were Pied Pipers. One, then another, would erupt in exultation, speaking the Elizabethan mother tongue with West Indian tones and rhythms.

> O mighty Caesar! dost thou lie so low?
> Are all thy conquests, glories, triumphs, spoils,
> Shrunk to this little measure?

Carriacou's Pierrots combat each other by quoting Shakespeare. We were following one village's contestants, traveling down to the final contest in Hillsborough, where they would match tongues and memory with Pierrots of other villages.

In town, twenty Pierrots gathered. They milled and paired off, circling like prize fighters, then locking in a test of Shakespearean recitation. Onlookers cheered them on like schoolchildren at a playground fight.

One man stood out, a good six-foot-six, heavy in build, his body an odd match for the petticoats he wore. His eyes stared intensely through his mesh mask. As he spat out lines from *Julius Caesar*, he stamped his boots, jingled his bells, and danced to the language. His opponent, wirier in body and more piercing in voice, retorted with more Shakespearean verse. He must have misspoken, because the audience murmured and then the larger Pierrot whacked him, rubber switch on his cape.

No one was clearly crowned victor, although cheers from

the crowd declared the tall man their favorite. Voices dwindled, the Pierrots moved on. More people appeared, some in costume, some in everyday clothes. Costumed children were returning. Everyone was coming to town.

Carnival would continue, but for us, it was time to go. We had seen the costumes, heard the music, danced through the streets. If we left the party behind still in motion, we could pretend it would never end.

"We could stay until tomorrow," David offered quietly.

"No," I answered. "This is the plan. We should go."

John and Alison first said their goodbyes. John let his arms hang, more hugged than hugging. Michael socked his biceps in a jovial way. Alison clung, especially to Becca, until we told her she had to let go. We sat on a picnic table, me, Michael, and Becca, watching David dinghy Kathy and the children back to *Hei Tiki*. It was hard to speak.

"I don't know how or when we'll be back here, but we will," I said.

"You better write," said Becca.

"For sure. You, too."

Another silence. The children climbed out of the dinghy. David started back for me.

"Dave says he wants to get a shortwave radio at home. Then we can call you."

"We'll miss you," said Michael. "Once you leave, it means we really live here. We're not cruising anymore."

"For us, it means we're going home." David surfed up to the water's edge. I hugged Becca, then Michael. David, one hand on the dinghy, tossed a salute fraught with feeling. He and I held hands as we motored back to *Hei Tiki*.

David sat at the helm. I pulled up the anchor. I glanced back ashore. Michael and Becca still sat on the picnic table. They were holding hands. The anchor pulled free. I signaled thumbs-up to David. I brought the anchor aboard, tied it down. We were moving northward.

Michael and Becca stood on the picnic table, slowly waving. I stood on the bow and waved, my eyes welling with tears. I climbed back down into the cockpit and took the helm. Everyone was crying. Alison, who always had a hard time at goodbyes. John, who never had cried at a goodbye before. Even Kathy was crying, close enough to all of us to feel this moment.

Only David's eyes looked dry. But then he stepped up out of the cockpit, walked up the deck, steadied himself on the rigging, and stood on the bow, all alone. He gazed back at Carriacou, at our friends, and at the furthest point away from home we had reached on our journey. I couldn't see his eyes, but I think he was crying, too.

16

Familiar Waters

The next morning, we heard the radio call as we left Union Island, sixteen miles from Carriacou. *"Hei Tiki, Hei Tiki."* Michael's voice, distorted by distance. I felt a twinge. David held the microphone, and all of us listened. "We really miss you guys already," Michael said. "We just sat there where you left us for a long time yesterday."

Everyone was feeling it—like parting from family forever. "We miss you, too," David said. Soon we sailed out of radio reach.

Going back up the islands felt different. We knew where we were. It gave a feeling of power, compensating for the insecurity of sailing without *Aerial*. We had already sailed from Nevis without them, but ahead lay long night passages—the Anegada and the Mona and the Caicos Bank all over again. I didn't want to do them alone.

"We just talk around and find others who are going our way," said David.

"It won't be the same," I said, and he knew it, too.

Kathy made up the difference for the time being. I felt a pride of ownership, showing her places we had been before. I

287

had talked up Wallilabu, and I wanted her to see the people and the rainbows there.

Two boat boys approached us well out at sea, long before we could see the bight at Wallilabu. "No, Kali helps us," I yelled them away. We passed Barouallie and saw the red-shirted speck of a person in a yola, hailing us with both hands over his head. He rowed frantically toward us. It was Kali. Our man. He had recognized *Hei Tiki* from a distance. We tied him up and towed him into the bay.

"I saw you leave early that morning," he told me. "I was bringing you some sorrel." It was Kali I had seen, then, the yola at dawn, silhouetted against the rocks.

We chatted about people as if we belonged. Garfield, who had offered us papayas, was in prison for stealing a neighbor's tomatoes. Roy, another boat boy, lost his dinghy and got his face slashed up in a fight. Five girls, including the one I had mistaken for Dyan's mother, swam out, calling for Alison. She joined them on the beach but soon returned, saying, "They kept touching me and putting land crabs on me."

Dyan appeared later, as we sipped cold drinks at the shore-side bar. She seemed to have grown taller and fuller in a month. "I am not supposed to be here," she whispered. "The man who own the store tell me, do not come here."

I ordered her a drink, figuring she would then qualify as my guest. She sipped nervously. "I go to school barefoot," she said quietly to me. "Would you give me money for shoes? Just five E.C." She was only asking for two dollars, but I didn't want to hand over cash, not sure who would get it or what it would be used for.

"I can't give you money," I said, "but I will send you something."

She wrote belaboredly on a restaurant coaster: Leticha Oliver, Kearton Village, Barouallie, St. Vincent.

"Leticha?" I asked her. "I thought your name was Dyan."

"Leticha my given name."

We hugged and she ran off, as if freed.

Second time through, Wallilabu felt different, no longer magical, more like real life.

As we sailed for St. Lucia, almost due north, the wind clipped at us from the northeast. We bucked through waves off the starboard bow. Kathy took the rocky ride in stride. By eight-thirty, she had on her two-piece and was slathering on sun cream. Alison followed suit: two-piece, sun cream, the pose of taking beauty seriously as she lay in the sun.

We anchored in Marigot Bay, crowded and upscale, dominated by a resort hotel. If not for Kathy, I wouldn't have visited the hotel gift shop. But as I waited for her to choose souvenirs, my eyes landed on a bright red two-piece. Strapless top, hip-hugging bottom. I had never felt able to wear anything so skimpy before. But now my body was taut and slender. I had had to buy new shorts along the way, clothing from home hung so loose on my hips.

I put on the bathing suit. I hadn't worn a two-piece since I was twelve. My midriff was tanless but firm. Some sense of power came from showing so much skin.

"It's you, Suze," Kathy said.

"Should I get it?" She nodded.

"You deserve it," David said when he saw the suit.

"Deserve it?"

"What I mean is, you can wear it now. You have slimmed down." He was bumbling through this answer. "You look great," he said, and smiled, wanting to leave it at that.

Our family of four had resolved to visit one volcano on this journey. St. Lucia's Soufrière was to be the one. We hopped a bus into Castries, capital of St. Lucia. It felt like a metropolis. Three-story buildings, traffic lights, cars churning by. People talking fast and walking quickly, pushing us aside. Unlike us, they knew where they were going.

It was Saturday, and the market spread out for block after block. As far as I could see, women on stools under big, black umbrellas, fruit and vegetables spread out beside them. The smells of citrus and meat smoke mingled with the din of talk, chatter about prices, gossip about life.

Surrounded by bunches of banana and plantain, an elderly man lifted a green coconut and whoosh! with a single slice of his machete lopped its top off and held it out for sale. For a while I lost track of David, then I saw his shock of white hair, his hand beckoning to me. He had found the bus to Soufrière.

We piled into a rattletrap van with four banks of seats, most already filled. People squeezed over and tucked market bags under their knees to make room for Kathy and John up front, David behind, and Alison on my lap in the middle. The driver revved the engine and turned up the music.

We climbed hairpin curves. The road banked left, and I got shoved up against the window. Then the road banked right, and I got shoved up against the lady sitting next to me. Lean and aging, she chatted without a smile to the woman sitting next to her. The cadence was West Indian; the phonemes French. I heard an occasional *mais oui*, an occasional *bus station*, but try as I might, I didn't understand this St. Lucia creole at all.

Out the window, I saw a road sign: SOUFRIÈRE, 21 MILES. It was the longest twenty-one miles I have ever traveled. During the first third, we zipped along modern pavement, passing acres of banana grove, crossing a bridge and looking down at women spreading their laundry out on rocks in the river. Then we passed through miles under construction, sharing the road with bulldozers that kicked up vast billows of dust as they pushed around boulders larger than our van. Past that, we traveled on unreconstructed roadbed: crumbling asphalt, one-and-a-half cars wide, with steep walls of fern swooping up on our left and down on our right. The driver swerved to miss a pothole, and my heart leaped. The island bass line throbbed nonstop. It took two hours to travel twenty-one miles.

Days later Kathy broke out laughing as she browsed through a travel guide. "In bold type yet," she said: "Do not plan to travel by road between Castries and Soufrière."

As we walked toward the volcano, every sense told us it was near. The smell of sulfur. Crumbling yellow rock under our feet. Hot, wet, mineral air. Steaming pools of sludge, bubbling, boiling. A guide chipped off a rock and struck a match to it. It sizzled and burned, giving off noxious fumes.

"Please stay behind the railing," the guide warned, telling of a visitor, some years back, who walked too close. The crust gave way beneath him, and he fell into the steamy slurry.

Still, we could lean out and look. We could breathe in and smell it. Here, the earth lay bare its turmoil beneath. What now just burped and bubbled once blew high and could, I supposed, do so again. Solid ground seemed ephemeral. The sea, with all its motion, seemed more reliable, more firm.

"Okay, John, notebook and pen," I said the next morning.

"I have to write?"

"Open your notebook," I nodded. "Write for five minutes about what happened yesterday."

"What did happen yesterday?"

"You tell me."

"I don't know."

"You were there."

"*Mom.*"

"*John.* Bus ride, Castries market, ride over the mountains, Soufrière, volcano."

"Oh. That."

He wrote for five minutes. Ten. Fifteen.

"I'm done."

"Look at the clock. How long?"

"Mmmm . . . seventeen minutes."

Yesterday we went to sulphur springs. There were a lot of minerals in the rocks. The sign said that the main europion eropted 40,000 years ago. We walked around the creater. There was sulphur that been bubling for 40,000 years.

When we put minerals in 175° digree water (FH) it turned
black. The sulphur smelled bad like old hard boiled eggs.
Some of the minerals were green, some were yellow, other
were orange. Our tour guide showed us a rock that burned
and it spead a toxin that could kill people. There was a
waterfall that had mineral water flowing threw. The name
of the volcano was "Soufriere."

He smiled with shy pride as I read the paragraph. I gave
him a hug. "Good job," I said, holding back on purpose. I
didn't want to make too big a deal of it. I wanted him to feel his
own pride. But what a milestone. Set him free, and he writes on.

We sailed on to Martinique, the island from which Kathy was
scheduled to fly home in less than a week. We headed for Fort-
de-France, the island's capital, and anchored across the harbor,
in among an international assortment of sailboats, all of them
anchored closer together than we would have chosen.

Fort-de-France really is a city, and a European city at that:
minicars darting through narrow cobble streets, businesspeople
swishing by in dark suits, carrying trim briefcases to important
appointments. It was a weekday, but the market still stretched a
full city block. Those who could not afford an inside spot spread
their vegetables on the sidewalks outside. Inside there were two
spice merchants for every vegetable merchant: burlap bags filled
with cloves, nutmeg, star anise, cinnamon bark; row upon row
of jars with powders and tinctures.

I heard a commotion from another direction. In the midst
of it, Kathy called my name. "Suze, help. What's she saying?"

A lanky black woman threw her arms akimbo, her eyes
wide with anger, yelling at Kathy. A man watched with interest
from behind, his machete atop the huge half carcass of a tuna.
The woman blurted out words. Between anger and creole, I
could only catch the drift.

"She says you should have asked before you took her picture," I said. *"Pardonnez-nous,"* I muttered, and hustled Kathy
away through the crowd.

For the weekend before Kathy flew home, we sailed up the coast, back to St.-Pierre. We roamed the Saturday market, so much smaller and sweeter than the one in Fort-de-France. We ate breakfast in a little café, looking out at the stone ruins of the theater, considered the Opéra of the Antilles before Pelée erupted. We ordered strong coffee, rich pastries, and pineapple juice for the kids. John said he was thirsty, even after the juice.

"No soda," I said, second-guessing him.

"I don't want soda. I'm really thirsty."

"Have some water then."

"You ask." He looked at me imploringly.

Time for a French lesson. I whispered the words, then he whispered them back to me, back and forth until he had them. He walked up to the woman at the bakery counter.

"Un peu d'eau, s'il vous plait," he said like a metronome.

The woman beamed. *"Un peu d'eau? Quel joli garçon. Mais oui, mais oui."* She recited the phrase like a schoolmarm repeating her lessons—*"Un peu d'eau, s'il vous plait. Un peu d'eau, s'il vous plait. Très bien"*—and rewarded John with a tall, icy glass of water.

We set out for the Gauguin Museum, a tiny collection recollecting Gauguin's few months in Martinique. Alison drew me into another room, to an exhibit that was even more fascinating: collages made from the remains of the Pelée eruption. "I like this one best," she said, pointing to a landscape constructed of shards of patterned china.

We had planned to go next to a zoo, but Kathy walked off in a different direction. "The zoo is that way," I called.

"I want to go to this butterfly garden." She pointed to a road sign—LA VALLÉE DES PAPILLONS, MERVEILLE NATURELLE—and kept on walking.

It was hot. The road was asphalt, a steep, dusty incline. Alison was dragging. David was hobbling, his feet cut again by his swim fins. I felt strung out between plans and spontaneity, between my family and my friend. I looked to Dave for sympathy, but he just shot me a glance as if to say he considered me party to Kathy's plan. We kept walking in her direction.

We arrived at Butterfly Valley. Entry fees were outrageous— more than forty dollars for the five of us. "No way," I said. "I'm just going to sit down."

John moaned that he wanted to go to the zoo. Alison complained that she was thirsty. David had walked out of sight. We were all disgruntled, and it felt as if it was all Kathy's fault. "I don't even know why we are here." I spoke testily. "I thought we had agreed to go to the zoo."

"Well, I changed my mind," she said, shirking it off. "Can't a person change her mind?"

I had no answer. Kathy could so easily pull off what I had been struggling with this whole journey. She was doing what she wanted to, no matter whether it made the rest of us uncomfortable, no matter whether it made the rest of us mad. Of course a person can change her mind. It was hard to allow myself that privilege, but I couldn't fault my friend for claiming it.

It felt ceremonial, slicing up tomatoes, peppers, onions, and pumpkin bought at market yesterday. Vegetable soup, Kathy's last dinner with us. It hadn't all been easy, yet she fit in like family. No hard feelings, no big surprises, and a lot of fun.

She and I sat on the foredeck, sipping the last of a bottle of French red wine, talking about life on the boat, life at home, and what we could make of it all.

"Thanks for taking care of business for us at home," I said. "Rent, bills, mail."

"No problem. It's my boarding pass." She smiled. "This has been so good for me. I haven't relaxed like this in years."

We looked out at the water. Lax waves lapped up against the boat.

"Work is intense, then I get home and Dad needs constant attention. It's a lot to juggle." She leaned back, eyes closed. "This has been great. I just hope I can carry some of it home with me."

"I keep wondering about that myself. What's it going to be like for us?"

"The kids have really changed. So strong, so independent," said Kathy.

"I think David has changed, too."

"He seems a lot calmer," Kathy agreed.

"Calmer?" I asked.

"He's a pretty intense guy, Suze," she said. "He needed it."

"Do I seem calmer?" I asked. I was so curious to see us from the outside.

"I wouldn't say calmer," Kathy said. "Maybe stronger." She paused. "You sure lift that anchor like a pro." We laughed. "You and David are more of a team. The whole family operates more like a team. I think it worked, Suze. You got what you wanted." She spoke as if the journey was nearly over.

"One thing worries me, Kath," I said. "Sometimes David talks as if he never wants to go home, he likes it so well out here."

"It will be interesting to see what happens when you come back," said Kathy. "Things will be different."

"I can't imagine. A house. A garden. Driving a car."

"Just promise me you *will* come back," Kathy said.

To affirm our friendship, I promised.

Monday morning before sunrise, David motored Kathy to the dock of St.-Pierre, where she would board a bus on her way to the Fort-de-France airport. The children and I watched wistfully as the dinghy putted away, as David handed Kathy up her bags, as they walked up the dock together. We all felt sadness at her leaving. She had been a good friend and fellow traveler. Yet there was also that sense of release, that feeling of being back to four again.

After Kathy's departure, we had to get serious about sailing home. We were already one week into March, and Granddad wanted the boat by the first of June. Three months. We had taken six months sailing down. We agreed to take it as fast as weather would allow. One night in Dominica, one night in the

Iles des Saintes. Guadeloupe, Montserrat, St. Kitts. There were islands to visit, but we would have to keep moving on.

The weather cooperated until we reached Basse-Terre, Guadeloupe's capital city. Northerly winds had blown up kicker waves. All night long we twisted and turned, rocked and slopped on the anchor. Stiff waves kept pummeling us from one side, then the other, depending on how the wind swung the boat around. David kept getting up to check the anchor line. Anchored nearby was a Panamanian motor-sailer, at least seventy feet long, decks ten feet above ours.

I darted awake. David was cranking up the motor. He didn't say a word, just pointed to the motor-sailer, not twenty feet away. We had to move fast.

Thick clouds absorbed the cold, gray light of the moon. The wind whipped my nightgown flat against my body. I worked the anchor line, pulled and pulled, leaning back to give it all the strength I had. Dave yelled and gestured from the cockpit. He thought the line had wrapped the propeller, the boat was hanging at such a strange angle.

It didn't feel that way to me. I kept on pulling, and finally the anchor let loose. I shot Dave a thumbs-up and strong-armed the line, chain, and anchor onto the deck as fast as I could. As soon as we came free, David drove forward, circling out and away from our hulking neighbor.

The wind kept howling as we moved up the Guadeloupe coast. We perched in the harbor of Deshaies until our next leap, across the Guadeloupe Passage to Montserrat. The wind blew thirty knots, but this harbor gave more protection. Still, for safety's sake, David wanted to put out a second anchor.

"I'll do that," Alison said. She seemed confident in her movements, so I stepped back. She leaned back with her whole body to set the anchor. She wrapped the line on the deck cleat and looked out, satisfied. Soon, in less than a month, Alison would turn seven. Her slender body had gained muscle. She had toughened over these months at sea.

The next morning, the winds were right, so we turned off the engine and set sail for Montserrat.

17

Blown Away

I HAD A CREEPY FEELING ABOUT MONTSERRAT from the start. We only stayed in Plymouth, its capital, for two hours—checking in with customs, buying lunch and stamps—but in that time I saw more signs of decay than I had on any other island. Derelicts draped themselves over park benches. Traffic moved too fast through the central square. A little gray-haired street sweeper, eyes to the ground, held out his hand as we passed.

"What did that man want?" asked Alison.

"He wanted money."

"Why?"

"I guess he needs money."

"I want to give him some."

"We don't have to do that."

"But I want to." I gave her an E.C. quarter. She gave it to the little man. He dropped the coin in his pocket and kept on sweeping.

Montserrat is shaped like a teardrop, with Plymouth on its southwest curve and very few protected harbors. We sailed around to the lee, heading for the one chink in the coastline. Old Road Bay: not much of an anchorage.

A dozen boats had already nosed into the shallow crescent. It was a pretty scene, with a broad stretch of black sand beach and courses of green above it. Grandiose houses dominated the hills, each with expensive landscaping and a sunset view.

What protection this anchorage gave came by virtue of its being on the lee side, but the trades were blowing fiercely out to sea and the waves came wrapping round, kicking up two- and three-foot surges that rolled into the anchorage. A couple of longhaired guys were actually surfing onto the beach. As every wave rolled through, *Hei Tiki* swooped forward, then settled back on the anchor line. It was a good thing we didn't plan on staying more than a night.

We awoke to howling winds and stinging mist coming down off the mountains. The waters were rough, but we set out to sail, destination Nevis or St. Kitts, forty or fifty miles northwest. All that lay between was the island of Redonda. We could just see its arrowhead silhouette on the horizon. Redonda was once inhabited, but people soon gave up on making that chunk of rock home. To us it could be a milestone, not an anchorage.

"We'll go a ways out, then have a family vote," said David. After fifteen minutes of seesawing through four-foot waves on the stern, we looked behind. Montserrat seemed a lost haven. We looked ahead. Cold, hard Redonda. Wisps of cloud brushed the sky. Maybe the jib sail would settle the movement.

"I'll help," Alison said, dashing up to the foredeck. She was feeling chipper, despite rough seas.

It all happened quickly. The boat plunges up and down. The wind blasts at us. The mainsail barely steadies us. The jib sheet comes loose and the sail starts flapping. The jib block rips loose and slaps Alison in the face. She winces and falls, cut near the corner of her eye.

"Hold her steady," David called to me. He climbed forward, stretched his body out, and collected up the thrashing sail. He gripped the deck with his feet and reeled in line and pulley from the drink. "We're turning around," he yelled from up there.

We already knew that. David tended Alison, who shivered as he held her. "Coming about," I called, and pointed the boat back toward Old Road Bay. The mainsail reversed itself. John worked the sheet and kept the boom in control. The sail refilled with a whoosh. Back to Montserrat.

Seeking some company, we climbed from the beach up to The Nest, an open-air bar perched over Old Road Bay. By the time I had ordered soft drinks for the children, David was deep in conversation with a guy I felt I would rather not meet. His face was swarthy, his clothes unkempt, his hair a snarl of auburn curls. In Virginia, I would stereotype him as an auto mechanic or a member of a motorcycle gang. Then the snarly headed fellow reached out his hand and said hello. Brouwer, he called himself.

"Those your kids?" he asked. Alison was dangling on the railing. John was chasing a lizard up the woodwork. I nodded.

"You like living on a sailboat?" he asked Alison. She nodded and reached toward me. John caught the lizard and brought it over in his fist.

"Man, you're fast," the guy with the hair said.

"Watch this," said John. He lifted the lizard up to his right ear. It grabbed onto the lobe with its little jaws. John let go and the lizard hung there like an earring.

We all broke up laughing. "Great kids," the guy with the hair said to me. I was beginning to like him.

The weather just wouldn't quit. From the boat, we would see clouds mounding up around the island peaks while blue skies still shined out over the water. In half an hour, a mist descended, then rain, as weather patterns pushed west. Gray moisture surrounded us, then lifted, and the cycle would start again. At times the air was calm, then a thirty-knot gust would plunge down out of the mountains, making it a struggle to walk from the cockpit to the bow.

Several other boats sat with us, waiting for the weather to turn. Brouwer and his German crewmate, Til, on *Faith Jones*. Cap and Kate, fast-lane Americans on *Sundance*. Oscar, a singlehander on *Take It Easy*. It quickly became habit for us to mingle for happy hour at The Nest.

Everyone was talking about a big storm in the States. Three

feet of snow as far south as South Carolina. This weather we were feeling was the storm's tail end, snapping through the Caribbean, adding force to the easterly trades. For the first time in months, I worried about home. How would the renters manage? What if they ran out of heating fuel? What if they drove off the road?

I found a pay phone and called Kathy.

"Your renters are on vacation. Spring break," she said.

"What's it like?" I asked.

"Four feet of snow. It's spectacular. Can't go anywhere unless you ski. I'll try to get over to your house in the next few days."

From the phone booth, I could see my children building sand castles, their skin sugar-coated with the charcoal sand of Old Road Bay. Any worry about the heat, the house, the few house plants I left behind, was a useless expense of energy. What happened would happen. Those were not my worries now. I was in a different world, a different home.

The waiting started getting to me. I didn't want to get to know another island. Even though Montserrat had its attractions— home of Radio Antilles and Air Studios, where the Beatles and the Rolling Stones had recorded—I didn't care. I wanted to move on.

But the weather played it differently and kept us in Montserrat for a week. We settled back into the rhythm of school in the morning, outings in the afternoon.

One day, the children and I rode in to Plymouth, just for diversion. A hotel minivan drove us along twisting hillside roads. We bought cheese and pasta at the grocery. We ogled expensive T-shirts. In a music shop, I bought a cassette of the "Mighty Sparrow," a legendary calypsonian. The bus returned us to the hotel, high above Old Road Bay. The children ran ahead, but I meandered, imagining what it would be like to pay hundreds of dollars a night to stay here.

I agreed to Cokes at The Nest before we headed back to *Hei Tiki*. I eavesdropped as the owner chatted with a customer. "I looked out and saw it heading straight for the beach," she said. "Swells are so big, must have broke anchor. Nothing I could do but just sit and watch. The guy seems to have it under control now. It was that one, over there, the little sloop with the blue deck."

She pointed to *Hei Tiki*.

My heart started pounding. The boat was anchored further out, back behind the others. David was on the bow, hauling back on an anchor line. I could tell by the way he moved that he was pressured and working hard. A new anchor line stretched off the stern. He stood, hands on hip, and looked at the forward anchor. His body loosened. He disappeared into the cockpit. He had reanchored the boat on his own.

I considered rushing out to help, but there was nothing left to do. Still, anxiety drove me—some irrational feeling that I should have been there. Or was it love—wanting to hold him, congratulate him, thank him, wanting to be together, wanting to know everything was all right?

"Drink up," I told the children. "Dad had to move the boat." We launched the dinghy through the waves, then worked hard to row across the anchorage.

"I was in the cabin, reading, and things started feeling funny," David told us. "Disorienting. You know how I can sense it when the boat moves the wrong way. I went up to check the anchor. I pulled on the line, and there was nothing at the end of it. The boat was surfing toward the beach." He kept his voice low and slow.

"And?"

"So I jammed on the motor and turned around as fast as I could."

"So where's the anchor?" I asked.

He nodded back over the water, toward the spot where we used to be anchored. "I'm going in for it right now."

"Right now?" Waves two feet high crashed up on the beach. They churned all around us. Even anchored stern and bow, our boat pitched.

"I made a note of where it was. I'm going in." He reached for his mask and fins. "John, get in the dinghy and row over to me." He climbed over the lifelines. Before I could say a thing, David had already swum through the anchorage. He dove down. This water was so confused, I couldn't see how he could remember where the anchor was, let alone find it underwater. His face broke the surface. He spat, gasped, and dove again. John kept the oars working, trying to follow his underwater father.

It seemed hopeless, but I was wrong. Not ten minutes later, David was heaving the anchor over the gunwales of the dinghy.

"I can't believe you found it," I said.

"I knew where it was." He stripped off mask, fins, and trunks and sat naked in the cockpit, fingering the frayed stub of anchor line still tied to the shank of the anchor.

"Not much to look for," David continued. "I kept diving down. Finally I saw a few loose strands sticking up out of the sand. The anchor was completely covered. John, get the twine and the splicing knife." He held the shaft of the anchor between his knees.

"John, you hold this taut," he said, handing him the strands of the old anchor line. "Susan, you take the spool when I hand it through." His hands started moving, and our hands moved along. Together, six hands as one, we wove a new connection between anchor and line.

The next day Brouwer, the guy with snarls in his hair, invited John to go fishing.

"He's nice," John said.

"Why is his hair like that?" Alison asked him.

"He wants to be a Rasta. A white Rasta."

"He looks weird."

"He's cool," John replied.

Brouwer bumped up alongside *Hei Tiki* in his heavy home-made dinghy, half again as long and wide as ours, made of hefty mill-cut lumber. "Climb aboard," he said to John. "Know how to drive an outboard?" They steamed off, John at the helm, Brouwer messing with the fishing line that they were already dragging off the stern.

———

As bad weather turned one day's stay into many, I was beginning to feel trapped.

Time moved so slowly. I had already scrubbed the cupboard under the sink. It was always a mess. I pulled out every bottle of cleanser, every scrub brush and sponge. Cleaned them and stacked them back as neatly as I could.

I had already done the laundry. Two inches of shower water into the dishtub. Small things first, since they didn't soak up much water, then larger things like T-shirts and shorts. I wrung everything vigorously. Every drop counted for fewer minutes on the line.

I dragged through another day of lessons with the children. John had worked up to LBJ in the book of presidents. He could read the words—war on poverty, student protests, Vietnam— yet did he understand the concepts? With every sentence, I had a story to tell. This wasn't history—this was my life. It made him mad. It was more than he was ready to absorb.

By the time it was Alison's turn for school, I was feeling all used up. "Why don't we just read some poems?" I suggested.

"Is that all we're going to do today?" she chided.

I bit my lip and breathed deeply. "Why don't you write a story?"

She sighed. From the way I draped myself in the cockpit, she could see that I didn't have much to give. "If I write a story, can we call that school today?" she asked. I nodded. She sat at the galley table and became industrious. Twenty minutes later, she brought me two sheets of paper, a story and its illustration. "Can I read it to you?" she asked. I nodded and sat up.

Sun tan Cay by Alison Watkins

She squirmed in her seat and read on.

Once upon a time
there was a villiagge
Named Suntan Cay Villigge.
The people speak Japanesse.

> The people eat Iguanas, Lizards, & pigs & Goats.
> There is a volcano it Erupte in
> 1972.
> There are two Stream the
> people
> Wash there Cloths in the
> Streames.
> the End

"See?" she said, pointing to her pencil drawing. "Here's the waterfalls, and the garden, and the pig, and the iguana." The clouds all smiled. Her creativity and her progress overwhelmed me. I felt ashamed that I had so little to give. I hugged her. "You wrote that all by yourself?" I asked.

"Johnny helped me spell 'Japanese,'" she answered proudly.

The children weren't bored. David was perfectly happy. It was just me who was feeling stir-crazy.

I started writing a letter to my father and Janet. It had been almost two months since their visit, so there were stories to tell. Wallilabu Bay, Carriacou. Finally something engaged me. I wrote so hard my hand cramped. I shook it and wrote some more.

David rowed up in the dinghy. "Hey, hon, grab the line, will you?" I wanted to say no. I held my writing in one hand and grabbed the line with the other. He kept on talking. "That Brouwer. What a character. But he knows sailing. He thinks this front's going to pass in another day." I kept on writing. I didn't want to talk. "That boat of his, *Faith Jones*? Used to be a shrimper's boat. What a cabin. Deluxe."

Finally he noticed I wasn't paying attention. "Am I interrupting something?" he asked.

"I'm writing a letter."

"Sorry." He climbed down into the galley and put water on to boil. For some reason, I couldn't let it lie.

"Can't I decide to write a letter rather than always listen to you?"

He looked up at me, face blank. I was picking a fight.

I kept on. "You have the right not to communicate in the

morning, when you're drinking coffee and smoking cigarettes and reading for hours at a time. Why can't I have the same right? I don't always have the energy to talk. Or to listen."

"I'll leave you alone," he said quietly. He made a cup of coffee, found a book, and stretched out in the galley. In twenty minutes, he was snoring. He seemed so damned satisfied, and I didn't even know what I wanted.

That night I tossed and turned. The wind whistled through the rigging. It was still dark outside when I heard David making coffee. I got up and made my own cup with the rest of the hot water. I looked west, where growing daylight glinted off endless rows of whitecaps.

"Wind keeps pumping," he said.

"Another day stuck in paradise," I said.

"We could give it another try."

"It's rougher out there now than it was three days ago."

"Mm-hm."

"This waiting is really getting to me," I said.

We sat in quiet together.

"You do a lot for me, and for the children," he said. "Maybe you need a break."

Maybe I did need a break—from David, the children, the boat, the wind, the feeling of rocking incessantly on the anchor, hooked here just because it was too hard to sail on. I looked out across the anchorage. It was so rough, I didn't even want to climb into the dinghy.

I got up my courage. I could do it.

"I think I'll take a walk," I said.

"Why don't you?" David said.

I made it to the beach, feeling quite nimble. I roamed, following island roads up and around. A trio of baby goats scattered in a bleating panic. Steeper still, a cabin tottered on the hillside, garden terraces striping the yard, growing flowers and vegetables on an incline one could barely climb.

The road wound into a village center, faded clapboard

buildings side by side. One trim white building burst out with people, men in black suits, ladies in white gloves and hats, craning their necks to see in. A hearse was parked at the end of the walkway. A loudspeaker fuzzed the voice of the preacher inside.

Here I was in shorts and sandals, hair a frizz. I turned away. A foursome passed me, walking toward the funeral. I nodded with reverence. They smiled with restraint. Hours later, back aboard *Hei Tiki*, I heard Radio Antilles report that the father of the minister of culture was buried today.

That evening, I went to The Nest just for something to do. John and Alison started up a game of hide-and-seek with two tow-headed toddlers. Their mother, Marisa, infant on her hip, told me she and her husband had sailed from island to island before deciding to settle in Montserrat. They hated the Virgin Island scene. They sensed violence in Dominica. They now owned mountain property above Old Road Bay.

"Are you making friends?" I asked. It was a question that kept haunting me. If it was hard for me to find cruising women, how would it be to move onto one of these Caribbean islands? I thought about Becca. Were there women in Carriacou that she would befriend?

"The local women and I do things together," Marisa answered, swaying back and forth to comfort her baby. "But it's not the same as my girlfriends back home in England."

She looked wistfully at the sunset. A disk of orange melted into the horizon, echoing in layers of peach, pearl, and lavender. The sea out there still tumbled with whitecaps.

"Think it's calming down?" I asked.

"Mackerel sky," she said, pointing to long mauve wisps. "Always means rain tomorrow."

After dinner, we heard the approaching roar of Brouwer's heavy dinghy.

"Come aboard!" David called. I had become fond of Brouwer. He was smart, funny, and unassuming. He was as interested in what I had to say as he was in David, and he had taken John fishing or surfing almost every day.

The moon hadn't risen yet. Clouds streamed across the stars. Wind still pumped through the anchorage at twenty-five or thirty knots. Flags flapped stiffly and halyards clanged.

"Baked some bread," said Brouwer, handing up a dense brown loaf.

"Rum and lime?" Dave asked.

"Don't mind if I do."

We told stories of our travels, first Dave and me, then Brouwer. John piped in with a detail here and there. Alison leaned back in my lap and fell asleep. We heard a whistle.

"That's Til," said Brouwer.

Whistle again.

"Jump in the dinghy and get him," David said to John. We had lashed our outboard motor to the sailboat deck, as we usually did when we expected rough sailing. All John could do was row.

"In this weather?" I asked. "Think he can make it?"

"He can take my dinghy," said Brouwer. "You've driven it before, haven't you?"

John, issued the challenge, assumed his deepest voice. "Sure." He stepped over the lifelines.

"I don't know about this," I said.

"Here, bud," said David. "Take this flashlight, just in case."

John settled in at the helm of Brouwer's dinghy. With one pull of the ignition cord, he started the engine right up.

"He's a pro," Brouwer said.

John revved the motor and drove the dinghy up the length of *Hei Tiki*, crossing just in front of our anchor line. *Faith Jones* lay no further out than we did, but a hundred yards away, one of the dozen other boats anchored in Old Road Bay. I tracked John by the voice of the outboard. It revved then slowed down, revved then died. From the sound of it, John had made it to *Faith Jones*.

Then I saw the flashlight. Moving out with the weather, fast. Scudding away from *Faith Jones*.

Then I heard the voice of my son, carried by the wind out to sea: "Dad! Help!"

Then he was nothing but a light moving fast into darkness.

Not a word. David tore free the dinghy line, leapt over the lifelines, and rowed away. I lost sight of him in the darkness. Brouwer and I stood, side by side, staring.

"I can't afford to lose my dinghy," Brouwer blurted. He jerked off his shoes, downed another gulp of rum, dove into the water, and swam toward *Faith Jones*.

"I can't afford to lose my son," I said to the wind.

I felt terrified.

I will recreate events based on what I later learned. It's a story best told from every point of view.

John desperately tried to restart the outboard motor. The wind quickly turned the dinghy around, so he faced into open water. He knew that the outboard worked as a rudder, but without power, it was useless. He tried once more to rev the motor. Dead. He shifted into the middle of the dinghy. Waves loomed behind him, taller and taller. That heavy dinghy of Brouwer's rode the waves roughly, jerking up a crest and falling into a trough with a bump. He pointed the flashlight back toward the anchorage. Those lights were growing smaller, fast. He let out a yell, but the darkness just absorbed it. He kept yelling anyway because he was so scared.

He heard a voice. His name being called. It was his father.

David had pushed beyond all limits to row out to save him. The wind was howling, so they had to shout.

"Take the line!" David cried. He threw a line across the water.

John stretched, but the line fell short of him. David reeled it in and threw it again.

John leaned over the gunwales, tipping Brouwer's boat off-balance, and grasped the line. Tied to the stern of the smaller dinghy, the line tautened and snapped. "Tie it on somewhere!" David cried. John jerked it around a metal cleat inside Brouwer's dinghy. Father and son were joined by a line. David pumped the oars, his muscles tensed with adrenalin. He strained to row two dinghies, but the wind and waves fought back. It was a losing battle.

He reached out and hauled himself up to John's dinghy by the line. Their eyes met. There were no words. John had stopped screaming. He was too frightened to be crying. David stayed in overdrive. "Hold on," he cried. John gripped our dinghy with all his power, and David climbed from one boat into the other. He tied the smaller dinghy more securely to the larger. All this, as the waves kept building and the wind kept blowing and the clouds still covered the stars.

David tried to start Brouwer's motor. Adjusted the choke. Pulled the cord, again and again. John flashed the light back toward the anchorage. The boat pitched into a wave. Cold salt water slapped the two of them down. David tried to start the motor again. No fire.

I felt numb and helpless. I could hear nothing but the wind, whistling through the rigging, and my heart, pounding in my chest. I could see nothing but that tiny light. I sighted its position by the compass: 335°. I knew nothing of what was happening out there, except that I was sure that my son and my husband were now together. The wind was ferocious, but it would have blown David to him. No way could they row back against it, but they were together. They were strong, they were smart, they were alive, and they were together. I check again: the light still shone at 335°. Then the light flickered and disappeared.

Brouwer sprinted up the ladder, sopping wet, yelling for Til. "John's blown out there in my dinghy! Up anchor right away!" He jammed on the switches. *Faith Jones* spewed exhaust out the back. Til threw on the hydraulic winch to get one anchor off the bottom. The winch jerked and wrapped the chain wrong. The motor strained. The winch wouldn't turn. Til jerked and heaved. He threw the lever on and off. "She's stuck," he yelled. Brouwer shoved on the chain, but the winch wouldn't budge. It was jammed. They couldn't use it to bring up either anchor.

"Pull the other one up by hand!" Brouwer shouted. Even two strong bodies together couldn't pull up a hundred feet of chain. Brouwer's mind raced. "We're going to have to dump it."

"Dump the anchor?"

"Grab a life jacket," yelled Brouwer. Brouwer threw a fast bowline knot, tying the float to the boat end of the anchor line. "Heave!" They threw out the life jacket. Cut loose from one anchor.

"We'll drag out the other one," Brouwer shouted. "Here goes." He drew a deep breath and threw the engine into gear. The boat steamed forward a hundred feet, then plunged in a nose dive. Brouwer clenched his teeth and kept the gas on. The boat lurched up, then dove down again. He felt a give. The anchor moved. The minute he could, Brouwer swung that boat around, making the smallest arc possible for a seventy-two-foot trawler. He felt the anchor drag, then bounce along the bottom, then break free. He throttled down to complete the arc, then pushed it as hard as he ever had, ploughing out between other sailboats, throwing a phosphorescent wake behind him.

The light returned. Still 335°. I stood and watched and prayed. "Oh God, be with us. Oh God, please be with us." Was that all I could do? My mind flickered through the possibilities. I could pull up anchor, I could turn the key, I could get the engine going. I could drive *Hei Tiki* toward that tiny light. But Brouwer was a far better sailor than I was, and I trusted David. Oh, how I trusted David. I knew he was with John, and that whatever could be done, he would do.

I pushed away all imaginings that they might drown together. I heard Jack on *Jim Hawkins*: "Boats are designed to survive." I heard David: "These Dyer dinghies move over the water." If things got rough, they would hold each other, and they would make it through somehow.

I glanced over at Alison. I was thankful that she was fast asleep—for her sake and for mine.

I turned on the radio. VHF 16. No voices. I wanted to call out for help. But what could I say?

My mind spun through mythic pictures of myself as wife and mother of seagoing men. I was pacing my widow's walk, watching the sea that devours sailors, watching, wondering, waiting for their return. It sounds ridiculous, but it gave me solace to think that others had felt this way.

I watched *Faith Jones* move out into open water. The tiny light hung steady in the distance. *Faith Jones* turned flank to me. I shuddered to think that they were doubling back, that they could not find them, that they would have to comb the ocean, search and search again, in the dark and the wind and the waves.

But then *Faith Jones* arced around, clearly heading back toward the anchorage.

"*Hei Tiki, Hei Tiki,*" a high-pitched voice called on the radio.

"This is *Hei Tiki,*" I stammered.

"Hi, Mom." Meek and quiet, like waking up in the morning.

"Is everyone okay?" I asked.

"Yeah, we're fine. A little wet." He had already learned his father's way of understatement. "We're having fun." His father's way of fending off fear with bravado.

"Hey, everything's cool," Brouwer cut in. "We're dragging a hundred feet of chain out here. Dave's helping us get that up, then we'll be back at anchor."

"Thanks, Brouwer," I said. I repeated it, emphasizing every word: "Thank you so much."

I made the bed. I tidied the galley. There wasn't enough for me to do, to calm my nerves and use up my energy. I couldn't possibly sleep. I wrote in my journal, and my hand was shaking. I said a quiet prayer of thanks and meant it more than I had ever meant it before.

Faith Jones dropped anchor in Old Road Bay, but it took another hour before John and David came back to *Hei Tiki.* They were laughing, drinking, jawboning—whatever it is that males need to do to rehearse the careless abandon with which they look back upon danger. When they returned, I wanted to shower them with love. They were nonchalant, on to other things.

"I got to use the radar," said John. "Brouwer let me steer the boat into the anchorage."

"Were you scared?"

"By the radar?"

"No, when you were out there in Brouwer's dinghy."

"Yeah, a little bit."

"How big were the waves?"

"I don't know. What do you think, Dad? Six feet?"

"More like four," said David. "Big enough."

I turned to David. "Did you try to row back?"

"No way that little Dyer could pull that monster dinghy of Brouwer's. I thought about cutting it loose. I might have been able to row back in just our dinghy. But that wouldn't have been very neighborly of me, letting Brouwer's dinghy drift out to sea."

"Brouwer's only words, before he took off to get you, were 'I can't afford to lose my dinghy,'" I told David. "You know what I said? I couldn't afford to lose my son." I poured out my fear, trying to cut back to the heart of the matter.

"Lose your son?" repeated David. "We weren't in any danger. Worst scenario, we would have landed at Nevis tomorrow morning. It's only forty miles, and I figure we were traveling a good four knots."

"How far out did you get?"

"Mile and a half, two miles."

"And you weren't scared?" I pressed a little closer.

"Wet and cold, yes. But scared? Nah," said Dave. He put his arm around John's shoulder and pulled him in close.

We stayed one more day in Montserrat. Three of the four of us were exhausted. But then the winds turned fair and the sun started shining. Brouwer and Til headed south toward Dominica. We set out early, going the opposite way. We opened sail and made good speed without a motor, north and west to Nevis, forty miles away.

18

Not There till the Anchor's Down

WE KNEW THE MOVES. WE KNEW THE ISLANDS. We anchored silently. We weathered tough sails and rough weather with a confidence born of experience. We were a cruising family, and we held together. We spent the whole sail back looking for sailing partners as tight as Michael and Becca, and we never found them. In the looking, though, we found that we could do it ourselves.

We screwed up our courage to reach St. Maarten by Alison's birthday, March 28. As soon as we rounded the corner of St. Kitts, heading toward St. Barthélemy, we ran head-on into thirty-knot winds and seas battering us port and starboard. If we headed for Barts, we faced weather on the nose. The jib tore free. David struggled up to the foredeck. The boat pitched and the waves threw David around. "Turn back!" he yelled, hugging the jib sail. I brought the boat about and we headed for Statia instead.

From Statia to St. Maarten, we faced stiff seas again. We started out one morning and turned back. The next morning we reefed the mainsail down and headed determinedly into waves so broad and tall, eight to twelve, that when we slid down into a trough, the next peak rose up above our heads. They were scattered and chaotic, tossing us fore and aft, side to side. A world

313

of flying fish—must have been a hundred—skimmed by, green and shimmering. *Hei Tiki* sailed on, and we reached Philipsburg before nightfall.

We celebrated March 28 in style. John wrote plans out the night before:

Alisons BirthDay
Wake up at 9 o'clock
Ring the bell
Shoot off the air horn
Alison puts up
the flags and mom &
dad sing the French
natoinal anthem.

We didn't quite do it that way, but we had as much fun. We did hoist signal flags, spelling out BIRTHDAY. Alison woke long before nine and opened presents before breakfast. We dined at the Golden Dragon, a red-and-gold Chinese restaurant. It was Sunday evening, and we had the place to ourselves. The waitress brought a surprise dessert: lemon tarts lit up with birthday candles.

My birthday came two days later. I was happy to spend it under sail. With the trade winds behind us, the Anegada felt like a dream. We rode the night as smoothly as a frigate bird soaring the currents. In dawn's light, I saw distant splashing. Couldn't be breakers out here, I told myself. Then a massive body thrust straight up out of the water—a whale breaching! I shook John, called to Alison. They awoke and ran to the bow. Another whale, and another. What a sight—animals larger than our boat, playing at dawn.

We pressed forward, through the Virgins and on to Puerto Rico, this time sailing with the wind behind. It's a different ride from sailing to windward. Seven-foot waves reared up behind us; we sledded down. We made good time, St. Maarten to Boquerón in a week. Waking early, sailing hard, anchoring, waking and sailing again—the rhythms came quite naturally. But it felt right to stay at anchor for a few days in Boquerón.

We hadn't been there a day before John and Alison made friends. Meg and Eric, eleven and ten years old, aboard the sail-boat *Serendipity*. By late afternoon, Eric was hoisting John up above his head, helping break off palm fronds, which the girls wove into lean-tos at the water's edge.

We caught up on lessons. John had been learning to count syllables. He was ready to do something creative with what he had learned. "Do you know what haiku is?" I asked him. I showed him the three-line pattern. We talked through one as I composed it.

Big fat groupers sleep
In dark holes in coral caves.
They look out at me.

We counted out the syllables one more time. "Five, seven, five. Get it?" He nodded. "Now you write one."

"Me?"

"Sure."

"About what?"

"Write about Puerto Rico. About the sailing we've just done. It's easy. I'll leave you alone."

He wrote:

In Puerto Rico
by 9 o'clock the wind howls
At night it whispers

"I love it," I said.

"I want to do another!" he bubbled.

Frigates what cowards
to steal fish from brown boobies
never getting wet

My son the poet.

We embarked on the Mona Passage. The sea lay remarkably calm. The air was so hot and windless that we stood on the bow several times that afternoon and dowsed ourselves with buckets of salt water. We sailed through a school of jellyfish that floated like iridescent purple bubbles on the flat water surface.

But weather started testing us by the time we entered Samaná Bay. A thunderstorm rolled out of the mountains. Rain plummeted all around us, so loudly we could barely hear one another. Landmarks were lost from view. Lightning cracked just off the port bow. I yelled at the children to get into the cabin. David stood on the bow, peering out, trying to discern any buoy or boat approaching. I could barely see him. He pointed to port. I turned, then saw just off the starboard bow the shore he was directing me to avoid. Lightning struck behind us. I cried out in fear. We carried on. By the time we had anchored, the storm had moved out to sea. We were wet, exhausted, and safe in Samaná.

A cold front settled over the Dominican Republic, socking us in for days. In that time I completed my last essay to send home. I knew I had to write about Montserrat. Not about John, swept out to sea—I wasn't ready to tell that story. Instead, I wrote about waiting for weather. The opening jumped right into my head:

> Here we are again, trapped in a tropical paradise, waiting for weather. We had planned only an overnight in Montserrat, but it's turning into a week.

I found a moral to the story.

> I vigorously clean the boat. I finish two novels. I spend more time helping Alison learn her vowels. We wait, and in waiting, we live here for a while.
> We look before and after, regrets Shelley: we pine for what is not. Waiting for weather, we simply have to be here now.

Was it a fiction to put this literate turn of philosophy upon that week of malaise? Maybe so, but it was my business. These essays were building toward a book.

Samaná welcomed us. *"Mi amigos!"* cried Chicha, our favorite boat boy, seeing us arrive. We saw Wally and Morgan at their restaurant. We bought another chicken at the market. We visited the waterfall one more time.

David sent John on a mathematical mission. "Take the dinghy and go around to every sailboat in the anchorage," he said. "Ask them for the length and the draft of their boats." John brought back twelve pairs of numbers, which David helped him graph, displaying that no matter how long or deep the boat, the ratio between the two is the same.

"Cool," said John.

My son the mathematician.

We slid between cold fronts from Samaná to Luperón, then sat another week, waiting for weather. Alison read *The Three Little Pigs* out loud to me. A light went on. That afternoon, as we walked the muddy streets of Luperón, I asked, "What are the houses here made of? Straw, sticks, or bricks?" We looked more closely. Many walls were woven of palm fronds, chinked with stucco or concrete. Many roofs were thatched, layer upon layer of palm leaves. The story gathered meaning.

As I wrote in my journal one afternoon, David and the children rowed together into the mangrove swamp. Two hours later they returned, forked sticks in hand. David trimmed them with the hacksaw, then showed the children how to whittle. When they had skinned the wood down to silken blond, David cut a rubber strap for each homemade slingshot. John took his back ashore and shot beach rocks into the water.

When we finally left Luperón, we sailed all night, right into Sapodilla Bay. We cheered to see the turquoise waters of the Turks and Caicos, and we reeled in a giant mutton snapper on our way into the bay. Something took a big bite out as we were reeling it in—probably a barracuda—but we still feasted that night on the front half of a prize catch.

John had perfected his ability to catch lizards, and Alison began to look on these animals as pets. By the time we left Provo, we had three sand-colored geckos aboard. The largest and most obliging of the three, she named Hercules. Hercules hid in the galley cupboards, among the herbs and spices. When Alison could catch him, she would hold him in her hands or let him rest on her belly. She talked to him. She worried that he was feeling seasick.

After only three days with us, though, Hercules met his fate. Alison found him during a bouncy sail, lying desiccated and eyeless in the port quarterberth. Apparently he had not seen the laundry basket sliding his way. Alison was heartsick, but she coped with her loss by finding a little box in which to lay his body and tossing the casket ceremoniously into our wake.

We lucked into companions for the sail to the Bahamas: Boots and Fred on *Recompense*—great name for a retirement catamaran. Halfway across the Gulf Stream, sailing from Florida, their Loran navigational equipment had gone dead. They could turn around and fix it in Florida or keep on sailing. Fred, a physics professor, welcomed the challenge. Boots knew these waters and didn't want to cut this adventure short. They had a buyer for *Recompense* back in the States. This was their last sail, and they planned to enjoy it.

They were silent sailing partners, never out of sight but rarely radioing. We sailed all day to Little Inagua, first of the Bahamian islands we would reach.

A sweep of turquoise water, a swash of white beach, the warm, sweet smell of island scrub in bloom. We were the only boats at Little Inagua. We were the only humans anywhere around. Only birds, crabs, lizards lived on this island. Underwater coral heads shimmered with life. David and John's hunter instincts took them into deeper water, but Alison and I swam right near the boat. She held my hand and pointed to a shy queen angelfish, electric blue and yellow. We circled around a coral head. So many variations on life, feathers and blossoms and whiskers and worms. A triggerfish tilted to look at us. We drank in these riches, shared by so few.

"Is Hogsty Reef as pretty as this?" I asked Boots that evening of our next day's destination.

"No comparison," she answered. "There's really no island

at Hogsty Reef. Fred and I were there once before. He liked it. I didn't."

"Why not?"

"I guess I just like to see some land nearby when we anchor."

"There's no land there?" I asked.

"Look at the chart," she said. "It's a horseshoe-shaped reef in the middle of nowhere. What land there is disappears at high tide."

I raised my eyebrows.

"It's not your typical anchorage," she said. "I'm glad someone's going with us."

It was a long haul from Inagua to Hogsty. We left before dawn. Sunrise turned into a steely sky that threatened rain but never delivered. The winds piped up over twenty and we kept driving, mainsail reefed way down, jib wide open, driving, driving, through gray-green waves with no land in sight.

If Little Inagua was a Bahamian paradise, Hogsty Reef was a Bahamian hell. Light was fading as we poled our way in. We were the only living boats to be seen. We weren't alone, though. Two hundred yards south loomed the ghost of an ocean tug, rusting away, trapped forever on this hard coral reef. A mile to the north loomed a sister boat, a freighter, also trapped aground. The two wrecks presided over the scene. In lighter weather, the reef might have offered protection, but it felt as if nothing could protect us from that night's blow, a steady twenty-five knots from the east. We struggled to put down anchors in a V off the bow. I felt as if the elements could blow us back into oblivion at any moment.

Fred called on the radio. "You people settled?"

"I think we've got 'er hooked," David said.

David and Alison fell asleep just after dark. John and I stayed up, talking about home. Then he fell silent, breathing deeply. I couldn't sleep. I tried to wedge my body into the galley settee. The boat rocked fore and aft, then it paused and promised rest, then it started tossing, side to side. Rattles and groans, squeaks and clicks. Everything aboard was shaking. I felt the strum of the anchor line. I bolted up. The boat started pitching again.

Up to check the anchor, I crouched, I crawled into the wind. The bow reared up and plunged down into the waves, as violently as it ever had during a windward passage. The anchor lines stretched so taut they were stiff. I struggled to stand, my legs spread for balance. Wind whipped my clothing. Breakers crashed all around. It was desolate and frightening. I crawled back into the cabin and fell into shallow sleep. By 2 A.M. the wind had dropped by five knots. By three, the clouds were parting. A shaft of moonlight swung through the cabin like a pendulum, prophesying blue skies ahead.

We sailed one more day with Boots and Fred, then parted ways. They were heading north to Crooked Island, we were heading west to the Jumentos. I felt no fear in sailing alone now, even though these southwestern Bahamian waters were as wild and unpeopled as any we had seen.

We wanted to set foot on Acklins Island, just to say we had been there. The coast was hard and rocky. We found a slip of sand and beached the dinghy. We walked across broad, hot rocks. A shrill call cut into the surf, the piping of a bird. My eyes followed the sound.

It was an oystercatcher: black body as big as a gull's, fading into a white underbelly, but long, tall, yellow legs and a sharp red beak. He stepped and squawked, fluttered up and down. Pip-pip-pip-pip. Clearly we were upsetting him.

Then I noticed his mate, hiding behind a rock, eyes on me. Her shape was the same, but she was brown and dappled. She squatted, curved open her wings, and scuttled along the water's edge.

Then I noticed their young. Two chicks, freshly hatched. Broken eggshells lay on a rock between me and the mother bird. One chick, dry and downy, had found shade under a rock ledge. The other chick, still wet, flopped around. We were disturbing a birth. I collected my family, back to our home.

Our stores were running low. Certain items we still had in plenty—cans of corn, corned beef, tomato sauce, all the things we were tired of eating. We had no bread, no butter, no rice, no eggs, no canned tuna or chicken, no fresh vegetables except a few potatoes, onions, and garlic. We had run out of paper towels. We were on our last roll of toilet paper.

We started fantasizing about food back home.

"Pork chops," said John. "Thick steak."

"Turkey," said Alison. "With stuffing."

"Ripe peaches," I said. "Green salad."

"Doritos!" John cried.

"McDonald's!" Alison added. The rhythm was building.

"You guys have a food fetish or something?" said David.

"It's to compensate for what we don't have here," I said. "You make dinner." And he did: corned beef cooked in ketchup, pearl barley and corn on the side. For anyone still hungry, David opened a cellophane pack of hard salami.

Fishing became more important with less food aboard. We were sailing up the Jumentos, a barely populated chain of little islands that curved up toward Great Exuma. We would see a sailboat here, a pleasure boat there, and we heard enough conversations over the VHF to understand that people came to the Jumentos to fish.

David brought back a lobster. John brought back a grouper. Even Alison went out with a spear in her hand and proudly returned with four glass-eye snappers.

We found shells in abundance, too. One beach was strewn with Turk's caps, pearlescent pyramids, spiral-striped in black and white. There were so many, we could pick up dozens and still leave behind many that others would call choice.

"Tell us a story, Daddy," Alison said. She and John piled on top of David as he lay, looking up at the stars, in the cockpit that night.

"Once upon a time there was a beautiful young lady named Alison," he began. "She searched the whole world over, and finally fell in love—with an underwater alien!"

"An alien?" she asked.

"He was so handsome," said David. "Handsomer than any of the boys Alison knew before. She accepted his proposal for marriage. Alison asked her best friend, the octopus, to be the flower girl."

"An octopus?" Alison asked.

"And a sting ray was the best man," John added.

"And a starfish was the minister," Alison pitched in.

"And the band played her favorite song," said David. He sang in his off-key way. "Now we will live forever together, forever together, under the sea."

All three laughed and hugged. "I love you, Daddy," Alison said.

"I love you, too. Both of you."

"Mom, too?" John asked.

"Of course," said David. "Mom, too."

I looked up at the sky. A shooting star swept by.

With the highs come the lows. Returning to George Town brought a lot of things back. Even as we sailed into Elizabeth Harbour, I found myself weepy. It had been a nerve-racking sail. We had poled through Hog Cay Cut, a hard coral pass with only five feet of water at high tide. It was not well charted, and you had to hit the deep spots just right to make it through without running aground. Then we miscalculated and overshot the harbor opening, backtracked at the wrong angle, and barreled our way in between two sets of breakers. We did fine, but it rattled me.

It was more than the sail, though. George Town felt like a rehearsal for going home. We were less than a month from the end of our journey, and we were close to the end of our money. Soon we would have to start making a living again. I had found work as a writer before, but I had clipped my contacts a year ago. Would I have any jobs when I got home? David was even less sure about how to make a living. He didn't want to go back into contracting. He would rather keep sailing, but that wouldn't make us money. It was hard to find engineering jobs at home that gave him the chance to build machines like he wanted.

All those worries that we had shelved for the past nine months now had to be dusted off and re-examined. Could we borrow some wisdom from our journey and apply it to our everyday life?

First thing Dave did in George Town was to call his father, to tell him we were back in the Bahamas and the boat was fine. "Dad said John and I are welcome to stay and sail with him," he said.

"He what?" I said. This was news to me.

"He's planning to turn right around and sail out to the Abacos once we get the boat back to Florida, you know."

I knew that. He sailed every summer. That was why we had to get the boat back by June.

"So I offered to help him cross the Gulf Stream," said David.

"What about me?" I asked.

"What about you?"

I felt jealous and abandoned already. I collected my thoughts. "How long would you be out again?"

"Month maybe."

I charged. "Leaving me with the burden of going home, moving back into the house, finding work, figuring out how to make money, taking care of Alison—" I couldn't believe his presumption.

He looked at me, and I could tell we weren't connecting.

John burst up the companionway, Alison right behind him. He was dangling Kelly the doll by her foot. He tripped over David and fell onto the binnacle. Alison laughed. David exploded. "How many times do I have to tell you, goddammit? You're going to break that thing, and that's the whole boat right there." The children retreated. I didn't know how to start the conversation again.

Ten minutes later, the children were back out in the cockpit, complaining about who slept where.

"John's slept outside for a week!" Alison said.

"I have not!" he shouted.

"Stop arguing," I said over their clatter.

"If you two don't shut up, I'm going to whack you." David raised the back of his hand.

"Stop threatening them," I said at his face.

"Don't you tell me what to do," he said. The children backed off, although magnetized by our argument.

I kept on going. "Hitting doesn't work. Saying 'shut up' doesn't work. Just saying 'no' to a kid doesn't work."

David kept on going, too. "You have your way, I have mine. Don't undermine me. If we did it your way all along, we would never have made it this far."

It sounded like the familiar refrain. I spat out some accusation along those lines, saying that I wished things would change.

"I have changed," he answered. "Now, when I see something I don't like, I say so. I don't withdraw."

It hit me like a bucket of cold water. We had gone through the same evolution. Each of us had learned to speak to the other. We were developing trust solid enough that we could display our differences. Say what we didn't like. Argue. Disagree.

For the moment, it hurt. For the long run, it helped our marriage. When we woke up the next morning, we looked each other in the eye, recognized we loved each other, and kept trying.

On May 24, our thirteenth wedding anniversary, we had made it to Nassau. Once again, we were waiting for weather. We had almost two hundred more miles to travel to get to Florida by the first of June. We were poised to sail, but we weren't going to break the rules we had learned through months of experience. Don't let the pressure of a schedule force a bad decision. Only sail when the sailing's good.

Nassau tried its city best to assault us. During the day, traffic noises rattled through the air: screeching brakes, honking horns, the roar of heavy equipment. "It's the first parking lot we've seen since Fort-de-France," said Alison. At night, corny nightclub music floated over the water. Cruise ships pulled in and out of Prince George Wharf, lit up all night.

Unwittingly, we had anchored a quarter mile from the dock where conch hunters from all around cashed in their quarry. A mountain of empty conch shells grew daily on that spit of land.

Winds sent the aroma our way. It was putrid, but so familiar I almost felt sentimental.

There was a poignant sense among all of us that our journey would soon end. The last shopping trip, the last chance to snorkel, the last time we fill the water tanks. One morning, after John and I had worked well together on parts of speech, for no particular reason he reached up and hugged me. "I love you, Mom," he said. I held him for a long time.

That same day, Alison told me she had a secret. She wanted to sit up on the bow, just the two of us. "What's the matter?" I asked.

She looked around, getting ready to tell me. Finally she cupped her hand to my ear and whispered, "I'm going to be sad when our trip is ending." She looked wistfully at me.

"We're all sad it's ending, Alison," I said. I looked at her seven-year-old eyes, realizing how long ago in the space of her lifetime it was since she last saw Virginia. "We have things to look forward to. There's Ahab and Pirate. They miss you, I'm sure. And our garden. We can plant tomatoes and green beans when we get home. Chris and Kathy. Your friends at school. They'll just be getting out for summer vacation." She sniffled and nodded vacantly. All of that seemed so unreal. "Do you know what I do when I'm sad to see a special time end?" She looked at me. "I write it down. You could do that, too." She pulled out her journal and wrote.

We have 4 More
Sails to Florida.
After That John
& Dad & Granddad
will go Back To The
BaHaMas. MoM &
Me will go Back home.
John & DaD will Be
on The Boat Longer
Then us.
I wish that I

Could Be on a Boat Longer.
I will have To go into School Next year.
I will miss my Family.

That night, against the Nassau night noise, David and I sat together in our little cockpit. Alison leaned against my chest, John against David's, and I read us another chapter in *The Wind in the Willows*. Water Rat (who just loved messing about in boats) had just met Sea Rat, who was urging him to take to the seas:

> We shall break out the jib and the foresail, the white houses on the harbour side will glide slowly past us as she gathers steering-way, and the voyage will have begun! . . . And then, once outside, the sounding slap of great green seas as she heels to the wind, pointing South!
> And you, you will come too, young brother; for the days pass, and never return, and the South still waits for you. Take the adventure, heed the call, now ere the irrevocable moment passes! . . . Then some day, some day long hence, jog home here if you will, when the cup has been drained and the play has been played, and sit down by your quiet river with a store of goodly memories for company.

I found myself near tears.

"I don't want it to end," I said quietly.

"It hasn't all been easy, but it has all been good," David said.

"I wonder how much we can carry home with us."

"We'll never lose it," he said. "The children will never be the same. Our family." Quiet settled between us, against the background of the city and, under that, the steady lapping of harbor waves against the hull of the boat. David spoke again. "I didn't realize how important it would be for me to be with the children. My mother always said that you do one important thing in your life, and that is to raise your children. I understand that now."

"I worry that we'll go back home and have to make money

and drive all over the place, and we'll get all wound up again and forget these feelings," I said.

"I don't think so," he said. He reached across the cockpit and took my hand. "Let's cover up the children and go to bed."

That night, we lay together in the forward berth. We moved slowly, tenderly, watching each other, as if we wanted to remember. David kissed my lips, and then he kissed my breast, and then his mouth moved down my belly and between my legs, sweetly tasting and touching, looking up at me to see my pleasure. I opened my body and felt the waves of love lifting up and through me. I danced on the water, I brought David in with me, he danced, we danced, and we held each other in our arms. The harbor waves kept lapping against the hull of the boat, cradling us as we lay together.

One week later, we anchored overnight at West End, the far northwest corner of the Bahama Islands. We thought we would spend a day of rest, then start across the Gulf Stream at sunset. It would be a comfortable overnight passage, and we would pull into St. Lucie Inlet by first day's light.

But November Mike threw up warnings of a tropical depression in the southwest Caribbean. David called his father. "Pack up," he said after the call. "It's coming over Cuba, headed this way. The old man wants his boat back. It's go now, or get socked in for five more days here."

"Where's the storm?" I asked.

"South of Cuba. Plenty of time. Might even help us."

In less than an hour we were underway.

Low, gray clouds striped the sky south and west of us all day long. Sometimes those clouds opened up into rainfall. We could see it streaking from heaven to sea, but it never fell on us. An occasional mist, a low rain all around, but never a downpour. What winds we felt came out of the southeast, behind us. Confused waves sloshed two to three feet all around, with a long ocean swell undulating beneath them. It was an easy sail, a sensual sail, a calming sail all day.

I stood at the helm, looking at this world around me, and I felt good about it. David was cooking our midday meal in the galley. The children were chattering away. I was moving from my center. My belly felt tight and strong. I knew I belonged here. I had made this life my own. I was sailing, and I had more sails to look forward to in the years to come. The second half of my life would not be a time of decline, but a time of new adventures.

"Look over there," said John.

A quartet of dolphins skidded alongside *Hei Tiki*. They skimmed the water and turned sideways for a look. One snorted, then they dove under.

"Look back there," said Alison.

Behind us, a rainbow arched high in the sky, subtle and numinous. It seemed the gateway out of which we were now departing. Without saying so, we all saw it that way.

I wanted to study the chart of St. Lucie Inlet before dark.

David pulled out a tattered guide. "It's pretty old. Nineteen seventy-five. Not very reliable."

"So we don't have a chart to get in here?"

"That's right," he said. "What do you remember?"

It was nine months ago that we left out of St. Lucie. How many other inlets, cuts, buoy markers, and passages since then? How different now was my understanding of the way one moves through water? "I remember it was tricky. Zigs and zags. I hope we can do it."

By the time we approached the inlet, a small rain was coming down, blanketing our senses. The GPS pointed us right up onto the outside marker, a red nun that whistled mournfully as we sailed by. We were close enough to land to be confused by all the lights. White lights, red lights, green lights, yellow lights. Traffic lights, headlights, brake lights. Lights inside and outside buildings. Two of them, we figured, must be channel markers, lighting the way in.

David spotted on the bow. I watched ahead, sensing the

water. I kept up speed as we sheered through the breakwater, past turbulent billows on either side. The water flattened. David pointed one way, then another. Squinting, I tried to make sense of shapes in the dark. The boat slowed down.

"There's a guy fishing right over there," said John.

The engine felt funny.

"Out of gear!" David yelled.

The boat oozed to a halt.

We were aground.

Now I began to make out the landmarks. Trees to our left. Water straight ahead. To the right, I could see an apartment building. And a beach, not twenty feet away. Two people stood on the beach, pointing at us.

David was trying to pole us off from the bow. "What time is it?" he called.

"Eleven-twenty," said Alison.

"Hour and a half till low tide," he said. "We've got to get off of here." Waves rolled in, pushing the boat over. David jumped into the water and started pushing back. I threw the motor into reverse and tried to drive out of this mess. The boat was stuck.

I could jump out and push with David, I thought, but that would leave the children alone on the boat. They were wide awake. Alison reached for me. John shivered with worry. I looked back at the breakwater. A twenty-foot opening in a hundred-foot rock pile. It scared me to think how easily we could have missed it.

"Everybody get a flashlight!" David called. "Try to figure out where we're supposed to be."

We swept beams across the water. All I could see were the waves. "There it is!" John cried. His light silhouetted a channel marker south of us.

"Anchor!" David yelled. Alison held the anchor locker open as I hauled out the smaller Danforth. John had the wrench ready. He screwed the anchor to a line and we handed it to David, still in the water.

David walked the anchor fifty feet out, back toward the

breakwater, in up to his armpits. He ducked underwater and set the anchor by hand. John fed the anchor line through the chock on the bow, then brought it back to the cockpit. Alison wound the line around the jib winch. John pulled the line hard. Alison set the crank in the winch and the children cranked together. The bow budged. I reached over and tailed the line. The boat leaned, bottom scraping. "More!" I yelled. We all gave one more heave. The boat teetered. We were afloat. I nudged the motor into gear. "Keep pulling!" We drew the boat up on the anchor line. David sloshed toward us and climbed aboard. "The minute we're over the anchor, turn," he panted. "John, keep a light on the mark."

I edged the boat on. David pulled in line as we went. He and Alison heaved up the anchor. I spun the wheel around, looking for John's flashlight beam. The boat lurched, hitting sand again. "Drive it off!" David yelled. Reverse, burst of gas. Forward, and the boat was moving.

"Drive straight for that marker and don't stop if you hit the bottom," David said, coming back beside me. "This is that old Florida mud. You can slide on through if you have to."

We made it to that marker, and past the next one, too, bumping the side of the channel as we inched along. Finally we dropped anchor. It was one o'clock in the morning, the first of June. A whippoorwill, whistling in the darkness, sounded so American. Alison tuned in Coast Guard weather on the radio. The tropical depression had dumped six inches of rain on Cuba. It was cutting across the Straits of Florida, heading straight for West End. We had beaten the storm. We had made it back to Florida. We had brought the boat back safely, and on time.

"This calls for a celebration," I said, pulling out a bottle of champagne that had been stashed deep in the galley ever since our journey had begun. Alison passed out plastic juice glasses. John popped the cork.

We raised four glasses of lukewarm bubbly.

"To us," I said.

"Thirty-five hundred miles," David said.

"To our good luck god," said Alison, looking at Hei Tiki, dancing as ever on the cabin wall.

"To good fishing," John added.

We clinked plastic and took a sip.

Alison made a face.

"You don't like it?" said John. "I'll drink yours."

"No, you won't," she said. "I'm giving mine to Mom."

"Why?"

"Mom drove."

Epilogue

THE TRANSITION HOME WAS HARDER THAN I could have imagined. David and John did go back out sailing with Granddad for another six weeks. Alison and I—once I got up the gumption to drive fifty-five rather than five knots—hit the road and drove together from Florida to Virginia.

At first I cried and cried. I cried to see our family separate, two and two. I cried to watch those good times fade into memories. I cried because I missed the sky and the water and the boat. I cried because I knew that everyday life in America wasn't going to let us live so intensely together as we had lived for the past nine months.

The first two nights home, Alison and I stayed overnight with Chris and Kathy. The task of moving back into our house, the house David and I had built together, the house in which we had conceived and raised our children, overwhelmed me. We drove up the driveway. We opened the front door. The place seemed huge, empty, and dirty. Before we moved furniture back in, I scrubbed the walls and floors. Walter and Polly Moore came over and helped me paint the living room. Alison couldn't get used to the new spatial dimensions. She would sit in her bedroom and say my name, presuming that, as on the boat, I couldn't be more than a few steps away. But often I was in the kitchen, downstairs, at the other end of the house, and I had to shout, "Come talk to me down here."

Our garden was a weed patch. At first I didn't feel like digging in. After months without soil, in a world full of white sand and salt water, the red clay of the Piedmont seemed filthy. I didn't want to get my hands dirty. Then, slowly, perennial flowers blinked open. Daylilies. Coneflowers. Black-eyed Susans. Chrysanthemums. I pulled weeds and gave the flowers breathing room. I turned the soil. That familiar smell of earthworms and humus convinced me to plant a fall garden.

Slowly I reconnected with people. I drove over one morning to a dear friend's house. Just drove up and knocked on the door at nine o'clock in the morning. I didn't want to call her on the phone first. I just wanted to see her, face to face. At first she didn't recognize me. Then we fell into each other's arms. Talking, talking, about all that had happened in our lives since we last saw each other.

It was harder to reconnect with those I knew less intimately. Everybody seemed to have grown a little bit fatter. Some would ask questions like, "Back from your vacation?" or "Did you have a good time?" How could I answer? I just smiled and said "Uh-hunh." Some seemed not even to have noticed that we had been away.

The stores overwhelmed me. I couldn't stay long in Kmart, and I avoided the Walmart that had opened during the year we were gone. The land of plenty seemed the land of too much. Bright lights, glaring colors, too many choices. I got dizzy deciding which loaf of bread to buy. I felt more comfortable shopping at the little market in a black neighborhood in town.

I started trying to line up work. I called people I had written for in past years and told them I was available. I owed the magazine a column soon. I knew what I would write about, of course: coming home. One newsletter needed an editor. I went in for a planning session. Everybody talked too fast. "Here's a new phone number for your Rolodex," someone said to me. My what? My head was swimming.

For a while, I thought that if I could get a job—regular

paycheck, regular hours, health insurance, an office to report to—things might come more easily. I watched the want ads, and I answered a few. Always a candidate, never the final choice, I realized all over again that I was meant to be a writer, not an employee, and that I should just sit down and write.

David called late one night. "I miss you guys," he said.

"Where are you?"

"Nassau Harbor Club."

"At a marina?" I was amazed. In all our months of sailing, we had tied up at a marina only one night.

"It's a different crew."

"How's John?"

"He's in with Skip, watching TV. Don and Anne arrived yesterday. They've got a room in the hotel."

"If they have arrived," I said, "time for you to come home."

"You're right. The boat's too crowded already."

David started a job at the end of that summer. The work excited him—pure engineering design, a new tent for the army, then managing prototype construction. But the office was in Fredericksburg, one hundred miles away from home. We gritted our teeth and set into a year and a half of weeks apart. He slept three nights a week in a motel. He made good money. His skin turned pale. He finally left that job, two Christmases later, and said it was the first time he had really come home since our sail.

Both children glided right back into school, no question what grades they belonged in. Alison's teacher had lived two years in St. Croix. She knew the lure of the islands. She welcomed our slide show and shell collection. Alison's crowning second-grade achievement was the picture book she wrote and illustrated, titled *Sailing the Caribbean on a 34-foot Sailboat*.

On the other hand, I watched John's situation with concern. His teacher couldn't understand why all he wanted to write about were his sailing experiences. He was bored in class. Too often, his assignment was to help other children learn things he already knew. We filled out papers and qualified for home schooling. John knew how good learning could feel. He, as much as anyone, wanted something better than that classroom was giving him.

Four years later, it still matters. We can go for weeks without a reference to our sailing year, then some little thing happens and one of us says, "Watch-a yo dinghy," or David calls John "Juan," or Alison warns us that "We're not there till the anchor's down," and the impact of our journey washes over us again.

I can't say our life is perfect. We have our ups and downs. John still complains to me that David is too hard on him. Alison complains about being the youngest, and she still plays little games to get her way. Sometimes, when David works too hard, I remind him to come home earlier. Sometimes, when I pull into myself, David reminds me that we need to work together.

Each year, I inch closer to my dream of being a writer. I've had a lot of work over these past few years—writing newsletters and advertising copy, editing books and magazines. But the dream is to write from the heart. To live a life worth living, then to write about it. I'm getting there.

We talk about buying our own boat. We talk about a long sail again, this time around the Yucatan to Belize. David and John have sailed *Hei Tiki* to the Bahamas several times with Granddad, and all four of us sailed six weeks last winter, all the way to George Town for New Year's Eve. It was colder than we expected, and the children missed a Christmas tree. But the rhythms of the water drew us in as if we still belonged there. Alison got her whole head of hair braided in Nassau. John reeled in a magnificent mutton snapper. We snorkeled the Exuma waters and we reunited with our friends on *Scud*. I know the times will come when we will sail some more.

We keep in touch with the friends we made cruising. Michael and Becca still live in Carriacou. They sold *Aerial*, bought land, and write often, saying that the next time we are down there, they will have the guest house built. Claw, Mary, and Crystal sailed forty days from Panama to Hawaii, where they still live, aboard *Tir Na N'Og*. Last fall, Ed and Marge visited us in Virginia, on their way from Wisconsin to a winter in Isla Mujeres, aboard *Windsong*. Pat and Jack, on *Jim Hawkins*, send a Christmas card every year. Boots wrote, sadly, to tell us that Fred had died, but not before they had gone trekking in the Yukon. The ties that bind this cruising community seem to stretch over years and miles.

We went sailing because we wanted to recreate our family. We wanted something we would share for the rest of our lives. We needed more time to live together. We needed joy, and we needed challenge. We needed to make room for intimacy at the center of things.

Did it work?

Let me tell you a story.

Last month, to finish this book, I left home. I stayed for two weeks at the Virginia Center for the Creative Arts. Single bed, single room, my own studio, all meals prepared for me. I lived every writer's dream, and I got some work done.

I came home for one night in the middle of that time. We had dinner, we watched a movie, we all four snuggled. Later, David and I made love. Sunday morning, we went to church. We came back to a chilly afternoon.

"I've got a concrete truck coming tomorrow," said David. "Pouring a slab in the back for the garage. Thought we'd also make the patio bigger." That seemed like a good idea. "I could use some help," he said. "Let's dig up the sod around the patio edge and replant it over there, on the side of the yard, where we've never been able to get grass to sprout."

David worked a shovel, slicing sod out and clearing the way for the new patio he envisioned. I worked a rake, opening the soil up for new roots to grow. John pushed the wheelbarrow, carrying sod from its old place to its new. Alison picked up clump after clump of growing grass and clover and placed them, like puzzle pieces, alongside each other on the bare, red clay soil. We tamped the sod down with our boots. It's still a little lumpy, but over time, with the snows of the winter and the rains of the spring, we will have created a patch of green where last year there was only dirt.

In the midst of that project, I stood back and wondered at the spirit moving us. We knew how it felt to work together. Each had a task, and together the work was good. Whether we are apart, or whether, like that afternoon, we work together, we know the feeling of being a family. By sailing away, we have come about, and we returned in love with one another. This is the center, and it holds, and we will never forget.

SUSAN TYLER HITCHCOCK grew up in Ann Arbor, Michigan. She attended the University of Michigan and the University of Virginia, where she received a Ph.D. in English. She is the author of two books on wild plants. She, her husband, and two children live near the Blue Ridge Mountains in Virginia. They now own their own boat, *Kia Ora*, and sail as long and as often as they can.